REFUGEES OF A HIDDEN WAR

SUNY Series in Anthropological Studies
of Contemporary Issues
Jack R. Rollwagen, Editor

REFUGEES OF A HIDDEN WAR

The Aftermath of
Counterinsurgency in Guatemala

Beatriz Manz

STATE UNIVERSITY OF NEW YORK PRESS

Cover photo is of Ixil woman and child in the military designed model village of Salquil Grande, Nebaj, El Quiché. Photograph by Pat Goudvis.

Published by
State University of New York Press, Albany

© 1988 State University of New York

For information, address State University of New York
Press, State University Plaza, Albany, N.Y., 12246

Library of Congress Cataloging-in-Publication Data

Manz, Beatriz
    Refugees of a hidden war.

    (SUNY series in anthropological studies of contemporary issues)
    Bibliography: p.
    1. Indians of Central America--Guatemala--Government
relations. 2. Mayas--Government relations. 3. Refugees,
Political--Guatemala. 4. Refugees, Political--Mexico.
5. Indians of Central America--Guatemala--Social
conditions. 6. Mayas--Social conditions. 7. Return
migration--Guatemala. I. Title. II. Series
F1465.3.G6M36 1987   972.81'00497   87-10169
ISBN 0-88706-675-5
ISBN 0-88706-676-3 (pbk.)

10 9 8 7 6 5 4 3

Contents

VI   Contents

Preface

Over two million people have been displaced as a result of political violence in Central America in the last decade. Underlying this desperate exodus are some broad social similarities, particularly an unyielding landed oligarchy confronting large numbers of impoverished peasants. Guatemala, however, has an important cultural difference: a large Indian population.

I first went to Guatemala to do anthropological fieldwork in the predominantly Indian highlands in the summer of 1973. At the time, the surface calm belied the intense suffering of most of the country's population as well as the escalating social tensions. Less than a decade later, an unusually ruthless and bloody military campaign drove tens of thousands to flee to Mexico and elsewhere, severing centuries-old ancestral ties to land and communities. I first visited some of these refugees in newly formed camps in the Mexican Lacandon forest next to the Guatemalan border in 1982, shortly after the mass arrivals began. Since then I have periodically visited both refugee camps in Mexico and Indian rural communities in Guatemala. Observing the situation on both sides of the border, I became increasingly interested in the long-term prospects for the refugees.

The immediate purpose of this research was to determine whether conditions existed for the repatriation of Guatemalans who had fled, particularly 46,000 predominantly Indian peasants living in United Nations refugee camps in southern Mexico. Answering this question, however, required addressing the continuing conflicts and future prospects facing Guatemalan society. Although the anthropological methods of the book concentrate on the microissues of community life, ultimately I feel this approach also provides important insights on the macroissues confronting the nation and the region.

This book has a limited focus, a probe into the aftermath of the counterinsurgency war. As such, it does not seek a comprehensive understanding of the dynamics of Guatemalan society nor does it deal with the insurgency itself and its impact on Indian communities, a topic that merits a study of its own. I do not want to leave the impression, however, that there was no insurgency or that the century-old lifestyle of the elites was not in reality threatened. Moreover, this book does not address the pivotal role of the United States in the region.

FIELDWORK IN GUATEMALA

The fieldwork in Guatemala for this book was conducted by a team composed, in addition to myself, of Celia Williams, Michelle Almen, Rachel Bronsky, and Janet Hall. A total of fourteen person/months were spent in the field. The core of the fieldwork, which forms the basis of this book, took place in El Quiché and Huehuetenango between June and December 1985. Supplementary fieldwork took place until June 1986. In total thirteen departments were visited, ranging from El Petén and Izabal in the north and east, to Retalhuleu, Suchitepequez and Escuintla in the south, including four of the six development poles. In El Quiché one or more members of the team collected data from six municipal towns and ten villages. In Huehuetenango fieldwork was conducted in eight municipal towns and three *aldeas* (villages). The stays ranged from two days to several weeks and, there were repeated visits. Information was also gathered about villages and regions not visited through discussions with secondary informants.

Interviews were conducted on both a formal and informal basis. In one community, sixteen primary informants contributed interviews lasting at least four hours and sometimes much longer as relationships developed over weeks. Numerous shorter open-ended interviews and countless informal discussions supplemented the primary informant interviews. In all cases a broad spectrum of people was sought, including distribution by age, sex, occupation, ethnic background, and religions. This distribution was not always possible. For example, men were frequently more disposed to speak than women, and officials more likely to talk to outsiders than the average resident.

Many secondary informants were interviewed in the departmental capitals and Guatemala city. These included members of the government and governmental institutions, the military, representatives of different religious organizations, and members of the press and nongovernmental agencies, both local and international.

Conditions for Fieldwork

Anthropological field work in Guatemala's highlands and northern lowlands as conducted prior to 1980 was not possible at the time of this study. Researchers could not count on extensive and unimpeded periods of research in a single community; nor was safety assured either for the researchers or the informants. The relationship between researcher and informant was difficult to establish, given the pervasive fear about the consequences of providing information or expressing opinions on social and political matters. Because the research team had no guidelines as to what could or could not be done, different methods were tried. In San Mateo Ixtatán research was conducted under the auspices of a respected community authority, assuring some protection and easier access to community members. Despite these optimal circumstances, collection of data was difficult. In the Playa Grande (Ixcán) development pole the fieldwork was done without prior contacts, a more difficult and dangerous situation for the researchers as well as the informants. In the Ixil development pole research was somewhat facilitated by the fact that many outsiders work or visit the area.

Given the fear and distrust of the informants as well as the uncertainty of procedures, we were well aware that flexibility in the field could determine success or failure. As such, frequent meetings of the research team proved invaluable to constantly evaluate the field data and methods, discuss preliminary results, make necessary modifications, and coordinate efforts.

Fieldwork in Mexico

Exploratory fieldwork in Mexico began in Chiapas in 1982 and continued in Chiapas and Campeche until 1984, during the period when the Mexican government was relocating the refugees. Additional field work was carried out in Campeche and Quintana Roo on two separate occasions: first there was a brief visit of all of the camps (Quetzal Edzná and Maya Tecún in Campeche, and Los Lirios and Rancho Uno in Quintana Roo) in the summer of 1985; and later, two researchers went to Campeche camps in early 1986.

During the Summer 1985 field trip, we spoke primarily with informal leaders; *i.e.*, educators, health promoters, and catechists, rather than with camp general representatives or group representatives. During the second trip, general and group representatives, informal leaders (especially educators) and refugees lacking special responsibilities in the camps were interviewed. A special emphasis was placed on interviewing women, though they hold no official positions in the camp structure, women have a particularly important perspective regarding daily life in the camps. Finally, we spoke with pastoral workers who provide assistance in the camps in Campeche.

Fieldwork was also conducted in Chiapas in the fall of 1985 in which interviews with camp representatives were carried out at the two largest camps, La Gloria de San Caralampio and Las Cieneguitas. Another visit was made to Chiapas in January 1986, to Poza Rica, where camp representatives, and both health and educational promoters were interviewed. Finally, Don Samuel Ruiz, Bishop of San Cristóbal de las Casas, Father Javier Ruiz, and other pastoral workers whose principal work in Chiapas is with the refugees, provided invaluable insights.

Interviews were conducted with Leonardo Franco and other officials from the United Nations High Commissioner for Refugees, Oscar González, Director of the Mexican Commission to Aid Refugees and many staff members of this agency, other Mexican governmental officials at the federal and state level, and nongovernmental organizations such as the Secretaria de Refugiados, and others.

Armando Vásquez Garibay contributed material on the Mexican legal system and Adolfo Aguilar Zinser on Mexican/Guatemalan relations. Gabriela González aided in research in Mexico.

ACKNOWLEDGEMENTS

This study was funded by a grant from the Ford Foundation. I would like to thank David Winder and Christopher Welna of the Ford Foundation Mexico office, for their support. The research was a collaborative effort and this team went beyond collaboration—friendship, mutual respect, and complete dedication to the research made this study possible. I am deeply grateful to Celia Williams and Michelle Almen, two former students and research assistants in this project, who collected field data under extremely difficult conditions and worked strenuously compiling the material on San Mateo and Ixil areas. I am particularly indebted to Celia for her continuous assistance from when this project was only an idea until the very end. And I am thankful to Rachel Bronsky for her deep insights about the overall situation in Guatemala and for the many inspiring discussions we shared. This book would never have materialized without the contributions of everyone in the research team.

I appreciate the enthusiastic response and perceptive and kind comments by the five readers selected by SUNY Press. Many Guatemalans and Mexicans eager to have the study available for discussion, made arrangements to have the first draft published in Spanish (Editorial Praxis, first edition, 1986). I am most honored by their interest. They, the subject of this book, are the final judge as to its value.

There are many people and organizations I have to thank for support throughout the research. The list is too long to mention them all. I am indebted to the faculty and staff at Wellesley, particularly my colleagues in the Anthropology Department. I am also thankful to my former and current associates at the Bunting Institute at Radcliffe College and the

Center for International Affairs at Harvard University. I was aided and inspired by students at Tufts, Harvard, and Wellesley. The close-knit Guatemalanist community in the United States, particularly the Boston committee, provided encouragement, and support from the early stages of the research. My husband and daughter, Harley Shaiken and Mariela, provided unstinting emotional support and encouragement. Finally, and most importantly, this research was only possible through the cooperation and trust of Guatemalans in the city, in the countryside, and in exile. To name some might lessen the value of the contribution of those who would not be named. While the subject matter was often grim, I have warm, happy, and unforgettable personal memories from the villagers and refugees I was privileged to meet.

1

Clash of Expectations

The most intense and brutal military repression in Guatemala's long history of political violence occurred in the early 1980s. This violence left thousands dead and resulted in the displacement of an estimated one million people, including two-hundred thousand who fled to neighboring countries, mainly Mexico and the United States.[1] This book focuses on a dual legacy of this period: the direct scars inflicted on individuals, families, and communities, and the nature and consequences of the continuing militarization of the countryside. I approach the subject through a detailed look at three predominantly Indian regions in northern Guatemala, seeking to reconstruct the devastation and its aftermath from the perspective of those who lived through it. I then look at the situation of Guatemalan refugees in southern Mexico.

The issue of repatriation has received considerable attention since Guatemala inaugurated a civilian president, the first in two decades. The Christian Democratic candidate, Vinicio Cerezo, won over one million votes in the final round of elections in December 1985. Cerezo pledged to end human rights abuses and promised domestic policies that harmonize (*concertación*) the country's polarized economic and social interests. The election and its accompanying political discourse raised hopes for democratic change in Guatemala allowing for a more credible claim that political and military violence can be brought under control, making possible the refugees' safe return.

Policymakers in the United States and Guatemala would welcome repatriation as a potent symbol of political stability and an end to human rights abuses. The Mexican government is anxious for the refugees' departure because their camps add additional tensions to a country already plagued with serious economic and political problems. Most of the refugees themselves would like to go back to their communities, but only under conditions that guarantee their safety and allow them to resume their livelihoods.

What, then, are the prospects for the refugees should they go back to Guatemala? Their safe return depends on broad yet currently unresolved political questions. Virtually all political observers agree that the military continues to exercise dominant power in Guatemala today, but the more important question concerns the direction in which power is flowing. Will the new civilian government slowly gain control over the military or will the military erode the limited existing civilian authority? Will the country continue to be the hemisphere's worst human rights violator, or will the initial political opening be maintained and even broadened?

I explore the central theme of this book, the aftermath of the counterinsurgency war, in the following way. I provide a context for recent events in the first chapter, beginning with a brief review of the rich ethnographic literature from the most affected areas. The goal is to establish a frame of reference for evaluating the cultural dislocations that have taken place. This discussion is followed by an overview of the last three decades, concentrating on the late 1960s through the early 1980s, and an analysis of the significance of the inauguration of a civilian president.

Chapter 2 discusses seven central issues affecting life in rural areas, linking conditions in rural communities to broader trends in Guatemala as a whole.

The core of the book, Chapters 3, 4, and 5, consists of three case studies of rural areas: the northwestern highland *municipio* of San Mateo Ixtatán, the central highland Ixil region, and the lowland rain forest area of Ixcán in the north of El Quiché. The site selection was especially important. The Ixil and Ixcán are development poles, a key component of the government's rural development plan. I selected the three Ixil-speaking *municipios* because they compose the military's most comprehensive development pole. In addition, the Ixil was one of the areas most involved in the insurgency and most affected by the counterinsurgency war. I chose the isolated and inaccessible Ixcán rain forest because the region was the most important land colonization area and the birthplace of the largest insurgent group. Moreover, the area has produced more refugees than any other single place and I had valuable base line data stemming from a research trip in the early 1970s.

Development poles, however, only encompass a small proportion of the population and are therefore not fully representative of conditions in rural community life. Consequently, I selected an area in northeastern Huehuetenango, the Chuj-speaking *municipio* of San Mateo Ixtatán. In San Mateo, the field team observed daily life and focused on new institutions, principally the civil patrol system. Given that the military has not specifically targeted this area for development, the region provides a view of the ways in which military-induced changes have penetrated the general rural society.

Chapters 6 and 7 provide a brief background of the refugees in United Nation's sponsored camps in Chiapas, Mexico and the impact of the refugee exodus on Mexico. The Mexican government relocated about half of the 46,000 refugees in Chiapas to the states of Campeche and Quintana Roo in 1984, and the book also examines conditions in these camps and the impact of the move on the refugees.

Chapter 8 provides an overall analysis of the issues and the book's conclusion.

AREA ETHNOGRAPHIES

A vast ethnographic literature exists on Guatemala. Because of its large Maya population, speaking twenty-two Maya languages, and rich history, ethnographers and archaeologists have studied few countries more intensively. Although these ethnographies generally pay little attention to the national economic, political, and social forces affecting Indian communities, they are nevertheless valuable for evaluating community-level changes in the last several years. The ethnographies from El Quiché, Huehuetenango, and El Petén, the areas most affected by the internal war and from which most of the refugees fled, provide a broad cultural framework, useful as a criterion for subsequent cultural transformations.

Army Presence

Since the Spanish Conquest, national central governments led by Spanish descendants have politically ruled Indian communities. These governments had laws and mechanisms at their disposal to extract taxes, conscript labor, draft soldiers and fill other needs.[2] Nonetheless, communities retained a degree of independence regarding local political matters of Indian concern, unless local decisions conflicted with National political aims.[3]

The most important political period of contemporary Guatemala, the democratic period of 1944–1954, had little direct political impact in the Indian highlands. As a result, the overthrow of Arbenz had few repercussions in most highland communities. In Aguacatán, Huehuetenango, for example, Brintnall asserts that political turbulence in the national arena simply did "not change the basic character of local politics" (Brintnall, 1979:152). National strife also had little impact on local politics in Cantel, Quetzaltenango, the site of a large textile factory with a unionized work force (Nash, 1958:89).

While *ladinos* (those culturally distinct from Indians, identified with the dominant western culture) almost universally dominated the municipal arena, Indians in the Ixil area of El Quiché "actively participate[d] in the government, primarily on matters relating to their fellow Indians" (Colby and van den Berghe, 1969b:119). Although subordinate to *ladino* systems of control, Indians had their own traditional political and ritual system, the "civil-religious hierarchy", which provided them with "[t]he basis of the social structure . . . , regulate[d] the public life, dispense[d] justice," and served as "the mechanisms by which all families, through their male members, [were] interrelated in terms of prestige and public service" (Nash, 1958:97; See also, Tedlock, 1982; Warren, 1978; Hawkins, 1984). These hierarchies were only set aside when there was the potential for positions of greater power. This was true in Aguacatán in the 1970s when Indians "affiliated themselves with political parties and peasant leagues, . . . [ran] their own candidates for local office, and won" (Brintnall, 1979:174).

Whether the civil-religious hierarchy predominated or whether more "ladinoized" forms of participation occurred, normal political life in the Indian villages involved minimal national supervision or control. Some communities were even by-passed for the military draft: "[a] significant aspect of political organization in T'oj Nam is the absence of national police or military personnel in the municipio . . . . The men of T'oj Nam are relatively unaffected by national military organizations" (Bossen, 1984:101). Since the national police were not stationed in the *municipio*, "policing [was] handled by local officials under the authority of the *alcalde* (mayor)" (Ibid:54).

The army is rarely mentioned in most Guatemalan ethnographies. While this omission might indicate methodological shortcomings rather than a military absence, more likely the army's presence was not enough of a concern to warrant emphasis in community studies. Other outside institutions played a more intrusive role in community life. Even when the army began to play a larger and more direct role in government after 1954, its role at the local level remained largely restricted to military affairs until the late 1970s.

Land

Land is central to Indian life and culture. "Land, the working of the land, and the inheritance of the land form a key to understanding domestic life" (Brintnall, 1979:87). Even in Cantel, where many Indians work in the factory, Nash found land considered essential to maintaining an adequate style of life (Nash, 1958:22).

During normal times each village kept its own inheritance patterns, altering them to accommodate pressure on the land. This separation from the national arena is illustrated in Shelton Davis's extensive study of land inheritance in Santa Eulalia, Huehuetenango, where he found that the national government had no say in land distribution unless the Indians themselves requested intervention. While the option of taking land disputes to the national judicial court did exist in Santa Eulalia, the Indians viewed it as their last resort, preferring to solve problems traditionally through local channels (Davis, 1970). When land pressure overwhelmed the traditional patrilineal inheritance pattern, Indians in many villages chose one or both of two strategies: Either restructuring land use patterns (see Morrissey, 1978; David and Hobson, 1982; Millet, 1974)[4] or migrating in search of new economic opportunities.

The army's current involvement in rural areas is so encompassing that even as fundamental a part of Indian culture as land use no longer lies solely within the purview of the family. The army's political considerations can determine access to land, and where and when cultivation takes place.

Labor and Service Requirements

Insufficient land has compelled Indians for decades to depend on wage labor or commerce to supplement peasant subsistence. To earn cash they have migrated to the lowland plantations, the city, or regional markets. Migrations have become woven into the pattern of Indian life. In the Ixil speaking municipalities of Nebaj, Cotzal and Chajul in El Quiché, for example, "many people contract themselves for six, eight, or more weeks, and since some stay away permanently or return only for vacations during fiestas, as much as thirty to forty percent of the able-bodied men may be absent from the area at a given time" (Colby and van den Berghe, 1969b:131–132).

Seasonal journeys to the southern coast plantations have been a source of discontent and dread. Although mandated by economic necessity, Indians in the past were able to decide when, where, and for how long to partake in the cash economy, subject to seasonal requirements and economic conditions. Forced national requirements of Indian time and service had not existed since the vagrancy law (1931 to 1945). Today practically all Indian men must donate time and service in the civil patrol system. This service requirement inhibits their labor options.

Prior to the militarization of the countryside in the 1980s, life was hardly idyllic. Indians suffered the effects of poverty, economic domination, social discrimination, and possessed little economic or political power. Yet the national government was rather indifferent to the cultural functioning of the Indian communities. Community members were able to decide matters affecting the community in accordance with their cultural norms. Most ethnographies emphasize ethnicity and the stability of distinct cultural and linguistic groups as central characteristics. The community was the stronghold of indigenous culture, a refuge from national economic and political dominance, a reinforcing place where Indian identity was formed and maintained. Today, the pervasive military interference in the most isolated of communities has violated and at times shattered this sanctuary.

Though anthropologists tended to overemphasize distinctive local cultural traits and underrate the influence of outside forces, an unmistakable cultural cohesiveness existed. Nash described Cantelenses as "people united by blood and custom, distinct both in their minds and in fact from their neighbors" (Nash, 1958:12). For the Ixil Indians, ethnicity is a factor "making for social isolation from other Indian groups . . . from the government, indeed from national society at large" (Colby and van den Berghe, 1969b:36). In Aguacatán, four groups of Indians live in separate areas and carry on differently organized, distinct lives (Brintnall, 1979:26). Local cultural traits were stable. Colby and van den Berghe, for example, state that "there has been very little change in the ethnic composition of the heavily Indian Western and Central highlands for the last quarter century" (Colby and van den Berghe, 1969b:170).

Although the cultural isolation between different ethnic groups began breaking down in the 1970s, the process was slow, voluntary, and largely self-organized. A strong sense of ethnic identity and cultural unity was maintained. Today, the role of the military and paramilitary organizations in even the most isolated communities has engendered divisiveness, fear, and mistrust. Not since the Spanish Conquest have the highlands seen such a general cultural breakdown. Moreover, although Indians were aware of their powerlessness *vis-a-vis* economic and political elites and the army, fear for their lives did not dominate their activities and consciousness.

THE LAST THIRTY YEARS: AN OVERVIEW

The Mass Movement

Political violence is not a new factor in Guatemalan society. The United States-backed overthrow of the Arbenz government in 1954 unleashed a campaign of violence in its immediate aftermath, inaugurating twelve years of continuous military government.[5] The level of repression rose and fell during this time, but ironically, the election of a civilian reformer to the presidency in 1966 was the prelude to more intense period of military repression. Although Julio César Méndez Montenegro occupied the presidential office, the military continued to exercise the real power. Instead of fulfilling the democratic promise of his election, Méndez Montenegro was unable to prevent the army and paramilitary right wing death squads from carrying out a bloody campaign against the civilian population. A military counterinsurgency campaign against several hundred guerrillas in eastern Guatemala escalated into an attack against all real and imagined opposition, resulting in from 3,000 to 10,000 civilian deaths.[6]

Méndez was succeeded in 1970 by Colonel Arana,[7] who declared a state of siege the day he was inaugurated. Following his term, Arana successfully supported the installation of General Kjell Eugenio Laugerud García as president, despite the 1974 electoral victory of the Christian Democratic candidate, former Army Chief of Staff General Efrain Ríos Montt. After eight years of harsh repression, Laugerud allowed a modest political opening, reflecting the military's success in eliminating dissent, their belief that political stability had returned, and the benefits of a decade of economic growth.[8]

The political relaxation benefited grass roots groups, some of which surprisingly were organized and survived during the late 1960s and early 1970s. These groups—peasant leagues, agricultural cooperatives, slum dweller associations, and labor unions—focused on improving the immediate living conditions of their members. Fueling some of these efforts were Catholic missionaries, many from outside the country, as well as members of the Christian Democratic Party and other reformist groups.[9] The aftermath of the February 1976 earthquake further spurred popular organization. International aid poured into the devastated highlands following this traumatic event, which left 20,000 dead. Residents, aided by voluntary organizations and missionaries, banded together to provide for basic needs and reconstruction. More important than any specific achievement was the sense of confidence and democratic participation these popular associations gave a new generation of Guatemalans.

These grass roots organizations generally sought to avoid directly challenging the government. Several factors, however, broadened their perspective and put them on a collision course. First, the political inflexibility of the system radicalized individuals and entire communities. Since the military and economic elites equated all reform with revolution, even modest proposals for social change met with a fierce response, making revolutionaries out of reformers. Moreover, the army's continuing hold on power, culminating with the disputed 1974 election, further undermined the confidence of many that reforms could be achieved through the system. Second, the Catholic Church was in the midst of deeprooted changes. The Second Vatican Council (1962) and the subsequent Medellín Latin American Bishops Conference (1968) sought new ways to meet spiritual needs in the midst of material deprivation. The Church began articulating a "preferential option for the poor" which was reflected and spurred by the experience of many church people. Some foreign priests had arrived in Guatemala following the 1954 counterrevolution, imbued with a strong anticommunist ideology and anxious to proselytize. These missionaries became involved in self-help projects which impressed them with the courage of the Indians in their struggle for survival and forced the missionaries to confront the iron-willed opposition of local and national elites to any reform at all.

The Growth of the Opposition

Peasants in the highlands in 1978 formed the Committee for Peasant Unity (CUC) which included agricultural workers from the southern coast plantations. The CUC would become the most formidable peasant organization in Guatemala's history, capable of leading over 80,000 plantation workers in a 1980 strike. The strike, which enhanced the visibility and reputation of the CUC, won a 200 percent increase in the daily minimum wage from Q1.12 to Q3.20 after paralyzing the sugar cane harvest.

Important opposition also arose in the industrial labor movement culminating in a number of independent unions and federations forming the National Committee for Trade Union Unity (CNUS) in 1976.[10] In addition, political parties organized around programs of moderate reform. The Social Democrats (PSD) and the United Revolutionary Front (FUR) reflected the desire of Guatemala's growing middle class for democratic change. The government responded by gunning down Alberto Fuentes Mohr (leader of the PSD and formerly the Finance Minister) and Manuel Colom Argueta (a leader of the FUR and previously Guatemala City's mayor) in early 1979. These killings, which occurred on Guatemala City streets during broad daylight, were accompanied by the assassination of dozens of other rank-and-file activists and middle level leaders.

Government violence was inflicting between 100–200 deaths a month by the beginning of 1979. The victims were peasants, leaders of cooperatives, students, rural organizers, labor leaders, political reformers, and church activists among others. At times, the victims were snatched off the street and never reappeared; in other cases mutilated bodies were dropped on roadsides; in some instances people were shot down in front of friends, family, or coworkers.

The Rise of the Armed Opposition

Parallel to the growth of grass roots organizations, a new generation of guerrilla groups was formed in the 1970s. There were three principal organizations, all with roots in the previous guerrilla movement that had been crushed in the late 1960s: the *Ejército Guerrillero de los Pobres* (EGP): the *Organización del Pueblo en Armas* (ORPA); and the *Fuerzas Armadas Rebeldes* (FAR), the group with the closest ties to the guerrillas of the 1960s. Today, these groups comprise the Guatemalan National Revolutionary Unity, URNG.[11] All three groups began operating in remote areas of the country, where the military had little direct presence and the geography favored clandestine warfare. Strategically, the three sought to transform people's immediate concerns into a commitment to armed opposition, and slowly began developing roots among the peasant population. The EGP and ORPA concentrated on predominantly Indian areas to avoid the isolation from this critical social base faced by the guerrilla groups of the 1960s. FAR located in a region primarily composed of *ladino* colonization projects. The three groups also began building a base in urban areas, principally Guatemala City.[12]

During the Lucas Garcia (1978-1982) regime the guerrilla groups expanded their membership and broadened their base of support. In its zeal to eliminate or at least subdue any independent organization, the army precluded peaceful reform, driving activists and even entire groups over to the armed opposition. Massacres, such as one in Panzós, Alta Verapaz in May 1978 and one at the Spanish Embassy in Guatemala City in January, 1980, outraged large sections of the population.[13] Meanwhile, with a base of support in Indian communities, the guerrillas increasingly began to appear as the only alternative to the military. Moreover, the Sandinista victory in 1979 made revolution seem possible in Central America.

By 1981, guerrilla groups were conducting daily operations in nine out of twenty-two departments, carrying out sporadic operations in an additional nine departments, and fielding daily actions in Guatemala City. The guerrillas were capable of inflicting heavy casualties on the army, and seizing sections of the Pan-American highway. The insurgents took over municipal and, at times, departmental capitals and destroyed vital parts of the transportation infrastructure, impeding commerce and threatening the army's mobility. It appeared that the insurgents would soon permanently control sections of the Indian highlands. Most importantly, the army sensed the guerrillas had tapped into a deep reservoir of popular discontent and that each insurgent victory could encourage latent supporters to become active combatants. Unlike the 1960s, the guerrilla "fish" were no longer in an isolated pond but rather swimming in a very large sea.

Military Corruption

The Lucas García regime was making little headway against this expanding opposition. In part, financial enrichment appeared to be distracting senior military men. At the beginning of the 1970s, high level officers began plundering state resources in a way that far overshadowed previous instances of military corruption. The process culminated in the unusually corrupt and repressive Lucas government. Lucas and his associates siphoned off millions through the creation of bogus programs, reshaped national development plans to enrich themselves, and simply extorted funds from other projects.[14] A powerful new economic elite began to emerge.

As a result of excessive greed and political ineffectiveness, the regime began to lose its base of support. The traditional elites viewed the military's wholesale appropriation of state resources for private gain as "unfair competition", and were concerned about the army's performance against the guerrillas. The middle class also objected to the corruption, and felt the impact of intensified state brutality. Junior officers became alarmed that the scale of financial manipulation was undermining the war effort, since the attention of senior officers and the resources of the state appeared more directed to personal gain than to the welfare of the soldiers in the field.[15]

In the March 1982 election 60 percent of the voters abstained, amid unusually extensive fraud. Oblivious to the erosion of his base, Lucas sought to install a hand-picked successor, General Aníbal Guevara, provoking outcries from across the political spectrum. Two weeks later an army coup ended sixteen years of formally though not necessarily fairly elected governments. General Efraín Ríos Montt emerged as the new leader, lasting in power only sixteen months before General Oscar Mejía Víctores replaced him in a second coup.[16] Junior officers achieved new power in the shake-ups, providing increased vigor and sophistication to the counterinsurgency effort.

War against an Unarmed Population: The Period of Mass Terror

During the 1978–80 period, the army sought to crush the increasingly popular grass roots organizations, in what Amnesty International has called a "government policy of political murder." The military viewed these groups as providing the insurgents a broader base of support, future recruits, and greater legitimacy. Targeting first individuals and groups who worked openly and legally, the military attempted to decapitate and destroy the mass movement.[17] These tactics successfully decimated groups capable of effective opposition, whether sympathetic to the revolutionaries or not, and left in their wake a generation of dead or exiled secondary and national leaders.

At the end of 1981, the army moved into a different strategic phase: an eighteen-month campaign whose scope was so bloody and pervasive, it must be distinguished from what went before and what has come after. To emphasize the horror of this period I will refer to it as the time of mass terror. The army waged war against the civilian population as well as against the elusive guerrilla units. No distinction was made between combatants and civilians, no rules of war were followed, and there were no prisoners of war. The campaign was so violent that whole families and even entire communities fled their villages to survive, depopulating large areas.

Since the military lacked the resources simultaneously to attack every area in which the guerrillas operated, the high command targeted the most vulnerable region—the territory controlled by the EGP. The EGP posed both the greatest threat to the army and was the weakest link in the insurgency. On the one hand, the group had the largest base of any insurgent organization and near insurrectionary conditions prevailed in areas of the highlands. On the other hand, the EGP was winning people to its cause faster than they could be armed or integrated. Consequently, the group was overextended with an increasingly vulnerable Indian periphery.

Destroying the insurgents' base of support after 1981 was no small task. An estimated quarter of a million people in rural areas supported the guerrillas to some degree, by making available food, shelter, and providing communication links. The worst excesses of previous periods such as the occasional massacre of an entire village became more common. Families were burned alive in their own dwellings, women were frequently raped, and old people and babies were hacked to death. Physical destruction also occurred: a scorched earth policy led to burned crops, leveled homes, and some 400 destroyed communities. The violence left an indelible mark on those who survived.

The particularly grisly nature and extensive scale of the campaign indicate a deeper purpose than combating the guerrilla forces or disrupting their social base. The purpose appeared to be eliminating future capacity for opposition, insuring that new seeds of revolution would not soon take root. As part of the campaign, the core of Indian community life was attacked by desecrating symbols and sacred places as well as destroying the *milpas* (corn field) on which subsistence depended. In the process, the military disrupted traditional patterns of respect, authority, and power.

A Military Conception of the Indian Question

As the army was carrying out widespread and indiscriminate destruction in the countryside, some officers were giving thought to the sources of the guerrillas' success. Impressed by EGP accomplishments in the Indian regions of the country, these officers were seeking ways to emulate the EGP's tactics as another means of maintaining the system. A 72 page military document, authored by Captain Juan Fernando Cifuentes and published by the Military Academy (Centro de Estudios Militares) in late 1982, provides an insight into the way some more sophisticated officers were grappling with understanding the roots of the EGP's appeal in the Ixil area. The document (Cifuentes, 1982) acknowledges that "the EGP was successful from the very beginning offering the Guatemalan Indians a hope for dignity, something they had not been offered during more than 400 years of humiliation and misery." In contrast, governments have always "viewed and treated the Indians as a sub-group, backward, and brutalized by ignorance and alcoholic consumption." Rather than proselytizing about Marxism or Bolshevism, concepts the Indians would find little identification with, the EGP addressed real issues in the Indian communities, according to this military analyst:

> What [the Indians] do understand is that they are poor and that they are so because they live miserably, their work tasks are exhausting and the exhausted land yields little. The temporary migrants to the coast also are aware that the product of their labor does not constitute a remuneration that would get them out of poverty.

The document appears to recognize that without a successful economic alternative offered by the military, the Ixiles' support for the EGP will objectively continue.

> As a consequence of the general situation and fear, the agricultural, commercial, and migratory activities have been affected to such a degree that the misery threatens to lead the population to desperation, giving the opportunity to the EGP to recruit followers with the hope they offer as an alternative.

The EGP is credited with understanding the culture of the people and speaking their language, which has enabled the guerrillas to "win the confidence of the population." In contrast, the document states "the civilian population shuns and refuses all collaboration with the military." The document elsewhere elaborates that "in general the Ixiles do not provide military service, mainly because recruits are found in other regions of the country where the character of the Indians is more inclined to military discipline."

The author estimates that the EGP had recruited about 1,200 people in the region although its political cadre was probably not over 100. Nonetheless, "potentially 50 percent of the population collaborates with the enemy in incidental activities of espionage especially about our movements." These activities on the part of the Ixiles disprove, according to the document,

> those that thought and asserted that "our little Indians [inditos] would never be communists due to their submissive characteristics, religiosity, respect of the military officer, customs and more than anything due to their resignation of accepting their destiny."

An important aspect of the document is a discussion of three broad courses of possible military action concerning the Indian question. These three alternatives are: First, "the ladinoization of the Ixil population so that it will disappear as a sub group distinct from the national mode;" Second, a contrary proposal "based on respect for the Ixil identity, its customs and language;" and, finally, an option that would not deal with culture at all but rather would "turn all government effort to improve the living conditions of the Ixil population." The document then systematically analyzes the pros and cons of each course of action. Paradoxically, even when the second alternative is considered, an "ideological war" and a "psychological campaign" to change the Ixil's perception of the nation is at the core of this approach.

The first alternative, ladinoization, means "the imposition of the Spanish language [castellanizar], eliminating the distinctive dress and other visible differentiating signs of the group." The Ixiles would then "cease to think of themselves as such and accept all the abstractions that constitute the concepts of nationality, fatherland, etc." Moreover, "once ladinoized the Ixiles will enjoy the benefits of our civilization." This course of action, however, is seen as having a doubtful outcome.

> During 400 years the Ixiles, more than other ethnic groups, have resisted the imposition of the Spanish language [castellanización] and consequently the effort could be useless since their thinking and their cosmological concepts will continue being the same even if they do not have differentiating exterior characteristics.

While it frankly considers the option of the cultural demise of the Ixiles, the author favors the second option on pragmatic grounds. Given the historical difficulties of ladinoization, a new effort in this direction would simply not work and in addition would put the army at a "disadvantage in relation to the enemy (EGP) who in order to approach [the Ixiles]. . . .have learned their language and apparently respect their cultural traits."

> Knowing the history and idiosyncrasy of the Ixiles it is estimated that this is the only way to convince them that they form part of a great Guatemalan nation with a pluralistic society more or less as is the case in Switzerland where the national identity of the groups that constitute the country has been respected.

This approach would not only "neutralize the strategy of the enemy, utilizing their own procedures" but with considerably more resources at the disposal of the army. The army, however, recognized as an obstacle to the successful implementation of this approach the intransigency of the *ladino* population, who would resist improving the working conditions and social relations with the Ixiles.

The document shows an understanding of the deep roots of the Indian culture and presents a way by which the army can win the loyalty of the population. It shows an appreciation of the EGP's efforts and successes and a recognition of the objective causes of that success. Nonetheless, there was not an adherence to an approach that would respect the Ixil or other Indian cultures. Instead, the military pursued a coherent strategy of quick and total domination over the Indian population, after which elements of the discussed plan could presumably be introduced.

Military Consolidation

The army brought the countryside largely under control by 1983, leaving a disoriented, disorganized, and relatively powerless population, with many grass roots leaders dead and local organizations destroyed. While wholesale massacres became largely unneeded, a continuity of murders and torture keeps alive the memory of the consequences of challenging the system.

With the civilian population subjugated, the military moved more aggressively against the guerrilla units. This proved to be the army's least successful effort. The guerrillas offered resistance, despite the fact that their urban network was in a shambles and their rural base of support shattered. To survive, the guerrillas have had to retreat to strongholds in remote parts of the country, underscoring their inability to achieve victory anytime soon and depriving them of the active collaborations of many.

By early 1984 the military sought to consolidate its gains and move toward a more stable, constitutional rule. As part of this process, the army began embedding its presence in the Indian highlands and lowland colonization areas through three institutions: regional centers of development or "development poles," civil patrols, and Interinstitutional Coordinating Committees.[18]

At the core of the development poles, located in areas singled out for their strategic importance, are "model villages". These settlements physically concentrate dispersed hamlets into larger and more easily controlled units. The civil patrols brought one million men into a paramilitary structure at the community level, enabling the army to physically leave many villages and retain control by proxy. Finally, the Interinstitutional Coordinating Committees were intended to link the activities of all agencies, governmental and nongovernmental, involved in any aspect of development work.

The degree of militarization varies widely, depending on the intensity of armed conflict and popular support for the insurgents. In some places, the army finds it necessary to exert control through its own physical presence. Increasingly, however, rural communities adjust to new military institutions, though not necessarily accept them, as a condition to carry on their daily activities. The years of open, violent conflict and the ensuing militarization have also provoked mistrust and divisions in numerous rural communities.

Elections for a constituent assembly were held in July 1984. The new Constitution, the country's fourth in thirty years, codified the heart of the army's strategic consolidation program, including the civil patrols, the development poles, and the Interinstitutional Coordinators.

GUATEMALA 1986: WHAT DOES THE FUTURE HOLD?

Whether the traumatic events of Guatemala's recent past will continue to characterize its future depends to an important degree on the effectiveness of the new civilian government. For that assessment it is valuable to explore the context and significance of the elections, and then examine the factors shaping the country's development over the next several years.[19]

The Decision to Hold Elections

An important initial question concerns why the military called for elections in the first place. Unlike countries such as Argentina where the military ceded power because of a debacle, the Guatemalan army was victorious in the field and chose to turn over the presidential office to a civilian. Two releated reasons appear to have motivated the decision: First, the military may have felt that formally occupying the executive branch entailed unnecessary political costs; Second, the army had embedded its authority in such a way that civilian rule would not undermine military power. In addition, international pressure further spurred the electoral process.

Consider first the cost to the army of retaining executive office. During the counterinsurgency campaign, the military wanted a totally free hand to combat an insurrectionary situation in the countryside. With success assured, however, formal participation at every level of government began appearing more of a handicap than an asset. The army was increasingly becoming a symbol of the country's economic and political problems. The economic elites may have tolerated a sliding economy when the alternative seemed to be revolution, but were anxious for a more competent and single-minded management of the economy with political order restored. Moreover, all social groups—peasants, industrial workers, the middle classes—were being squeezed by severe economic contraction. With more unpopular economic measures obviously on the horizon, the military was ready to shift responsibility for economic traumas and the resultant social conflict to a civilian president.

The armed forces were also aware that a certain legitimacy is necessary to govern successfully. The previous "social pact" based on the passive acceptance of poverty and political exclusion had broken down. Thus, the military and economic elites were willing to consider a new social pact allowing for somewhat broader political, economic, and social participation, within the framework of preserving their power.

Second, even though a civilian would occupy the presidential palace, new institutions such as development poles and the Interinstitutional Coordinators could provide the military broad control over key aspects of political and economic life, even in the most isolated of villages. Moreover, fundamental reform was excluded from the political agenda for the elections. The Christian Democrats (DC), for instance, publicly stated that land reform was not a viable possibility. In the final case, the continuing autonomy of the military combined with the political history of Guatemala in the last thirty years underscores who retains final authority. The military would clearly remove a civilian government that sought to fundamentally challenge its power or to restore "order" from social "chaos".

The fact that clean elections were held and a Christian Democratic government actually installed is evidence of the army's confidence in the results of its earlier counterinsurgency activities.[20] The necessity for elections, however, reflects a broad consensus throughout Guatemalan society that the previous system no longer worked and some more meaningful political activity should be allowed. But this is largely a consensus against what was, rather than a unified perspective on what should be. In fact, the underlying thrust of the country's political process in the coming years will be to shape a new social pact that defines the relationship between the country's diverse ethnic and economic interests. Some fundamental and contentious issues remain to be worked out. For example, what are the limits of reform? What formal and informal role will the army play in political life? Will the civilian government expand its power or remain peripheral to important areas of political and economic life?

The Christian Democrat's "National Project, 1986–1991"

The Christian Democratic Party's "National Project, 1986–1991" defines the party's political vision for the future. The overall approach seeks to harmonize diverse interests through a process of consultations with representatives of various social sectors. The hope of the Christian Democrats is that over time the democratic process will become institutionalized and slowly expand, thereby enlarging the scope of possible reform. Their fear is that pressing too forcefully or too rapidly against the existing political constraints would cause them to contract rather than expand.

The project lays out both a process of governance and an economic agenda. The approach to governance emphasizes securing the individual and societal rights defined in the constitution; developing new representative organizations and interest groups such as cooperatives and including them in the formulation of government policy; and decentralizing political influence away from the capital through strengthening local and regional government. The economic program seeks to lessen social tensions and to spur development. On one level, a central goal is to establish a more stable democratic base by strengthening the middle class and minimizing the gulf between rich and poor. The specific mechanisms include promoting small and medium-sized businesses through reorienting credit and introducing other facilities, and redistributing wealth through tax reform and the restructuring of services. On another level, the economic program stresses agro-industry as a central engine of modernization (Democracia Cristiana Guatemalteca 1985a and 1985b).

The Christian Democrats' proposal avoids the question of who holds and exercises power and the structural basis of their power. At most it questions how power has been exercised. It seeks to institutionalize greater flexibility and participation without changing the fundamental relationships between the country's social sectors. Consequently, there is no talk of agrarian reform or any other fundamental reforms for the problems underlying the country's glaring inequalities.

The plan is what Cerezo and his party would like to do. What they will be able to do is another matter.[21] No matter how circumscribed and cautious the party may be concerning challenges to existing sources of power, its rhetoric and policies could raise popular expectations and set in motion grass roots activities that might spark a reaction from the military or economic elites or both. While the first months in office are far from encouraging, a series of factors are worth examining which will certainly influence the new government's possibilities for achieving more integrated development than in the past.

Factors Favoring the Christian Democrats

There are a number of factors in the Christian Democrats' favor. First, Cerezo won with an overwhelming majority of the popular vote in clean elections, and the party has an impressive base both in the national assembly and in municipal offices. Cerezo himself is an astute professional politician who could skillfully utilize whatever resources are available. Internationally, the U.S. has given important support to the constitutional process that brought the Christian Democrats to power, recognizing that a "centrist, democratic" government in Guatemala strengthens its own position in the region. Moreover, Cerezo's party is part of an international network of Christian Demoractic Parties, providing his government with almost automatic diplomatic alliances. These factors provide Cerezo some margin to exercise and even expand his still limited powers *vis-a-vis* traditional elites.

The Christian Democrat's impressive electoral showing does not necessarily indicate deep-rooted support for the party's platform. For many it was more a vote for "hope" and a vote against the army (Jorge Carpio, the other major electoral contender, was rumored to be close to the army) than a vote for the Christian Democrats per se. To carry out their programs, particularly measures that could provoke conflict from traditional economic or military elites, the Christian Democrats need to build an organized and active base. This base would spread the party's influence through a broader grass roots movement whose activities would be both more supportive of the government and subject to its control. A number of factors will undoubtedly facilitate creating this base: The DC has a long history of neighborhood organizing and community development work in most of the country; it is a structured party with trained cadre and considerable international support; and it is the party in power at a national level, with access to state resources for its programs.

Further aiding Cerezo is a general tacit agreement among private sector and military elites that new attitudes are needed in the country's development.[22] In addition to the "scare" from the near insurrectionary situation of the early 1980s, factors encouraging new attitudes include: the gradual transformation of the country's productive system over the past thirty years, the inheritance of family enterprises by a new generation educated in Europe and the U.S., more willing to introduce new investments and to moderate traditional labor relations, and the pressing need to diversify the country's economic base (even though it will still be export oriented).

The consensus that past policies have failed provides Cerezo a certain margin for action. In its first year, the National Project stresses political matters, especially establishing and securing the institutions defined by the new Constitution (Presidency, Congress, Courts, the Constitution itself). To consolidate its political position, the party has sought to assure those who wield real power, the private sector and the military, that the Christian Democrats will be "responsible"; *i.e.*, advocate reforms that operate within rather than challenge existing power structures. Only after the political situation is consolidated might the Christian Democrats try to implement measures that could require more important "adjustments" on the part of the elites.

Problems Facing the Christian Democrats

The problems and the obstacles for the Christian Democrats are more numerous. Three domestic areas stand out: political instability, the economy, and continued human rights abuses.[23]

Politically, the Christian Democrats may become caught between the rising expectations of their followers and the unwillingness of the private sector and military to allow fundamental change. In part, Cerezo's national consensus rests on two contradictory pillars: the expectation of many followers that he will provide more far-reaching change sometime in the future and the expectation of economic and military elites that he will contain fundamental reform. As various sectors of Guatemalan society demand action on their agenda, Cerezo's room to maneuver could shrink.[24]

Should other groups in the society seek more far-reaching changes, the military and economic elites will likely demand that Cerezo contain the situation. If so, precisely those measures that are necessary to placate the elites will alienate his followers and potential base. Instead of harmonizing diverse interests, his policies could further polarize these sectors.

Two social movements are providing a major test for the new government. The first, a loosely-knit group led by a Catholic parish priest, has mobilized fifteen to twenty thousand landless peasants and agricultural workers on the south coast and nearby areas. Father Andrés Girón is thought to have close ties to the Christian Democrats, an impression

Father Andrés Girón. Sitting behind him (with sun glasses) René de Leon Schlotter, Minister of Development and First Lady, Lic. Raquel Blandón de Cerezo, July 1986. Photograph by Pat Goudvis.

reinforced by the fact that First Lady (Licenciada) Raquel Blandón and other government officials greeted both of the major marches he has led. Girón insists the movement is independent of any political party. He initially requested that the government purchase two large abandoned plantations to subdivide and sell to landless workers. More recently, he has begun to call for land reform. "I will not stop until there is an agrarian reform in Guatemala. No one can stop me, unless they kill me. We are not going to be intimidated, because we are not doing anything illegal."[25]

The other important movement is the Mutual Support Group (GAM), a 1,250 member association of relatives of the disappeared, with clearly no ties to the Christian Democrats.[26] GAM has centered its demands on locating the disappeared and demanding that their captors or murderers be brought to justice. Nineth García, the president of GAM, summarized her position on the Christian Democratic government by stating "we cannot build democracy on a foundation of corpses."[27]

Both these social movements are presenting specific demands with obviously broad appeal. The demands, however, challenge the core of the existing power structure, the landed elites and the military. The plantation owners, for example, view the most modest call for land reform as incendiary because of the precedent it sets and the expectations it raises. Demanding trials for military officers responsible for human rights violations would challenge the unrestricted authority of the army and subject its activities to civilian control. In addition, the trade union movement is becoming revitalized and poses important challenges to the government.

Complicating matters considerably, Guatemala is in the midst of its worst economic crisis in more than fifty years, the result of both internal factors and international economic problems. Falling prices for major export goods, diminishing foreign exchange reserves, skyrocketing debt, scarce new investments, devaluation of the national currency, negative economic growth, sharp inflation rates and increasing unemployment are all part of the panorama in a country long known for its economic stability. In 1985 the per capita gross domestic product plunged to 1971 levels, 40 percent of export earnings were being used to pay the foreign debt, and unemployment had increased five-fold in relation to 1980.

The extent of the economic collapse affects the ability of the Christian Democrats to realize their program. The government must implement measures that alleviate some of the worst effects of the crisis to build even a limited social base. To address the crisis in this way means advocating measures such as structural tax reforms, a more even-handed policy for labor-private capital conflicts, controlling prices, facilitating small business access to credit, creating jobs, and appropriating resources for social services.[28] But measures such as wage increases and price controls would provoke sharp conflicts with business elites whose willingness to have Christian Democrats head the government is conditioned on avoiding measures that restrain their enterprises.

The ongoing repression also continues to plague efforts to implement democratic reforms. The level of violence has risen since the inauguration, particularly in the capital and at times approaches the height of previous levels.

Prospects

The Christian Democrats obviously have a difficult road ahead of them. In their first six months in government, they have made little progress beyond winning approval for an economic package similar to one proposed the year before by the military government. Cerezo stresses, however, that his government is a transitional one, slowly and painstakingly implementing democratic institutions, and that one should not expect rapid change. In line with this, the Christian Democrats might be more successful with the economic policies than in taking steps toward meaningful political or social modifications. Yet without these modifications, the fundamental social problems of Guatemala will not be resolved. The danger is that the Christian Democrats will increasingly be put in a position of carrying out military policies rather than the other way around. Vinicio Cerezo's ability to harmonize a deeply divided and economically polarized society will be greatly tested during his tenure in office.

President Vinicio Cerezo and from left, General Jaime Hernández, then Minister of Defense (now retired); Colonel Roberto Matta, Chief of the Presidential Staff; General Héctor Gramajo, then Army Chief of Staff, currently Defense Minister. Army Day, June 30, 1986. Photograph by Pat Goudvis.

Conditions in Guatemala: The Central Issues of Repatriation

In this chapter, I briefly explore seven issues that together provide a broader context for the three case studies and also offer a framework for assessing the current conditions and future prospects for Guatemalan society. These issues are human rights; military power in civilian spheres; economic conditions; land; the 1985 elections; attitudes toward refugees; and dissent and resistance. The selection of these issues emanated from questions raised by the refugees themselves, interviewed in camps in Mexico.

HUMAN RIGHTS

Guatemala has long been infamous as the hemisphere's worst violator of human rights. As a result, the most fundamental issue continues to be the right to life and safety. For the refugees, whose flight has marked them as suspect, the existence of this right is not an abstract issue. Some sources place the total number of deaths at 50,000 to 75,000 for the period 1978 to 1984.[29] Guatemalan government sources estimate that 100,000 children lost one or both parents to political violence in the early 1980s.[30] And approximately 35,000 people have disappeared at the hands of government security forces over the past two decades.[31]

Since the end of the mass terror under Ríos Montt, repression has been more selective. I make no attempt to comprehensively catalogue this violence here, since the nature and extent of these abuses have been amply documented elsewhere. Nonetheless, the grim results of military terror run through the case studies, threatening at times to overwhelm the reader with the sheer number of incidents. Quite obviously "selective"

GAM demonstration on independence day, September 15, 1986. Photograph by Pat Goudvis.

is a relative term. What is selective compared to Guatemala's past would hardly be considered selective even compared to countries known as the worst human rights violators in Latin America.[32]

The army does not acknowledge involvement in a single murder or disappearance.[33] Nonetheless, among its last acts, the Mejía Víctores government decreed an amnesty to be applied to anyone who was responsible for or committed politically motivated or related crimes during the four years of de facto military government (March 23, 1982–Jan. 14, 1986). Consequently, members of the army and other security forces may not be brought to trial. President Cerezo's position is that the past should be laid to rest: "this is a time for reconciliation, not revenge." In this vein, GAM accuses the new government of taking no major steps to investigate the 1,467 writs of *habeas corpus* (all disappeared family members) submitted by GAM to the Supreme Court as of May 31, 1986.[34]

Some argue that conditions have improved with the inauguration of a civilian government. Available data, however, does not confirm this positive assessment. The threat of violence remains a serious concern since the inauguration of the new civilian government. The risk is real, grave, and persistent. Between January 14 and July 1986, the *Washington Post* reported 700 murders occurred, with the exact number contested as to political motivations and common crime.[35] Some crimes undoubtedly are related to the economic crisis or the social disintegration stemming from decades of governmental violence.[36] Much of the current violence, however, appears politically motivated. In some cases, the far right may be seeking to destabilize the new government. In other cases, indications are that the military continues to utilize torture and political murder as a tool of its counterinsurgency drive.[37] Consequently, much of the violence follows familiar patterns: disappearances; tortured and mutilated bodies left in ravines or along roadsides; public executions on city streets; and no known investigations into the crimes.

Outside the capital reports continue of violence carried out by the army or civil patrols. A June 30, 1986 letter to President Cerezo from the parish of San Pedro, El Estor, in the eastern department of Izabal, feared for the fate of eighty people who resettled a village in March 1986, persuaded by the democratic opening. Since then, three people have been kidnapped; only one has reappeared. One man was killed, and soldiers took seven as guides on a sweep and these men have not been seen again. In addition, an undetermined number of women and children have been murdered, according to the parish. Moreover, there has been a marked increase in killings and disappearances in the south coast after the peasant march to the capital in May 1986.

The macabre nature of many killings fill press accounts. *Prensa Libre*, for example, reported on April 28, 1986 the discovery of a body in

Nueva Concepción whose head and arms had been cut off by machetes. In some cases, the press reports that not all body parts are found. A week earlier *El Grafico* told of the discovery of four bodies in an area of Escuintla. One body was riddled by seven bullets, another by five, and the last two had their heads beaten in as well as being shot. *El Gráfico*, May 22, 1986 related that three disappeared women were found strangled in San Marcos after evidently being tied for a long period. *Prensa Libre* (April 28, 1986) quoted a villager as saying: "The assassinations we're seeing are typical of those carried out by the government of Lucas García."

Disappearances and assassinations continue in the capital as well. While fewer nationally and internationally known leaders have been killed, these murders and disappearances still occur. For example, a fifty-three year-old municipal workers union leader, Justo Rufino Reyes, was knifed to death in the center of Guatemala City on July 23, 1986.[38]

Some operational differences have been stressed by the new government. First, the Christian Democrats are trying to extend civilian influence in the police force and other sections of the Interior Ministry in an effort to counterbalance military domination of the country's security forces.[39] Without subordinating the army to civilian control, however, these steps will at best be limited. Second, there is greater latitude for grass roots organizing, despite the continued repression. While individuals, labor unions, and landless *campesinos* have taken advantage of whatever opening might exist to organize and seek solutions to their grievances, they do so in a continued climate of fear.

Personal Freedoms

The military exercises more subtle forms of control through restrictions on personal freedoms. A well-educated Guatemalan woman with a government job in the capital commented in the midst of an interview: "I never say what I think. In Guatemala, in order to survive, we are taught never to say what we think." A teacher in an elite artistic profession said:

> I wonder if I will ever be able to behave and speak freely again. In my profession we can't be creative. It is psychologically devastating. Perhaps it will take a whole new generation to feel free again. I don't think I ever will. The fear is overwhelming.

She admitted that fear, desperation, frustration, and the resulting deep depression has led her to depend on valium. She said that even when she attends international meetings she is constantly assessing who she should see and what she can say.

In the countryside, military control is more direct and the restraint more pronounced.[40] The military has limited the right to travel and move freely in some areas of the countryside, political expression and religious activism are fraught with danger, and independent collective actions have become associated with "subversion." Moreover, certain Indian communities are subjected to military indoctrination.

Freedom of Movement

The right to travel and move about freely is not uniformly respected, but rather depends on who you are, where you are, and where you are going. If the person is properly documented and going to an unrestricted area, travel is unrestricted. If the person is from Saraxoch, a tightly controlled model village in Alta Verapaz, travel may not be allowed at all. Restrictions on the right to travel for most fall somewhere between these two extremes. In various parts of the country, travellers are stopped to have documents checked or to be questioned regarding their destination or the purpose of their trip.

Passes are required and strictly enforced on all civil patrol age men traveling beyond many municipalities. In some places, residents must go to the municipal office and pay ten cents for each permission slip. In places such as Santa Cruz Barillas, the pass sytem is unusually strict; signed permission is needed to travel virtually anywhere within the municipality.[41] Traveling beyond the municipality, men from Barillas are subject to extra scrutiny at all patrol and army checkpoints. In one observed instance, the army detained a man in Soloma for not having his signed pass, although his friends tried to vouch for him. The risk in not having one's "papers in order" is substantial; there are at least twenty-six potential checkpoints on the bus route between Barillas and the department capital, a distance of about 120 kilometers.

In the Ixcán area, both the army and patrol commanders must sign papers permitting travel or excusing one from patrol duty. As described in the case study, Ixcán residents are consistently subject to thorough army checks. No one travels at night under any circumstances, not even the soldiers, according to residents.

Residents of Ax'ctumbal ("La Pista") stated that permission was needed to travel even to the neighboring marketplace in Nebaj. In the Ixil, patrollers routinely checked all men's papers at roadblocks and sometimes searched luggage as well, and residents are especially self-restrained regarding their movements. Peasants in Acul mentioned that those with lands far away know that they are "not allowed" to travel there and that certain hillsides are off-limits to gather firewood. Informants reported that army representatives, whether uniformed or not, were always present in the markets and on roads leading to conflict areas to monitor the amount of food carried by any one person.

Peasants throughout the country claimed travel at night was dangerous, although less so than during the mass terror, when "the streets were absolutely empty by 4:00 or 5:00 pm." In Santiago Atitlán (department of Sololá) informants maintained cultivating fields far from town was dangerous in late 1985; two men had disappeared collecting firewood earlier in the year.

Travel restrictions affect women differently than men. Women are expected to carry passes and papers but are checked less often.[42] Despite this relative leniency, women face the additional fear of rape and other sexual abuse by soldiers, especially if they are traveling alone or in isolated areas.

Freedom of Political and Religious Expression

Guatemalans are more willing to comment on the economic situation than on political matters. Even during the height of the 1985 election campaign, people were generally reluctant to state their political party affiliation or candidate preference for local or national elections. Informal party meetings went on in San Mateo, but involved mostly the close friends of the local candidates themselves.

In the Department of El Quiché, where the Catholic Church had been most active in the 1960s and 1970s, many catechists — active lay church workers — still feel vulnerable (14 priests and hundreds of catechists have been assassinated) and Catholic services are said to be monitored by military informers (Americas Watch, 1983:253). Typical of military sentiment, an Evangelical church worker cooperating in government-sponsored community work accused Catholics of "sowing bad seeds, from which you can only expect bad fruit." The military's stand on religion seems to be that "there will be guarantees in religious profession so long as it does not go against the interests of the State" (Cifuentes, 1982).

Other Restrictions on Activity and Time

Membership in various associations is considered dangerous. Trade unions have traditionally existed in the capital city but were severely repressed, leaving many union leaders dead or in exile. Although the labor movement is slowly reviving, members remain apprehensive.

Army recruiting can blatantly violate notions of due process regarding conscription. The army comes to major market towns to round up the young men who come for the market day. In one case, soldiers boarded a highland bound bus to abduct two young men traveling home.

The soldiers yelled to the surprised but helpless witnesses "tell their mothers they're in the army now." In another instance, soldiers patrolled the streets and stopped outbound buses following the high school graduation day in the departmental capital of Huehuetenango, seizing young men of likely age. Only through exceptional means, such as the intervention of a school official or an authoritative religious person, can forced conscription be averted.

Many people commented on the personality transformation during military training. Young Indian boys conform to boot camp and return to their communities hardened (*duro*), troubled and discontented. A common problem is alcoholism among former soldiers and an inability to reintegrate into the community.[43]

Government Imposed Ideological Education

As a sophisticated component of its counterinsurgency program, the army carries out psychological operations, including required "re-education" —political/ideological indoctrination activities directed at the local population. These activities are especially widespread in the Ixcán and Alta Verapaz (Playa Grande and Chisec development poles). One army document recommended that public education in the Ixil should "include a 50 percent [emphasis on] civic struggle (lucha cívica) and ideological war, in the instructional programs in the area." Along with that the military should also "investigate the ideology of the teachers in the three *municipios*" (Cifuentes, 1982). Given that the Ixiles do not feel a part of the Guatemalan nation, the document goes on to suggest that it is "imperative . . . to adopt an intense, profound and well thought out psychological campaign that would rescue the Ixil's mentality until they are made to feel a part of the Guatemalan nation." Another useful tool is the "establishment of a radio that transmits, in the Ixil language, programs of interest to the region and of course [programs that include] elements of civic character."

The S-5 section of the army, in charge of these and other "civilian affairs", runs daily programs for all men of civil patrol age in targeted villages. The S-5 specialists discuss anticommunism, patriotism, civic duty, and the fallacy of the guerrillas who lied to people and brought about their misfortune. Attendance is mandatory, and men fear missing the programs.

The army produces large quantities of propaganda with the basic message: "the army is your friend". Newspapers and T.V. carry stories designed to improve the army's image, such as soldiers distributing goods to *campesinos*.

Although personal freedoms, particularly physical movement, have improved as the war in the countryside has subsided, most respondents fear a return to compulsory duties or a strong army presence.

MILITARY POWER IN CIVILIAN SPHERES

The Guatemalan army has penetrated community life as never before throughout rural Guatemala. Its control is maintained both through its direct physical presence in a community and through institutions it has created. The main institutions are the *Patrullas de Autodefensa Civil* (PAC or civil patrol), the system of *Polos de Desarrollo* (Regional Centers of Development or development poles), the *Coordinadora Interinstitucional* (IIC or Interinstitutional Coordinator), and networks of informers that report to the military. Army control is such that the local military officer and his civilian proxies can determine the entire tenor of daily life in a rural village.

Civic act at Saraxoch, an "Antisubversive Village, Ideologically New," Alta Verapaz, August 1986. Photograph by Pat Goudvis.

Although the army has held formal power in Guatemala for most of the past three decades, until recently its presence was comparatively weak in most rural communities. The *comisionado militar* (military commissioner) a local civilian charged with filling the local draft quota and involved in passing intelligence information, served as the principal military representative. Highland towns and villages were able to maintain a degree of autonomy in their economic and social organization, employing traditional Indian power structures to resolve conflicts and manage village life. Local civil authorities such as the mayors were elected or chosen through discussion and community assent. Moreover, voluntary organizations such as the Catholic Action movement and cooperatives and peasant leagues began appearing in many villages in the past thirty to forty years.

The army has sought to penetrate and control highland communities involved in strong grass roots organizing or suspected of providing support for the armed insurgents. Since the early 1980s, the military has established garrisons and outposts in some communities with which they previously had little contact. The army base is situated in the center of town in Nebaj and Barillas; in others it is located just outside the village, often on a hill overlooking it, as in Cotzal and many of the model villages.

Civil Patrol System

The civil patrol system is a critical military instrument for retaining control of the population in the countryside. Formally, the justification for the civil patrol is that it allows the villagers to protect themselves from the guerrillas. The system, however, serves primarily to control the men who have to participate and to monitor the activities of the rest of the population, allowing the army to concentrate on other military activities.

Since patrollers must show up for duty and report travel to the civil patrol commander, their own activities are closely monitored. As a result of patrolling, work details, and periodic sweeps in conflict areas, two to three days a week can be spent in supervised activities. Moreover, civil patrol commanders admit spies are placed in patrol groups to inform on subversive tendencies.

While a few supported the official position that the service is voluntary, evidence indicates the service is mandated.[44] The usual twenty-four hour shift falls anywhere from every five days to every three months, depending on local circumstances. Enforcement, which varies throughout the country, is strictest in conflict areas, especially when the army is not present at all times. In the eastern part of the country, for example, the civil patrols are relatively "flojo" (not strict) while in the Ixcán, and other development pole regions, the obligation is rigidly enforced. In one

Army detachment in Sacapula's main square 1983. Sign reads: Only he who fights has the right to conquer, only he who conquers has the right to live. Photograph by Christian Garcia.

major army-occupied town in the Petén, the duties barely exist, while in the surrounding villages the army rigorously enforces patrol service.

The army or civil patrol commander must give permission for a patroller to miss a turn, ostensibly to "make sure that when someone leaves, the village will enjoy adequate protection." When permission is granted to leave town, the patroller must find a replacement and return within the allotted time. More often than not, slots are traded with kin or friends given the economic situation. If no one can do it, patrollers pay the replacement from one *quetzal* (daily wage for agricultural work in the highlands) to five or more *quetzales* per turn. Punishments for missing a turn without permission vary with the civil patrol commanders. Sometimes the offender is made to do petty tasks or must spend a day or more in jail. A common punishment in 1982 and 1983 was to be placed in a pit of water for several hours.

Typical patrol duty consists of guarding the town or village entrances, checking the identification and belongings of everyone entering and reporting anything suspicious to the civil patrol commander, who in turn reports to the nearest army base.[45] Additionally, periodic sweeps are carried out through the surrounding countryside to route out guerrillas.[46]

There have been some reported cases of the army forcing patrollers to use violence against their neighbors or lose their own lives. Several unrelated sources in the Ixil reported incidents in which the army ordered patrollers to burn houses and crops and to kill refugees. A refugee from Rabinal tells how the army killed a man for refusing to rape the wife of his neighbor. At other times, civil patrol violence can stem from personal conflicts or greed.

A requisite of the job of civil patrol commander is literacy. These commanders are directly accountable to the army and must make weekly reports on the local situations to the closest army installation. The time-consuming duties of the post limit other activities and constant contact with the military pressures such men to keep their communities "in line." This pressure may cause them to act in repressive ways against their own people, which delegitimizes previous community roles such as religious advisor or community arbitrator.

The civil patrol commander, as a proxy for the army, has wide-ranging powers. He decides whether and how to punish a patroller who misses a turn, and his endorsement of a claim that someone supports the insurgents can be equivalent to a death sentence. The impact this post has on a specific community depends a great deal on the individual who fills it. Some civil patrol commanders and military commissioners take advantage of their power to enrich themselves on the land, animals, or goods of those who have fled, been murdered, or are too frightened to complain. Some make use of the power to rape women without fearing reprisal.

The military rarely takes action against its appointed representatives in the civil patrol, even when their abuses are excessive. When punishment does occur, informants complained of light sentences. In Sololá, a group of military commissioners had practiced extortion, denouncing more than fourteen people who the army subsequently killed. Despite attempts by these commissioners to terrorize them into silence, the people of the town protested and the men were finally brought to trial. The army, however, sentenced them to less than two years in jail and has now cut back on the punishments, releasing several of the guilty. One informant said: "The army puts them in and takes them out, then decides on their replacements. The people don't matter at all."

Guatemalans in the countryside prefer not to discuss the military or political implications of the civil patrol. Since the system is officially in place to protect them from the guerrillas, criticisms could be construed as an expression of support for the opposition.

Informants claim that patrollers may be taken to the city to seek out and denounce refugees from their home communities. In late April 1986, a displaced person living in the capital was dragged from his home in the early morning. His wife recognized one of the abductors as someone from their home village, according to informants. Using the civil patrol in this way adds to the climate of distrust and fear.

A worker for a private development agency contended the civil patrol system and other work requirements have caused an increase in hunger in the highland communities. Less time is left for men to work the fields or seek paid work in the area. Moreover, travel restrictions and the high cost of finding a replacement for missed patrol duties have disrupted migration to the coast.

The army instituted a variety of involuntary work projects in addition to patrol duty in the highlands in 1982 and 1983. The leading project was road construction and maintenance, clearing the forest for 100 meters on either side of the road. These tasks involved hundreds of villagers for months, since the work had to be done with basic hand tools. In the development poles, people have also been put to work building model villages.

When these plans were put into effect, the work was to be rewarded with food in the *Alimentos por Trabajo* (Food for Work) program. While some food appears to have arrived sporadically in 1982 and 1983, the forced work continues in some places but without compensation. Villagers are compelled to fix roads, labor at military bases, build latrines, repair cemeteries, create parks, make community wells (*pilas*) and shelters for washing clothes, pick up garbage in the streets, or any other task the commander may want done. An army commander in Huehuetenango commented that these projects keep villagers from "lounging around".

As major infrastructure projects are completed (roads, model villages), and the civil patrol system is well under way, some of the harsher service requirements usually have been loosened. The army is moving out of certain areas, cutting down on the forced labor and allowing civil patrol groups (*pelotones*) to divide so that the men serve only half as many turns. But in the Ixcán and the Ixil areas and other places where the armed opposition appears strong, the civil patrols and work brigades are stringently enforced.

Since the 1985 presidential and congressional elections, the civil patrol has come under criticism, most consistently by the congressman from Chimaltenango. He claims that the patrollers "are forced to do vigilance turns . . . without arms or adequate equipment . . . Many have died due to inclement weather." He has called for a dissolution of the entire system. The press reported that the Congress was discussing making the service "voluntary" in response to these demands. The army holds, however, that "It is almost impossible that the civil patrols disappear, at least for the next few years because for many peasants it is their security. Without the civil patrol they are left to the mercy of the guerrillas" (El Gráfico, May 13, 1986).

Development Poles and Model Villages*

As part of the six *Polos de Desarrollo* (Regional Centers of Development), the army has planned forty nine model villages. Thirty three were either under construction or completed as of early 1985, housing about 40 percent of a projected 60,000 people. These villages are newly constructed, generally on the sites of villages destroyed in the counterinsurgency campaign. They are under army supervision, including the layout, the assigning of residences, and the provision of building materials[47] and the army is generally present or able to reach these villages rapidly.[48] Physically, the new villages are quite unlike those that have been destroyed. In a typical community the houses were spread throughout a valley or hillside, each surrounded by a field of corn; the model village houses lie on a centralized grid with streets running between rows of two houses.

The development poles are situated in the zones where the insurgency was strongest and generally serve as relocation sites for the displaced and will likely house the refugees returning from Mexico. In the Ixcán, where most of the former residents were either killed or are refugees in Mexico, many of the inhabitants are new settlers, lured by the promise of land.

---

*See also Appendix D.

The model villages are designed to regroup the population in more concentrated and easily controlled population centers. A further goal is to address the problems that fueled the strong social movements of the last decade and to rechannel these energies into the army's model of development. The military claims this program will modernize the agriculture of these "marginal" areas and link them to the national economy. The reality, however, has fallen far short of these goals. In fact, the inhabitants of the development poles are noticeably impoverished even within the context of Guatemala.

The residents of the model villages enjoy little fredom: the location of their homes is drawn from a hat, they often are prohibited from going to the land they once farmed or traveling freely in search of work or markets. In the Ixil area, the army continues to forcibly bring in internal refugees and settle them in the new villages. There, as in the Ixcán, people may be restricted from leaving the villages to resettle in their original sites.

Because of the destruction and threat of further violence, it is difficult for the residents of these villages to be self-sufficient. Families must often rely on handouts from governmental agencies or the generosity of a few religious workers permitted to operate in the regions.[49] A heavy dose of paternalism permeates many projects. One government employee remarked:

> We must force the Indians to work on our projects or else they will never appreciate what we are doing for them. But they are so stupid. Even when they have slaved away building a playground, they still, the very next day, steal the tires we used for swings to make themselves sandals.

The most striking aspects of the model villages were the regimentation and lack of resources, even in those used as "models" for the foreign press corps.[50] Compared to their previous lifestyles, villagers enjoy *less* access to land and resources, personal freedoms are curtailed, participation in community matters has decreased and cottage industry which might allow self-sufficiency is lacking. The army cites physical improvements such as roads, electricity, and potable water, but these changes hardly compensate for broader deficiencies. As one Indian woman said, "What do we need electricity for? So we can watch our children starve to death at night?!"

Interinstitutional Coordinators

The system of Interinstitutional Coordinators (See Figure 1) potentially allows the army to oversee all development work taking place throughout the country, although it has not always worked in practice. These coordinators are committees charged with directing the resources of public and private agencies toward activities in rural communities. As such, the army is informed of and can channel the distribution of the funding and materials provided by both governmental and private (including international) agencies and has veto power over the implementation of almost all development projects. To more effectively execute these responsibilities, the army has formed a new department parallel with intelligence, operations, logistics, and personnel. The national head of this new section, termed Civilian Affairs and Local Development (ACDL), presides over the highest level of interinstitutional coordination, along with the army's chief-of-staff.

In each of the country's twenty-two departments there is another coordinator, presided over by the local military commander, generally a colonel heading a battalion. The secretary is the commanding officer of the ACDL company of that battalion.[51] On the municipal and rural levels, the hierarchy changes: mayors preside over the coordinators with the local military commander serving as secretary. The aim is to decentralize development administration and incorporate representatives from the community, private development and service organizations, and public-sector personnel. In this way, the army claims it is involving local community members in decision making and breaking with the paternalism of the old civic action program. Supervision and evaluation of the entire program, however, remains a military responsibility.[52]

The military maintains that the IIC is the "most effective tool in the government's work." Although in theory the Interinstitutional Coordinators function in the entire country, to date their work has concentrated on development poles located in the most conflict-ridden departments. It also contends that the development poles and "the voluntary civil defense patrols will protect [the people], and the Interinstitutional Coordinators will make them progress. In sum: Security and Development." (Ejército de Guatemala, 1985a)

In the areas studied, the primary decision-making power lies with the departmental coordinator. At this level, and in some of the towns, the Coordinating Committee meets on a weekly or monthly basis. The local army representative or the army-appointed mayors preside over the meetings. In Huehuetenango the newly installed commander was beginning to "sit in" on the meetings rather than openly direct them, but participants were convinced that projects he vetoes would not be carried out.

In San Mateo Ixtatán, Cotzal and many smaller towns and villages, the coordinating system has been reduced to infrequent meetings of the powerful men in the community. Once government pressure to submit development proposals waned, the structure of the IIC seems to have col-

FIGURE 1
GUATEMALA: INTERINSTITUTIONAL COORDINATORS, 1985

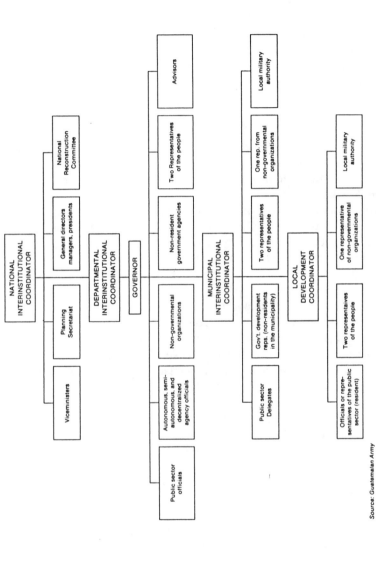

Source: *Guatemalan Army*

lapsed. Since the election, the government has announced that department governors will head the department coordinators. The change, however, may be largely cosmetic. Given the power and presence of the military, they will likely continue to be informed of all activities and could determine the course of development. As an S-5 (Army Civilian Affairs) captain said in an interview: "After the elections, we shall be able to maintain our influence through the Interinstitutional Coordinators and the National Reconstruction Committee, since we control the funding."

Military Presence

In towns and villages where the army is present, the local military commander usurps the responsibilities traditionally held by civilian powers. As a religious worker said, "Whoever the commander is, he becomes a little tyrant, involving himself in everything. Not even our shadows fall outside his domination. He puts himself in charge of everything—social, civil, or judicial." As the arbiter not only of official power (until January 1986 the army *was* the government), but physical power (commanding troops and weapons), the local army commander is effectively the ultimate authority.

Villagers are often uncertain as to what is acceptable under a certain official. One resident military commander, for example, may carefully investigate any denunciations brought before him and spend most of his time organizing soccer matches between the army and the civil patrol teams. The following month, his replacement may view missing a civil patrol turn as an offense meriting a beating or an even stricter punishment.

The army has pulled out of villages and towns, where it feels its control is secure. Nonetheless, these areas are still subject to periodic military occupations and spot checks.

ECONOMIC CONDITIONS

The health of the Guatemalan economy is critical for social stability and the issue of repatriation for two reasons. First, economic instability means political instability, and thus the likelihood of increased repression. An unhealthy economy exacerbates the already considerable political tensions and conflicts in the country, forces the government into increasingly unpopular measures, and provides the rationale for the army to become an implementer of supposed order. Second, the economic crisis slows the reintegration of refugees into the economy by providing few employment opportunities and poor markets for what the refugees produce.

The 1960s and 1970s were decades of impressive economic growth. The production of goods and services expanded over 5 percent annually (in real terms) and the real domestic product per capita, slowed by a 3 percent population growth, climbed 50 percent between 1960 and 1980. Despite economic expansion, Guatemala saw increasing inequality in income distribution. The income share of the poorest 20 percent slipped from 6.8 percent in 1970 to 4.8 percent in 1984 (see Table I).

TABLE 1
Income Distribution (in percentages)

	1970	1980	1984
Wealthiest 20%	46.5	55.0	56.8
30% above the mean	29.3	25.0	24.9
30% below the mean	17.4	14.5	13.5
Poorest 20%	6.8	5.5	4.8

Source: Inforpress, 1985:19

Today Guatemala is in its worst economic crisis since the Great Depression, squeezed between a collapse in exports and a weak domestic economy. The result has been negative economic "growth" in three out of four years between 1981 and 1985. In 1986 gross domestic product per capita slid back to the level of 1971, eroding half of the growth achieved since 1950. The public debt (internal and external combined) was over Q5.3 billion and the cost of living, according to the Minister of the Economy, jumped 38 percent (*El Gráfico*, May 28 and 29, 1986). The foreign debt alone exceeds Q2.6 billion and will require over 40 percent of the value of the country's exports to service in 1986. At the same time, Guatemala has lost Q1.2 billion in projected export earnings (*Prensa Libre*, May 7, 1986 and *Latinamerica Press*, December 19, 1985).

Guatemala sold most of its gold reserves in mid-1985, unofficially devalued the national currency several times, and lifted consumer protection ceilings on many basic goods. The price of oil skyrocketed, nearly prompting a coup d'etat in June 1985. In addition, increases in urban bus transportation, milk, and bread contributed to riots and government worker strikes in September of the same year. Prices of basic staples have soared (See Table II).

Under these circumstances funding for social programs will be difficult to generate. In addition, seeking funds through major tax reforms presents problems. Only 18 percent of the federal budget is covered by direct tax revenues, one of the lowest in the world.[53] Despite raising tax reform during the campaign, Cerezo, at least for now, has limited his efforts to imposing a one-year windfall tax on export earnings.[54] His need to maintain already tenuous private sector support has made him reluctant to pursue a bolder economic program.

TABLE II
Prices of Staples (in pounds)

	1975	1985	1986	1985–1986 % increases
corn	0.11	0.16	0.25	56%
beans	0.20	0.45	0.65	44%
rice	–	0.25	0.45	80%
sugar	–	0.20	0.35	75%
chicken	–	1.29	1.65	28%
salt	–	0.12	0.20	66%

Source: El Gráfico, May 4, 1986

International loans present other problems, especially in the medium and long-term, as the debt burden expands. Although the government recently received congressional approval for $287 million in new foreign loans, business generally opposes measures that increase the country's indebtedness. In addition, IMF conditions, which influence many governmental and private loan decisions, include reduced social spending, eliminating public subsidies, wage controls and policies that favor the export sector (at the expense of the internal market in countries like Guatemala), precisely the kinds of measures that exacerbate the effects of the crisis for the poor. While the government has refused so far to cut public sector spending, it has met other IMF demands, namely, lifting a variety of protectionist measures and devaluing the *quetzal*. Nonetheless, loans have been less abundant than hoped for, in part because the U.S. has other priorities in Central America.

Guatemala's social indicators are grim: 35.7 percent of the population does not satisfy its basic needs and an additional 39.9 percent have less than a minimum diet, leaving only 24.4 percent above the poverty line (see Table III). Moreover, 82 percent of children under five are malnourished, and Indians suffer an infant mortality rate of 134 deaths per 1,000 live births, as well as a life expectancy of only 41 years (compared to an average of 59 years for the overall population) (Oxfam, 1984).

TABLE III
Standard of Living[55]

Less than minimum diet	39.9%
Not satisfying basic needs	35.7%
Not poor	24.4%

Rural Guatemalans have always relied on a variety of means to produce necessities and to generate enough income for survival, including farming, weaving, seasonal migration, and selling goods in the market. The economic crisis combined with the counterinsurgency and its aftermath have disrupted these activities. The most common complaint voiced throughout the country is "there is simply no work." Even if Indians could migrate to the south coast as often as they wished, there are not enough jobs on the plantations to absorb them. The south coast is flooded with landless and displaced people who form a permanent labor pool. While some plantation owners continue to contract laborers from the highlands, others rely on the local landless *jornaleros*, or day laborers.[56] In addition, lands have been taken out of production, and others transferred from coffee or sugar cane to less labor intensive activities such as cattle or corn production.

Wages are either down or at best have remained constant. The highest wages on the south coast are Q3.00 and Q4.00 per day, if transportation and food are not provided, although informants frequently reported wages of Q2.00 a day.

This lack of cash means foregoing essentials such as medicines, tools, and even beans, and certainly "luxuries" such as coffee, meat, or new clothing. With real income down, many described cutting back on their normally minimal variety of food, reducing the daily diet at times to corn tortillas, salt, and *hierbas* (wild greens).[57]

Although employment statistics tend to be optimistic and unreliable, the economic crisis has obviously taken its toll. Between 1980 and 1984 underemployment rose from 29 percent to 32.9 percent of the work force

Girl selling in the Chinique market, El Quiché, 1983. Photography by author.

and unemployment has soared from 2.2 percent to 10.5 percent (Inforpress, 1985:18).

In the past, the purchase of chemical fertilizer was one way to increase yields. Skyrocketing prices, however, have made it prohibitive for the vast majority (fertilizer is now five or six times 1984 prices). Increases in tool prices, transportation costs, and travel restrictions further limit access to profitable markets. Moreover, the loss of one or more harvests during the period of mass violence still burdens displaced or resettling families.[58]

In the area hardest hit by the counterinsurgency, the peasants are operating from a smaller than average material base. The army, for example, slaughtered or stole many domestic animals. Replacing resources is difficult, given the drop in real income. The general economic deterioration has also meant that peasant families are more likely to sell their remaining animals, lowering their consumption of meat, milk, and eggs.

Survival increasingly depends on formerly auxiliary activities. In forested regions, firewood gathering can net seventy-five cents per day, but army travel restrictions can limit this possibility. Coveted government-sponsored roadwork is rotated among communities in fifteen day stints (for a total of Q38.00). Women who previously wove traditional fabrics and clothing only for themselves and their families, now produce to sell in already saturated markets. Women also sell tortillas and *atole* or their own *huipil*.[59]

Temporary migration to the capital city is an option increasingly relied upon by highland communities. Domestic servants and petty trading are two common occupations. Neither is reliable or lucrative. Those peddling gum, sweets, or pens, take a risk since anyone caught without the proper license (difficult and costly to obtain) is subject to fines. If one has been displaced for political reasons, arrest can have serious consequences.[60]

The overall economic situation is particularly acute for widows. In larger towns and department capitals displaced widows swell the ranks of the unemployed and underemployed seeking work. Their choices are limited by few skills, many children, and the stigma of having lost a husband "in the violence." In addition, the coastal environment is especially difficult. A religious worker observed: "The women hate to go, recognizing they might lose a child because of the tropical climate and insufficient food, but they find themselves with absolutely no alternative."

Rising oil and gasoline prices inflate prices both on basic goods and transportation.[61] A bus ride to the department capital from San Mateo is Q9.00 round trip and Q17.00 round trip to Guatemala City. As a result, travel whether to settle a bureaucratic issue, visit a relative, or sell woven goods, is a significant financial burden.

Other services remain insufficient or nonexistent. The credit cooperatives of the 1970s have vanished and BANDESA, the government farmer credit institution provides limited assistance. A National Reconstruction Committee (CRN) official observed: "The required collateral to receive credit from BANDESA is land, and BANDESA does not grant credit to buy land, therefore there is a vicious cycle that never permits access to credit." Moreover, advances from locally based contractors for future work on coastal plantations is generally no longer available.

Resource shortages and military imposed restrictions can converge, causing a further erosion in the standard of living. In the town of Xix (municipality of Chajul, Quiché) the military instructed the population not to rebuild their destroyed town until they could do it according to the army specified model village plan for the area. Without the material resources to comply, the population was forced to live in marginal, temporary, and crowded housing for all of 1985.

LAND

Land in Guatemala is crucial: the rural population depends on land for survival, and land is the basis of the country's export economy. The distribution of land, however, is so skewed that the United States Agency for International Development (1982) characterized the inequality as "more serious than in any other country of Central or South America." Farms of 450 hectares or more, 1 percent of all holdings, accounted for 34 percent of cultivated land, according to the 1979 data. In contrast, 54.2 percent of all holdings, 288,083 parcels of under 1.4 hectares, account for only 4.1 percent of farm area.[62]

Present land holdings continue to decline. Access to arable land per capita declined from 1.71 hectares in 1950 to .79 hectares in 1980. As a result, 88 percent of farms were sub-family size, or too small to provide for the needs of a family in 1979.[63] Moreover, an estimated 309,119 agricultural laborers were landless. Another estimate has put that number at 419,620 landless laborers in 1980, a figure that has likely grown since then (U.S. AID, 1982:83 and Inforpress, 1986).

The landless have become concentrated in unprecedented numbers in the south coast. An estimated 100,000 peasants, displaced by violence from their communities, have settled there. In addition, between 260,000 to 400,000 peasants continue seasonal migrations to the coastal plantations each year. Not surprisingly, the "March for Land" in late April

1986 began in the department of Escuintla, the heart of the south coast.

The AID study indicates that there are 369,467 hectares of land available for distribution, mainly in the isolated lowlands of El Petén and El Quiché. Ironically, the amount of *idle arable* lands on large private holdings was approximately 1.2 million hectares, (U.S. AID, 1983:52) while the land needed for the landless population is 1,205,566 hectares (*Ibid*: 83).

Within the land tenure context, the field research points to several different patterns in the holding and use of land in the Indian regions following the large-scale displacement of the early 1980s. These patterns affecting the refugees, fall into the following broad categories:

1. abandoned land available for the original owner (or anyone else) to claim.

Peasants in the south coast, at a Nueva Concepción rally demanding land, July 1986. Photography by Pat Goudvis.

2. land farmed by relatives or neighbors from the same community. These new people may consider the land on temporary "loan," or may consider it permanently theirs.
3. abandoned land, classified as "off-limits" by the army.
4. land seized by army officials, local authorities or others.
5. land used by the army to resettle abandoned areas and repopulate villages.

1. Abandoned Land, Possibly Available

This situation is the least troublesome and unfortunately the least common for returning refugees wishing to regain their original holdings. In northeastern Huehuetenango, many villages remain abandoned although some villages (such as Poblado) are unlikely to remain abandoned much longer.

2. Land Farmed by Relatives and Neighbors of Original Occupants

A general finding in the field research is that others within the community or nearby relatives utilize land belonging to those who were killed or fled. People commonly stated this land was farmed on loan (*prestado*), because it had original owners. The possibility remains, however, that the borrowers may not want to cede the land to returnees for reasons either of need, prejudice against those who fled, or simple greed.

In San Mateo villages, small groups of three to ten families have been able to return to their lands without problems. The key factors were an absence of only a few months and a return during a period of demographic flux, a time when no suspicion was cast on anyone who had fled temporarily.

3. Land Marked as "Off Limits" by the Army

The army has prohibited the cultivation of large tracts of land located in conflict areas. This prohibition applies to areas in the nothern part of the Ixil, sections of Ixcán, and parts of the Petén. In the municipality of Nebaj, the army permits access to only six villages out of an original thirty.

Unofficially, many restrictions exist regarding access to land throughout the highlands. Informants would often explain that certain lands were considered too far away and therefore unsafe. Given these restrictions, peasants were unlikely to venture alone to lands declared off limits. In several villages in the municipalities of Nebaj and Cotzal, people were allowed to travel every day to plant fields, yet had no permission to resettle. Sometimes civil patrollers would accompany them.

Some "off-limits" land is becoming accessible once again, especially in the Ixil area. In the municipality of Nebaj, an enthusiastic local official reported the army had just declared Palop open for resettlement. This meant that it was now "pacified" territory which the army felt adequate to "protect". He predicted that Palop residents who fled as far away as Huehuetenango would shortly get word and return.

4. Land Seized by Army or Other Officials

Rumors abound of recent land seizures by large landholders (*finqueros*), special police forces (*judiciales*), or the army. Because of the difficulties of obtaining accurate information only several cases could be documented.[64] In the model village San Felipe Chenlá (Cotzal, Quiché), the president of the local reconstruction committee (the base level of the Interinstitutional Coordinator structure) sought to obtain 100 *cuerdas* of land to pass on to his children. This individual, not originally from the town, apparently threatened former residents who might return from Mexico. In Pojom, an infamous civil patrol commander rearranged land holdings to take advantage of the best coffee land. He is accused in the death of at least six returning refugees who he denounced as "subversive" to the army base in Ixquisis.

5. Land Is Part of Army Resettlement Campaign: New Occupants Are Living on the Land

The army has undertaken an extensive campaign to resettle abandoned lands with several objectives. Resettlement improves the military's image (the national press highlights army land distribution) and relationship with people in need of land. INTA (the National Institute of Agrarian Transformation) reportedly has awarded some 2000 titles "to peasants in the most conflictive areas" (Latinamerica Press, December 19, 1985). Moreover, resettling deserted or destroyed villages helps "cover up" physical evidence of the large-scale violence. Finally, analysts cite the deliberate mixing of ethnic groups as part of the larger counterinsurgency strategy (Black, 1985). As one informant said, "[these lands] are being deliberately resettled by the army with those they have handpicked, who will stay there on army terms and replace those who the army considered 'troublemakers'."

The government is currently implementing this policy for the most part in the Ixcán and Petén regions. In some cases, a nationwide call has gone out for new settlers, advertised mostly by radio, and other times a specific target population is approached via direct contact through the auxiliary mayors.

In Río Seco, a village of San Mateo Ixtatán, the original inhabitants fled following a massacre in 1982, and have remained in Mexico. The army invited residents from another San Mateo village to resettle in late 1984 and these villagers have done so. The municipal mayor asserted the original owners should have the right to the land, but rumors maintained the army was giving new residents documentation, complicating the situation if the original inhabitants return.

Chacaj, municipality of Nentón, was a village destroyed and rebuilt as the department's only "development pole". Although the army intended the town for 10,000 returning refugees from Mexico, presumably including Chacaj's original inhabitants, the project did not succeed as planned. By early 1985, new settlers were being recruited in villages throughout Nentón and San Mateo. Lured by promises of free land, housing and electricity, many such villagers went and some remained.

The entire population of Xalbal, a village settlement in the Ixcán region, fled during the widespread massacres throughout the area. The village was resettled in 1984 with new residents from different parts of the country, typical of abandoned villages throughout the Ixcán. Seven or eight language groups may now live side by side in the area.

Other Observations Regarding Land and Land Policy in Study Areas

Most of the refugees' land officially being resettled was colonized national land. Articles 114 and 115 of the INTA bylaws state that land claims can be lost if the land is "voluntarily abandoned" or if a settler "abandons indefinitely the home without justified cause." A study done by the *Programa de Ayuda para los Vecinos del Altiplano* (PAVA), (1984) notes potential problems for refugees wishing to return because of INTA guidelines stipulating that "land that is abandoned for more than one year, automatically becomes property of the government."[65] This observation is confirmed by a May 1986 article in the Guatemala press stating that INTA would be giving away land in the Ixcán abandoned for more than one year (La Palabra, May 6, 1986).

Another problem for the refugees in reclaiming land is the lack of titles or other documentation. For many, titles were never necessary and seldom procured. For others, municipal records of such titles were lost in the destruction of government buildings during the violence, making the trace of these records in the departmental capital or offices in Guatemala City a difficult endeavor.[66] In the Ixcán region, many government titles were issued in the name of cooperatives which no longer function, but whose surviving members might lay claim to those lands (see Ixcán section).

ELECTIONS: CAMPAIGN, CANDIDATES, AND VOTING

Vinicio Cerezo Arévalo, a Christian Democrat, was elected president in a two-round voting process and inaugurated on January 14, 1986.[67] During the fieldwork, the elections were constantly apparent and their conduct on a local level gives some sense of the extent of involvement or lack of it in the communities studied. Eight parties in all were represented, the major contenders being the Christian Democrats (DC), the Union of the National Center (UCN), the Democratic Party of National Cooperation/ Revolutionary Party (PDCN-PR), and the National Liberation Movement/Democratic Institutional Party (MLN-PID). In the second round of elections for president the field was narrowed to the UCN and the DC.

The presidential candidates' propaganda penetrated even isolated villages, where children picked up the parties' theme songs from incessant playing on the radio. The candidates, especially from the major parties, visited most of the larger towns in the country. Beforehand the public relations workers would place announcements and fliers all over town to attract a crowd. At the rallies, the presidential or vice presidental candidates along with local candidates would make speeches promising benefits such as paved roads and improved schools. None of the speeches witnessed were translated into the local languages.

Despite the deluge of publicity afforded the presidential elections, people rarely spoke of them unless questioned directly. Respondents generally reflected an awareness that change was necessary but also a sense of personal powerlessness. Most restricted criticisms of the military government to its economic blunders. A shopkeeper in Huehuetenango proclaimed: "A civilian government is what we need to help the economy. The military doesn't know how to manage the economy. They don't know how to govern, only how to make soldiers." A peasant in the same department remarked, "the economic crisis is really bad. A new government will change it. Anyone who gets in has got to be better than what we've had."

Informants predicted a clean and fair electoral process, though widespread doubt was expressed that the elections would alter their situation in any meaningful way. One informant complained, "Politicians never do anything for the *campesino*. They are like a hoe; everything gets pulled toward them. They promise and promise and then forget us as soon as they're in the Palace." Others recalled the voting for General Lucas García in 1978: "Lucas came up here and mumbled a few words in our language and said, 'Look, I am an Indian like you, vote for me!' and many people believed him and voted for him, and what did he do but kill us?" A middle class man from the capital said, "The army controls all the power and all the wealth. They like it that way," and a municipal official said, "The government has always lied to us. We have suffered a lot of deceit." When a *ladina* shopkeeper in Quiché was asked if she would vote, she laughed and said no, she didn't care which thief was in the Palace. Interviewed shortly after the 1985 earthquake in Mexico, she said, "You know who would make the best president for Guatemala? One of those dogs that are saving people in Mexico City!"

Massive leafletting by most of the political parties led to houses displaying the propaganda of three or four different candidates. Despite this, many people living outside the major cities, including military commissioners, could name only one or two, if any, of the national candidates. Official party platforms were not released until a few weeks before the voting and those that were published contained little more than generalized statements in favor of democracy and economic development. These platforms were generally available only in Spanish.[68]

The press routinely described the Christian Democrats as sympathetic to the left, some commentators accusing them of being communist. Although the party enjoys the support of many Guatemalans, the last six years of violence are never far from consciousness, thus many were unwilling to link themselves to it (or other parties) before the results were in. "If Vinicio wins or if he tries to do anything once he's in, there will be a coup d'etat, just like with Arbenz," complained a nurse from the highlands. DC candidates for mayor in various places including San Mateo, received death threats and in at least one town in Huehuetenango open threats were made against those who did not vote for the MLN–Guatemala's far right party.

Radio, newspaper, and television announcements reiterated that voting was the duty of every good citizen, and that failure to vote would constitute an "unpatriotic act" endangering the fledgling democracy. Refusing to vote or expressing reservations about the elections might appear *tendecioso* or sympathetic toward the opposition, particularly since the official line of the URNG (Guatemalan National Revolutionary Unity) held that the elections were a sham and that voting was only playing along. A teacher explained, "We don't talk about the elections. We are afraid. Many realize that the elections are worthless but if they don't vote they will be fined and perhaps viewed as subversive." Moreover, due to constant civil patrol and army checks of peoples' papers, lack of the voting verification stamp would be quickly apparent, raising the prospects of reprisals for those caught without it. Many assumed difficulty in obtaining other official papers without the stamp.

The confusion surrounding the electoral process reveals limited popular involvement. Although television and radio announcements as well as printed material were constantly available explaining the voting procedure (to those who read or understood Spanish), the majority of voters observed in rural areas seemed mystified at the voting table. The ballots showed the party symbol of all the presidental candidates, but many voters did not understand how to mark them. An election official described the people who came to his table: "They had no idea what they were supposed to do. Many people left it blank or marked all the boxes. For some this may have been a sign of protest to say 'I don't agree with any of this,' but others just did not understand at all."

Voting took place only in the municipal capitals and most people were required to vote in their municipality of origin. For some this could mean a journey of several days, plus travel expenses. The government required every literate person over eighteen to preregister and then vote or pay a fine of Q5.00. In one case the outgoing mayor told citizens of outlying villages the wrong date for the registration, leaving many of them unregistered. The villagers believed this was a deliberate action to keep them from voting because they would likely vote against the mayor's chosen candidate.

In some smaller, more isolated villages only twelve to twenty people were registered to vote, including almost no women or older people, in part, because nonliterate people were not required to vote.[69] A government official responsible for registering voters elaborated, "Women don't get checked at the roadblocks so they don't need the voting stamp on their identity cards."

Unlike the national election, residents appeared more involved in mayoral campaigns. Many looked forward to once again choosing their immediate leaders, as appointed officials had often misused their power. "The mayors we elect know we put them in power and can take them out again. They also have to live right here with us and don't want to make us mad." Mayors, however, will find themselves confronted with the army's institutional power and few resources at their disposal.

Throughout the elections the military maintained a careful distance and showed a lack of interest in the outcome of the local or national contests. The predetermined range of acceptable candidates and discourse might explain this apparent indifference. Army personnel in several interviews expressed the view that the activities of civilian candidates were of no importance to the military. Colonel Edgar Hernández, commander of Cobán, declared in August 1985, "The army also expects the civilian government will respect the military's plans against subversion." He elaborated that the army did "a professional job that has already marked out its future directions. The army believes the civilian government will inherit a solid organization. The proof of this is the Institutional Coordinators" (Inforpress, 1985). Colonel Byron Disrael Lima, commander of Santa Cruz del Quiché, referring to civilians entering government, said, "That doesn't mean military men will lose their ultimate power. Latins take commands from men in uniform." He added, "Civilians don't work until we tell them to work. They need our protection, control, and direction" (Wall Street Journal, October 30, 1985).

ATTITUDES TOWARD REFUGEES

Two distinct attitudes concerning external refugees are prevalent. The first, voiced primarily by army officials and *ladinos* living in larger towns, holds that the act of fleeing is an admission of guilt. The second, more common attitude expressed by refugees' fellow-villagers, maintains the refugees fled unspeakable terror.[70] This section examines three situations: refugees returning from Mexico to Huehuetenango: internal refugees taken to the Ixil development pole; and displaced persons hiding in populated centers.

Relatively few of those who left Huehuetenango at the height of the violence have returned. While there are cases of refugees returning safely and even regaining access to their land, the general perception is that returning is dangerous. Informants related stories of killings, either in the army base or after refugees returned home, and rumors describe neighbors denouncing returning refugees with fatal consequences.

Those who returned to surviving family face fewer problems in regaining their land and are considered less suspicious, especially if they came back under the army's aegis. A group of some thirty people, originally from a village of San Mateo, returned from Mexico in December 1984. The civil patrol escorted them to the municipal capital where they were kept under observation for several weeks. Because they were known to fellow villagers the refugees were allowed to return. The people of the village considered them *honrado* (honorable) and the returnees have regained their land. Not long after, however, two men tried going back to the same village without informing the army. Pressure was placed on these men to leave and they finally resettled in the model village of Chacaj.

All informants agreed that returning refugees were watched closely not just by the army, but by the local civil patrol and even neighbors. One civil patrol commander admitted he especially kept an eye on the refugees and if they showed suspicious habits he would immediately turn them in to the army.

Informants commented on social and psychological rifts between refugees (many gone for over five years) and those who remained. Some spoke of bitterness because "We stayed and suffered, while they left." At times half a town fled while the other half remained. Additionally, as a religious worker pointed out:

Those who remained have been put through a process of militarization. They have been trained for the civil patrol, they have lived with the army in their villages, their values are changed. And then there are the problems over land. If we are to live together again, bridges must be built between these groups.

Those who remained have learned to adapt or reach a compromise with the military. The refugees have not.

Ixil Area, Internal Refugees

Many of the same problems affect those returning to the Ixil area after living in zones not controlled by the army. The army keeps these refugees in the local base for a period ranging from several days to several weeks, ostensibly for medical care. When they come out of the base, an informant related and others agreed, "They do not speak of their experiences. They are very sad and very frightened. More than anything they want to survive and to do this they must obey the law."

After the base, refugees usually go to a holding camp such as Las Violetas. The army claims that it provides for these refugees, but they apparently survive on private aid. Relief workers in the area described the situation facing Indian peasants as quite bleak:

There is nothing for them in the towns or in the model villages. They have lost everything. They will not be allowed to return to their land for a very long time, if ever. Their houses and the belongings not taken by the soldiers or the patrollers have been burned.

After passing through the base, refugees are officially allowed to return to their land if it is under army control, that is, part of the development pole system. This return occurs most frequently when a family member, already living in a village, agrees to take in the refugees, thus vouching for them. Refugees without family are also assigned to model villages, but are under especially close observation. "If they act badly or it is apparent that they lied and did not confess everything to the army, they will be punished," a catechist explained. Refugees may be forced to inform on others. The army immediately takes out men brought in from the sweeps, compelling them to show where others are located. Informants believed some of these men do not return, presumably because they did not collaborate.

Refugees forcibly returned to the areas under government control face a difficult situation. In addition to severe economic hardship, they are confronted with suspicion and insults. An informant related how children in Cotzal are taunted or even attacked for being refugees. Attitudes toward these people, however, are not necessarily negative. The Catholic sisters, who run a nutrition program for refugee children, recount with amazement the small charities of people in the town. They tell of one woman who had taken in two orphan children and would come to the parish bringing a basket with three small tortillas in it, willing to share the little she had.

Other Internal Refugees

The largest number of displaced persons have taken refuge in towns and cities throughout the country. They live in constant fear of continued represssion, after the traumatic experience of fleeing their homes and often losing family members in the violence. The south coast or larger cities, especially the capital, offer some anonymity. Nonetheless, hundreds of refugees in Guatemala City have disappeared in the last few years despite attempts to live dispersed and blend into the population by abandoning their traditional clothing and speaking Spanish instead of their native language. Several informants spoke of the government practice of bringing informants from villages to identify such people. Many are terrified of returning home, feeling they have no chance of surviving in their villages. Some fear their land is in the hands of others who would be willing to denounce them to retain it.

Economically their situation is desperate. As refugees, often without documentation, they cannot obtain work permits (to do street corner vending, for example) or make use of social services such as schools or hospitals. The only skill many have is working the land. A relief worker in the capital painted a grim picture:

> For everyone, but especially for the women, the prolonged horror, the fear that lives with them at all times, the memories of the rapes, the killings, the pressure of having friends perhaps turn you in, pressure on you to turn in brothers and neighbors and the lack of organization among the refugees, is too much. It is very bad.

DISSENT AND POPULAR RESISTANCE

The military has sought not only to defeat the insurgency and bring its supporters under control but to subdue the population in a manner that would prevent future opposition. As such, one of the military's pacification strategies has targeted the stronghold of Indian culture — the community — reshaping its daily functioning. The scale and intensity of the onslaught has taken a severe toll on the population, breeding mistrust and exploiting historical rivalries between ethnic groups in the process of establishing military supremacy. Within this context, however, incidents of resistance, although frequently isolated, do take place. Guerrilla activities, which demand a significant degree of local collaboration, continue in parts of the country—even the most militarily dominated. Grass roots protest activities occur, and some communities have defied army orders regarding civil patrol duties or found other ways of expressing dissent. In Guatemala's repressive environment, simple acts such as privately making fun of the army or coming a few minutes late to civil patrol duty can be symbols of defiance.

After the persecution suffered by Catholics, many withdrew from active church participation, although people were returning in 1985. One religious worker claimed, however, that "people are much more careful, they gather together in Bible study groups, but they only discuss the Bible without relating it to larger issues." Though some have abandoned their traditional dress in the city for security reasons they adopt another area's traditional dress to maintain their self identity as Indians.

Women have played an especially important role. The GAM, overwhelmingly made up of Indian women, has been cited for their brave acts of defiance. The organization's activities often dominate the daily press, at times putting the government and the military on the defensive. There have been women's resistance in other areas as well. In the model village of Chacaj, Huehuetenango, for example, an informant related that the army had attempted to organize the women into the civil patrol and they had refused. Women, too, were sometimes the most sympathetic in their support of those accused and persecuted by the military.

In a few areas, the army has not been able to mobilize an effective patrol structure, despite repeated efforts. In the town of Poptún, El Petén, there is not a civil patrol, although the army tried to initiate one. Poptún itself is host to a very large military base, and apparently the population would not accept the rationale that the patrol was necessary for its own "protection." The surrounding villages also had not participated very enthusiastically with the patrol structure and in late 1984–early 1985, the patrols had almost died out completely. Following increasing insurgent activity, however, the army reportedly "beefed up" the patrol system, visiting the villages and mandating that patrols be restarted whether the population liked it or not. In Cantel, Quetzaltenango, the people successfully organized against instituting the civil patrol and in Mataesquintla, an eastern area that saw little violence in the last decade, the village populations have essentially abandoned the patrols, insisting patrol duty is an unnecessary nuisance without insurgents in the area. Only when directly prodded by the military will they patrol and then only until the soldiers are no longer present to enforce the duty.

The army does not fully trust the civil patrols. In conflict areas officers demand that the civil patrols accompany troops in *rastreos* (sweeps), yet do not tell the patrols in advance when, where and for how long they will be gone, so the guerrillas cannot be warned.

The public requests calling for disbanding the patrol system have been cautious but persistent.[71]

The proposed 50 percent increase in urban bus fares and simultaneous increases in milk and bread prices sparked protracted demonstrations in Guatemala City in September 1985. High school students were the first in the streets, soon joined by the women of the city markets, university students, and more and more of the general population. For some the memories of the victorious 1978 urban uprising that blocked a similar attempt to increase bus fares proved more powerful than fears developed after years of bloody repression. Soon municipal workers and teachers went on strike, demanding increases in pay.[72]

Since then, other public demonstrations have taken place. Almost 2000 people spontaneously demonstrated in Santiago Atitlán following the arrest of a local resident. The 1986 May Day commemoration brought workers and supporters, though in relatively modest numbers, to the streets of Guatemala City. Landless peasants from the south coast, estimated at 16,000 strong, marched to the capital demanding access to plantation lands in their area.[73] Other smaller demonstrations have taken place, the majority focusing on economic or human rights issues.[74]

In addition, organizing reportedly occurs through clandestine channels. Networks are being reestablished within and between communities. People spoke of how others (they would rarely discuss their own participation) are organizing; to defend their land, to renew information and self-help networks, to have contact with those exiled from their communities.

Widely acknowledged but not well documented are the Guatemalans who are living inside the country but outside army controlled territory. Sometimes dubbed the "population in resistance," referring to the fact they are successfully eluding army control, these people are mainly concentrated in the mountainous and lowland area of northern Quiché. Estimates as to their number vary. Several people have visited the "population in resistance", placing the number at 20,000–25,000 total. The army marks them as subversives who support or are themselves guerrillas.[75] If such people are captured or starved out by the army, however, they are then heralded as "liberated captives" of the guerrillas.[76] Some familiar with their lifestyle say that after four years of living in hiding they have developed relatively stable and cohesive communities, growing their own food and, in some cases, residing in or near their original, remote villages.[77] Those who are sympathetic commiserate with the harsh conditions faced by this group that is continually pursued and harassed on the ground and at times bombed and fired on from the air. Still others see them as starved and sorry characters, driven by extremist politics to stay in the mountains, living in caves and eating wild plants. If the army discovers one of these settlements, the soldiers destroy the cultivation and any belongings left behind. Most, even the army, admire the tenaciousness involved in eluding capture for so long in one of the most militarized areas of the entire country.

Insurgent activity has increased substantially since 1984. Despite government claims in December 1985 that only "spots of subversion remain in a few areas," over 210 guerrilla actions were tabulated in the first ten months of 1985, representing a 40 percent increase over the same period in 1984 (Central America Report, December 13, 1985). Many military outposts have been attacked. Meetings in isolated towns and plantations, as well as roadblocks, have increased. The majority of insurgent actions documented in the press have taken place in the southern departments of Esquintla and Suchitepequez, in San Marcos, and Sololá (ORPA areas), and in the northern department of El Petén (including the short-term takeover of the famed archaeological site, Tikal, in October, 1985 by the FAR). One of the most noted actions was ORPA's January 1985 occupation of Santiago Atitlán, Sololá, for a few hours. A group of journalists who spent a week with an ORPA detachment in the central part of the country found them well supplied by the local population. The civilians did not betray the guerrillas, who receive "everything they need from the local peasantry . . . [who come] . . . with baskets of food or gifts of cigarettes or just to pay a friendly call."[78] Not regularly covered by the press (but alive through word of mouth) is the EGP activity in the Ixil area and throughout the Ixcán region, as well as Northeastern Huehuetenango.[79] Petén and San Marcos were also rumored to host much more action than the army or city newspapers would acknowledge. In May 1986 the Defense Minister acknowledged that the guerrillas are active in eight (of twenty-two) departments, and "there is not total control of the subversive movement."[80] In some areas, local residents said that guerrilla/army skirmishes (*enfrentamientos*) happened once a week or more, resulting in many casualties (information about casualties depends on who is doing the reporting).

Though much reduced from its peak, collaboration still continues between the population and the guerrillas. This collaboration can involve direct support, complicity such as providing information regarding army movement, or more extensively an indirect and passive collaboration—a tendency to "look the other way."

In general, discussion about the guerrillas is not an acceptable topic. Some would echo a major theme of army propaganda campaigns: the guerrilla tricked us, they fooled us into supporting them by giving us false hopes.[81] Still others would whisper that not only had most people actively supported the opposition but that many were still sympathetic although less inclined to outright collaboration.

Finally, one example that demonstrates resiliency — the ability not to be completely subdued by the militarization imposed on them — is the ability to joke about it. People are constantly deciphering the double meaning in a conversation, acknowledging the decoding with a responsive laugh or joining back with another coded statement. Much is communicated by body language and eye contact. At a check point, for example, when the military orders everyone to step out of a vehicle, the manner in which someone complies communicates their attitudes without a word being spoken. There are also many jokes about the army or about people carrying out or outsmarting army orders. The army's repression, and the compliance expected, has been so overwhelming, that by its very nature there is a built-in failure factor. The result is that any freedom of thought, expression or action, becomes an act of defiance and therefore a psychological victory for the individual.

3

The Case of Northeastern Huehuetenango

The years of intense violence (1981–1983) inflicted on San Mateo Ixtatán and other communities of northeastern Huehuetenango appear on the surface to have altered the region little. Nonetheless, our findings reveal significant modifications: the army and its proxies such as the civil patrols are now the institutions that most dominate people's lives, depriving them of former mechanisms for self-government and problem solving and limiting traditional means of generating income. In some instances, access to land and other key natural resources has been restricted or brought under new forms of control. These changes make it difficult to successfully reintegrate refugees into their communities of origin in this area. Additionally, evidence suggests that the safety of returning refugees could be compromised if they return to this region.

GENERAL BACKGROUND AND INTRODUCTION

The municipal capital of San Mateo Ixtatán lies 2,540 meters above sea level, high in the Cuchumatán mountains in the department of Huehuetenango. It borders on Mexico to the north, the Guatemalan municipalities of Barillas to the east, Santa Eulalia to the south and Nentón and San Sebastián Coatán to the west. The municipal capital is 112 kilometers from the departmental capital of Huehuetenango on an unpaved and difficult road. The trip requires five hours by jeep and approximately nine hours by bus.

The residents of the area are primarily Chuj Indians. In Santa Eulalia and Barillas the people are Kanjobal, as are some of the villages of San Mateo. While some rivalry exists between the two groups, it is not uncommon for Kanjobales to live in Chuj areas and vice versa, and many Chuj speakers also speak Kanjobal. The 1973 census showed the population to be 15,914 for the entire municipality, with 1,834 people living in the municipal capital. In the municipality 14,754 were Indians, and only 1,537 claimed to be literate.

The climate in most of the San Mateo municipality is cold, and the earth is not very fertile. The slopes are steep and the land tends to be rocky. Corn, wheat, beans and some vegetables are the main crops grown in the region of the municipal capital, with peanuts and fruit trees sometimes planted as cash crops. The villages to the north, nearer to Mexico, are hot lowlands with fertile, flat ground suitable for cardamom and coffee. Two crops a year of corn, beans and other staples can be produced.

Most people are small land holders, owning anywhere from two to one hundred *cuerdas* (a *cuerda* is a unit of land measured in *varas* [one *vara* = 33 inches], may be either 25, 30, 36 or 40 *varas* square. The most common is 25 *varas* square). Land is generally inherited and subdivided among offspring so that the resulting small parcels produce only enough food to last six to nine months. Nutritional deficiencies are a continuing problem. According to health workers many illnesses are related to malnutrition and water contamination, such as the widespread occurrence of worms and parasites. Tuberculosis is common. Unable to survive on their tiny plots (*minifundia*), many families must migrate temporarily to the south coast at harvest time to work on the large coffee, cotton and sugar cane plantations of *fincas* (*latifundia*). People also migrate to Mexico and sometimes to the lowland plantations in Barillas in search of work. The land shortage in San Mateo caused many Mateanos to take advantage of the cooperative land ventures carried out in the Ixcán area in the late 1960s and early 1970s.[82] Others go to Huehuetenango or Guatemala City hoping to find work in the informal sector (petty trade or domestics). This migration to the city is sometimes the only alternative for single young women, although the wages they earn are low and sexual abuse by employers common. Local agricultural day labor and felling and gathering wood from the surrounding pine forest also brings in income, and some earn money by producing and selling salt, evaporated from the water collected at nearby salt mines.

Much of the commerce in San Mateo relates to Barillas, which lies in the lowlands and produces bananas, *panela* (crudely refined brown sugar) and other more tropical products. In early summer when the area harvests begin to run out, corn and other foodstuffs grown on the south coast are imported to the local markets. In San Mateo many people sell a little of something: *huipiles* (women's embroidered or woven blouses), and other artisan products, tortillas, rice, *atoles* (grain beverages most commonly made of corn), secondary trading of bananas and *panela* from Barillas, *cuxha* (bootleg liquor), etc. Villagers have also traditionally raised sheep to sell the wool.

In northeastern Huehuetenango, the municipal structure consists of a mayor, who also acts as justice of the peace and chooses the municipal staff (a vice mayor, a secretary and assistant, a treasurer and two treasury assistants, the police chief, and in San Mateo, a person to run the salt mines). In the villages an auxiliary mayor, generally chosen by the people of the village and authorized by the mayor in the municipal capital, deals with minor problems such as petty thievery and drunkenness. Larger problems go to the town mayor who may set up a commission to investigate accusations. The municipal staff deals with land boundary problems, animal robbery, rape, and other violent crimes. Until 1982 mayors were chosen by popular vote. After that year's coup, Rios Montt appointed mayors in all municipal capitals. In 1985 mayoral elections were reestablished.

The political and religious power of other traditional positions such as *alcalde rezador, principales* or members of *cofradía*, while once strong, has been eroding over the last years in San Mateo. This erosion is less true for the villages which remain more isolated and less influenced by outside forces than the town of San Mateo itself.

The penetration of outside religious influences was relatively weak until some thirty years ago when Catholic missionaries began working in the area. Resentment toward those who first converted from the *costumbre* (traditional) religion remains deep in some areas.[83] Evangelical Christian sects have also gained ground in Huehuetenango, although not nearly so much as in the Ixil area. Many of the villages have at least a few families who have converted. Three sects are represented in San Mateo. Tensions often run high in communities among *costumbristas*, Catholics, and Evangelicals.

Foreign clergy in the San Mateo region, both Catholic and Evangelical, often have access to resources from their home countries and have instituted projects that draw followers to their religion. The clergy are asked to loan money, help obtain material goods, or intervene with mayors, governors, army, and civil patrol commanders. Many religious workers accept the fact that some members see their Church as a means to an end, *i.e.*, to obtain material advantages, to learn Spanish or to gain power within their community.

In many spheres, the traditional and new ways vie with each other and overlap. Many refuse to go to a doctor, but will buy injections in the market, trusting that one shot will make them well. Catholics will simultaneously entrust their families to the church clinic in San Mateo and recruit the *costumbre* elders to appeal to deities to stop the sickness.

By the mid-1970s, community organizing projects became quite popular in San Mateo. A group of health promoters was trained with the help of the Catholic Church. Production, credit, and service cooperatives were formed. And a number of social promoters, primarily young people, worked on community improvements and setting up a night school for adult literacy. In general, the founders and leaders of these movements were all Indians.

In the late 1970s, the EGP began to organize and make its presence known in the municipality of San Mateo, primarily in the outlying villages. Several people who had gone to the Ixcan colonization projects joined the guerrillas there and then returned to the San Mateo and San Miguel area to talk to fellow villagers about the cause. The EGP was widely accepted in the area and, while traditional municipal authorities continued in place, the guerrillas militarily controlled the municipality for much of the time between 1979 and 1982. Throughout these years, the army was reluctant to enter the area, allowing the guerrilla flag to fly for several weeks along the road rather than going into San Mateo to take it down. Nonetheless, the reasons for and depth of support varied. Some entered into wholehearted collaboration with the goals and methods of the armed insurgency, either joining the ranks or supplying food and information. Others apparently joined the guerrillas as a means to personal power or because it happened to represent the ruling force at the moment. And still others cooperated out of fear. While opponents of the insurgents reportedly existed, they were not very powerful at the time.

Conditions have changed markedly. During the fieldwork, there was little or no guerrilla activity in the region, although a resurgence has taken place since.[84]

THE ARMY AND POWER

Prior to 1978, the Guatemalan army was seldom, if ever, present in the area. In the 1970s, a troop contingent was stationed in the nearby town of Barillas, but informants say that they were "harmless" and never came to San Mateo. Today, eight years later, the army may well be the single most important institution in people's lives, whether through its direct presence in a community, indirectly through the omnipresent civil patrol system, or via its dominating influence on the Interinstitutional Coordinators.

To regain control over the region the army garrisoned itself in municipal capitals and in strategic towns, undertaking grisly campaigns against unarmed communities, using mutilation, rape, torture, and large scale massacres.[85]

Control Mechanisms

As one way to establish military authority, the army formed forced labor details. In San Mateo, villagers recall soldiers ordering them to form work details to cut down the almost-sacred forest (because it offered sanctuary to guerrillas or civilians who had fled their communities following army massacres). Moreover, the army commanded extensive road work and the overnight construction of a wooden kiosk in the town square, a whim of the base commander.

In early 1982, the military began setting up civil patrols in virtually every town and village in the area. On July 2, 1982, troops arrived to organize patrols in the town of San Mateo. They summoned everyone to the town center, where the heavily-armed soldiers read out a list of names of those supposedly appointed as patrol leaders who were to receive special training. Nine people responded out of a list of forty, and a tenth man volunteered. They were taken away on the road to Barillas. Halfway there, according to witnesses, the soldiers made them get out of the truck and began to chop off their hands. When one tried to fight back they chopped off his arms and then killed them all, leaving the bodies on the road.

Since then, the civil patrols have become the most important institution for extending military authority. In the beginning the army supervised the system directly, which it still does in key localities in northeastern Huehuetenango, such as villages near the military base in Ixquisis, close to the Mexican border. In other areas where the civil patrol system is strong, the army has begun reducing its permanent presence, instead appearing for a few months at a time or simply arriving for a day or two before moving on.[86]

Orejas

It is widely believed that the army has established broad networks of informers, *orejas*, in most communities.[87] Prior to the counterinsurgency campaigns of the early 1980s, local military commissioners and their assistants primarily carried out and coordinated army intelligence activities. Now the military directly coordinates a more elaborate informer network, probably through the G-2 (military intelligence). The common perception is that those who act as *orejas* are trying to clear their own names from suspicion or are paid for the information they pass on. The system stifles dissent, and sows distrust in the community. While the extent of the informer system is impossible to assess, virtually everyone *believes* that informers are everywhere and might be anyone. Several people remarked that women and even children are now beginning to act as *orejas*.

Villagers are extremely careful in their conversations, both regarding what they say and to whom they say it. In the main squares in the north of Huehuetenango, people would fall quiet if they noticed a few small children listening to the conversation. A parochial house that gives free lodging to people in need turned away two elderly women because the workers didn't know them. During the 1985 elections people were afraid to meet together to discuss the voting, fearing the military might get wind of it and punish them.

The *oreja* system is effective, according to informants and field observations. Control is also maintained in more subtle ways than it was during the period of mass terror. This subtlety is only possible, however, because the threat of violence is still omnipresent.

The Highest Authority

In virtually every locale visited, informants stressed the importance of local and departmental army commanders: their decisions are effectively the law during their tour of duty (a period ranging from a few months to several years). In San Mateo, residents characterized each of the past few years according to whether the commander was "good" or "bad". If the commander allows soldiers to steal sheep or decides to set up work details there is no higher authority.[88] Army decisions are rarely challenged, due to fear of reprisal, and abuses perpetrated by officials or soldiers under one commander will rarely be punished by a successive commander.

While family problems and land disputes are still generally taken first to the civil authority, if the losing party wishes, the matter can be taken to the army base and appealed before military officials. Especially in cases in which a community wants to replace a local authority, its members go to the nearest army commander to seek a solution. Sometimes the army responds favorably to a village's request; other times the answer is no or enough of a runaround so the request is abandoned.[89] A lawyer in Huehuetenango explained that his office never deals with land problems because land issues are within the army's jurisdiction, and it would be dangerous to get involved.

The army vests its authority in civilian proxies: military commissioners and civil patrol commanders.[90] While patrol commanders have taken over some liaison functions with the military, the commissioners remain important. In addition to intelligence gathering, their main function is helping to fill the army's quota of recruits.

Military commissioners claimed it had become more difficult to leave quotas unfilled. The army has new lists of all male inhabitants in every town, drawn up upon the formation of the civil patrols, eliminating the excuse that not enough men can be found to fill the quota. While most commissioners willingly complied, some look for excuses,[91] aware that once a boy is taken for the army he may never return home.[92]

Relief Work and Interinstitutional Coordinators

With the immediate danger of a popular uprising contained by 1983, the army began altering aspects of its activities in the zone. While acts of violence still occur with some frequency, no massacres were reported during fieldwork and the dreaded, large-scale forced labor details are rare.

In its current attempt to win over the population, the army distributes food and other assistance to those who come to them in need. In fact, the military has become something of a clearing house for community needs. For example: the army supplies its own marimba band and helps provide the party materials for town fiestas at a minimal cost; a schoolteacher appealed first to the army base to procure a new roof for the school; municipal officials spoke of forwarding requests to the base when they themselves did not have sufficient resources.

In one instance, a group returning from Mexico was escorted home in an army truck after "treatment" in the base. An informant claimed the army had given them the animals and other things they had:

> The army takes advantage of people coming back to do their 'big friend' routine, bringing them in on their trucks, giving them animals and things to get started with again. They even take people to the hospital and give them free medicine.

To systematize its involvement in relief and development work throughout the country, the army set up the Interinstitutional Coordinator system. In general, informants in Huehuetenango view the IIC as an instrument of military control. Because even the smallest project must be presented for approval to the IIC, little occurs in the department without the knowledge and consent of the army commander.

In the departmental capital of Huehuetenango, the IIC is well institutionalized.[93] It has regular meetings, with a set group of representatives attending, and has carried out a number of projects. Informants who are participants claim that the army is unquestionably in control of the process, running the meetings, setting up the agenda, and controlling the resources. One informant told of a project proposed by lay Catholics to help returning refugees. When it was brought before the coordinator for approval, the army suggested two alternatives. One, do the project under the supervision and evaluation of the army's National Reconstruction Committee, or two, give the money they raised for the project to the NRC and allow the committee to carry it out. As neither were acceptable to the participants, the project was dropped.

One participant described the meetings thus:

> The commander may claim to be an uninvolved observer but he has all the control. He comes to the meetings with his body guards and his secretary. What they mostly do is drink coffee and tell jokes. Private people and organizations have to go so it will look like they have input, but we know that the army controls the whole thing. We have to tell them everything we do.

When the local coordinating committee was first organized in San Mateo and the outlying villages, teachers, religious, and other NGO people participated with representatives of state agencies, and presented projects. A few were carried out initially such as building a bridge and fixing a small landslide. Nonetheless, the army-appointed mayor and the military commander ran the IIC and determined which projects would be carried out.

When the coordinator was first beginning, *ladino* representatives from Huehuetenango would come to San Mateo to encourage them to send projects down to the department capital. It was to little avail, however. At one point, a dispute erupted between the mayor (an Evangelical) and the civilian sector (the religious, health and educational organizations) over plans to build a roof over the basketball court, which would have destroyed the facade of the Catholic church (one of the oldest) in Guatemala). After this incident the mayor and military representative began to phase out the participation of the other sectors. The mayor claimed the priest or the schoolteachers were always out of town. These people, however, counter that they no longer received word of meetings. Nonetheless, they expressed relief, as they had found the meetings a waste of time.

The coordinator in San Mateo now consists of the municipal staff, the patrol commander, and the military commissioner. The IIC has done little in 1985 according to residents. The village-level coordinators also lack organization. There was no evidence of any scheduled meetings or previous accomplishments by these groups. Requests from the outlying villages for roofing materials, food supplements for school children, supplies for the festivals, etc., were generally sent by the group that needed them (teachers, for example) directly to the army base in Huehuetenango.

As a further aspect of this "developmentalist" strategy, the army is redistributing lands abandoned by refugees or left unoccupied by the massacres. Thus, the landless recipients, who had previously been unable to support their children, are now landowners as a result of the army's help. They suddenly might have an interest in supporting the military.

In the department capital informants expressed concern that people were forgetting what the soldiers had done to them. In contrast, some recipients of the new generosity were claiming that army personnel, from the troops in their town on up to the president, had completely changed since the worst violence and thus could not be blamed for past atrocities. Others were convinced, however, that many villagers were just taking advantage of free supplies in the context of increased economic hardship.

Fear Persists

In numerous conversations the threat of potential army violence surfaces. A common pattern persists: someone is denounced to the army, then subsequently punished, disappears or is killed. A denunciation may come from an army informant, a neighbor, civil patrol member, or even a relative. Many inhabitants still fear the arbitrary and random nature of violence which they feel could strike at any moment. While acknowledging that the situation is calmer now, informants expressed concern the lull may be only temporary and the fierce violence of "before" could return at any time.

CIVIL PATROLS

The civil patrol system has been a part of daily life now for over four years throughout the Guatemalan countryside. All men from the ages of eighteen to fifty-five must patrol, although in isolated rural villages duties can officially begin at fourteen, and even younger boys sometimes substitute for their fathers or older brothers. In Barillas, young boys are selected on the basis of height rather than age. Moreover, older men are often active well beyond the age of sixty.

The patrols man checkpoints at key places in town or along the roads leading in, monitor people's identification papers and travel permits, patrol the streets, and accompany the army on sweep missions. In addition, the system keeps tabs on the activities of all adult males and creates a sense in the community that everyone is being watched. In northeastern Huehuetenango, villagers seldom miss their turn without first seeking permission. Few people could describe the overall structure of the civil patrol in their community, or knew how many *pelotones* (patrol squads) are active each day or how many guard posts are manned. Thus, the following description of the civil patrol in northeastern Huehuetenango is based on field observations as well as on the information obtained from a large number of informants.

Patrol Commanders and Squad Leaders

In most municipal capitals there are two or three *comandantes de patrulla* (patrol commanders), although generally only one is really in charge. Under these men are the *jefes de pelotón* (the squad leaders), each responsible for a shift of duty. Each squad is assigned to a guard-post and other specific activity to be covered in a twenty-four hour period. The *jefes de pelotón* oversee the distribution and return of weapons used during their shift, and together with the primary commander, grant or deny permission for *pelotón* members to leave town or miss a turn because of illness or travel.

The military chooses the primary commander of the civil patrol, who has become the most powerful person in some communities.[94] In all cases in the fieldwork, the patrol commanders, Indians and *ladinos*, were men who had served in the military; in some cases they may have been the local military commissioner. In smaller villages lacking men with military experience, catechists are often selected as commanders. In part this may be because they can read and write and are already community leaders. Nonetheless, some feel the appointment is designed to put them under closer surveillance by increasing their contact with the military. *Jefes de pelotón* are chosen by the commander, with veto power held by the army.

The power of civil patrol commanders undercuts traditional conflict-solving mechanisms within the community. As in the case of the army commanders, this individual's personality and moral integrity can determine the tenor of life in a community. Corrupt commanders, who use extortion and violence or practice nepotism with friends and family, have an extremely divisive effect.

The commander in one town sees himself as a strict Catholic and refuses to denounce anyone, even people he thinks support the guerrillas, because he knows it would mean their death. He does not relish the task as it keeps him away from his family, but he sees the job as his obligation and has little choice in any case. The man named commander before him fled to Mexico to escape the responsibility.

In contrast, the civil patrol commanders in some towns have used their power with impunity to eliminate peasant landowners or other adversaries. In one village for example, the commander seized the rich coffee growing land of villagers who fled to Mexico and planted these lands with cardamom. In another case, the head of the civil patrol aided by five members beat a villager for two hours and then destroyed his land markers. Villagers are too frightened to bring charges against them, and those who could not bear the situation have left. One civil patrol commander has reportedly murdered eight men. A priest has reported the apparent murder of one villager who had gone to the U.S. to earn some money, and while he was gone the commander began raping his wife. When he returned, the commander reported to the nearby army base that the man had been in the mountains with the guerrillas, and that is the last anyone heard of him. The commander has now reportedly moved in with the man's widow. Another has publicly threatened to kill any who come back, declaring "if refugees return here, I will have them killed."[95]

It was generally not viewed as desirable to be a commander or *jefe*, except for those using the post for personal gain. Respected community leaders disliked acting as the mouthpiece and arm of the military against their own people. Moreover, informants holding these positions complained about the time it takes to organize the patrols and sweeps, supervise every turn, and be available for duties such as issuing passes. The economic costs of this unpaid position in time away from productive work can be even higher than for the average patroller.

Frequency

In San Mateo the civil patrol was organized by *cantón* (town section or rural subdivision). Every *cantón* at one time had a *garita* (guardpost) in addition to the ones at the roads leaving town. By 1985, the army consented to reduce the number of manned *garitas*. Within a *cantón* there are fifteen to thirty men assigned to each *pelotón*. The population size of the *cantón* determines how often one patrols. If there are enough men to form fifteen *pelotones*, for example, then one patrols every fifteen days. The same is true in the villages.

In some places, such as the towns of San Mateo, Barillas, and Sta. Eulalia, large groups have divided to patrol half as often, or to cut the shifts to twelve hours. In San Mateo this seems to have been the decision of the men themselves, with final approval given by the patrol commander. Generally the approval of the nearest military commander is needed for these kinds of decisions.

In the areas studied, patrol duty might fall as often as every five days, as in villages near Ixquisis in San Mateo and small villages in Barillas. In rare cases it falls only every thirty days, as in the capital of Huehuetenango, where patrol duty is now only at night. In some places the *jefe* is lenient enough to allow people to sleep part of a shift. Patrol duty, however, is generally performed in a *garita*, which is often only a roof with a few boards to make a low wall, and many men complained of the discomfort of the duty and their difficulty in sleeping. Much of the day following patrol duty is often spent recuperating. An additional annoyance is the presence of informers on most shifts, confirmed by several patrol commanders.

In addition to regular patrol duty, each patroller is on call for sweeps into the mountains. These sweeps generally last a day or so, but may extend up to a week. The longer sweeps are physically gruelling because of the difficult conditions in the mountain regions where they are carried out. Men are seldom told how long they will be away, and thus have virtually no way of knowing how much food, water, and other provisions they need to carry as these are not provided by the army. Sweeps are supposed to be scheduled once a month and are not announced beforehand, for security reasons.[96]

Missing a Turn

Few are officially exempt from civil patrol duty. Town authorities, however, were seldom observed doing a turn, although they are required to patrol. In San Mateo, teachers are unofficially exempt, while in other places like Barillas, they are required to serve.[97] Priests and Evangelical ministers are exempt (the latter due to a special decree by General Rios Montt). With these exceptions, however, everyone, including health workers, is required to patrol or provide a replacement.

The commander has the responsibility to grant permission to travel or to miss a turn. He may delegate that task to the *jefes* under him, while retaining the final say. Again, much depends on the attitudes of the *jefe* or commander as to whether or not permission to miss a turn for health or other personal reasons is granted. In the department capital, it was reportedly difficult to get out of a turn without a doctor's statement; in other places it was much simpler.

Most patrol commanders throughout Huehuetenango seem tolerant of the fact that people have to "*ganar los centavos*" (earn a living) by going to Mexico or the south coast and will generally grant permission to travel.[98] The usual limit for missing patrol duty, even when a replacement is provided, is a month (two turns). In most places a replacement is formally required, but sometimes the stipulation is ignored in the case of illness or until fewer than five people report for duty. Certainly, in most villages, replacements are not commonly paid simply because no one has any money. But in the department capital it is more common for better off people to pay a replacement rather than patrol. In the country a young son, relative, or friend will fill in, often in return for the same service at another date.

In general, in towns and villages where the army is present control over the civil patrol is much stricter. In the department capital, each *pelotón* has a radio and must maintain steady contact with the base, verifying that all patrol members arrived and are patrolling throughout the night.

The commander also metes out punishment to those who miss a turn without permission. In some villages, commanders ignore missed turns unless only two or three members of a shift report, and then only because they fear spot checks by the military or the municipal capital commander. In other places, if someone did not report, the *jefe* would send other patrollers to bring in the missing man if they didn't believe he was sick. If the problem was drunkenness, the man might have to spend a day or two in jail. Punishment for missing a turn without permission was rare in the town of San Mateo, although people generally reported it consists of a few days in prison and a fine of up to Q5.00. In other places, punishment consists of a verbal reprimand or work on behalf of the patrol, *i.e.*, carrying firewood for the *garita's* fire, improving the *garita*, etc.[99] Some patrol commanders punish people by making them run laps or hold a gun or heavy book at arm's length for several hours. When the army was stationed in Barillas (until mid-1985), if someone missed a turn or was caught drunk or sleeping on patrol, the army would often take the offender to a special cell at the base. There he would be thrown into a pit full of water and made to stand in it for hours on end. Informants say that the situation is more relaxed now that the army has left, but Barillas is still known throughout Huehuetenango for having one of the strictest civil patrols.

Economic Impact

As in all of Guatemala, civil patrol duty in northeastern Huehuetenango dramatically affects the ability of nearly all men to work as before. While the system has some flexibility, patrol obligations take time away from productive activities and restrict freedom of movement. Patrollers would often complain that the civil patrol made it much more difficult to earn a living. Some development workers claim that the economic costs of the civil patrol are increasing malnutrition in the highlands.

All migration has been disrupted, first by the period of violence and currently by the civil patrol system. Previously, villages migrated to the south coast or to Mexico for two or three months, until they had earned "enough". These wages have been essential to the survival of thousands of families in the study area for several decades. Entire families still travel in search of work, but the time limits the patrol system impose reduce earnings. Moreover, in areas where large numbers migrate at one time, replacements may need to be paid (one to five *quetzales*), further eroding a family's income. People involved in itinerant commercial activities who traveled from town to town for months at a time have also had to restrict their circuits.

In some cases, men were able to persuade the commander to permit longer leaves, providing they left a replacement. In the poorer villages of San Mateo, where the commanders are not as closely monitored by the army, most men have been able to leave for up to two months. At certain times, most of the young men migrate, leaving the elder men and boys to take their places.[100]

Women are also affected, since their husbands have less time to work in their own fields or to bring in income. Consequently, some women now work in the fields, which they had seldom done before in this area of Huehuetenango. In some cases, families send sons too young for patrol duty to Mexico seeking earnings necessary to survive.

The time spent patrolling, in recovery, and doing sweeps and involuntary community work drains the community. Even though much time on duty is spent inactively, patrollers are home less with their families. A health worker describes a "chain of revenge, with women suffering most. The men are angry at the civil patrol, and they take it out on the women." Alcoholism and wife-beating are not new problems in the highlands, but some health workers see an increase in problem drinking and domestic violence, as men vent the frustration they feel on those around them.

Villagers were extremely reticent to voice criticism of the civil patrols (their reluctance was greater only in regard to the army itself). Only informants of greatest confidence would say anything other than the civil patrols protect the town or the people now feel safe when they sleep at night. No one, however, made any attempt to support the claim that patrol service is voluntary, as the government claims. The response to questions about "voluntary" duty was most often a laugh. A number of informants recalled that when the patrols were first established, people talked about protesting and complaining. When those first resisters were killed or otherwise severely punished, others realized that there was little alternative but to comply. Secondary sources in the region emphasized that villagers consider the civil patrol a major burden and are angry at the government for imposing the system on them. Perhaps the sharpest comment came from a highly trusted informant who confided:

> People will tell you that they like the civil patrol, that it makes them feel safe, but that is only because they are afraid that they will be overheard

and word passed on. Then the patrol commander or the army commander will come and call us together and ask "Who is in agreement with the civil patrol?" And we will all raise our hands because we all want to survive. But no one is in agreement with it. We do it because we have to, and the minute we got the chance we'd stop. It is not voluntary. It is obligatory.

Control of Movement

Officially everyone in Northern Huehuetenango needs a pass to travel outside of their town, including women. Nevertheless, the system is not consistently enforced. In Barillas it is absolutely necessary to have permission from the civil patrol (this could mean seeing three local officials and sometimes paying a bribe) to leave or enter town. In San Mateo it was strongly advised that villagers carry a pass even to go to the outlying villages of the municipal area. Other places may be more lenient, but residents will generally solicit a pass to go anywhere for more than a routine trip to the market.

Men traveling by bus are routinely checked for passes and identification papers at some checkpoints, particularly where the army is present. If passes are not in order, the army or civil patrollers may detain the person. In one case, the army removed a man from the bus in Soloma for not having the appropriate papers. The passes of groups migrating to the coast are often checked as well. Information on destination, date of departure and return, and reason for the trip must be documented on the passes.

There are over twenty-six potential civil patrol checkpoints on the 112 kilometers between the departmental capital of Huehuetenango and San Mateo. On various trips over a several-month period, the bus was stopped regularly at eight of them, and the men had to get out and show their identification and pases at five. Women were seldom required to get off the bus or show identification, unless the army was going the check. Cars were seldom stopped in northern Huehuetenango, although they were strictly controlled only a year before.

The rigor of the inspections varies depending on the personal desires of whoever is in charge. At one stop a North American photographer was manhandled and had film destroyed for attempting to take photos of an army checkpoint. At the same place, others were given no problems.

Occasional disputes erupt between the patrollers, who would order everyone to get off the bus, and the passengers, who would loudly insist that "we all have papers" or "we were just checked." Either side may prevail depending on the circumstances, but there seemed to be a spirit of mutual understanding. If the patroller let them pass, the feeling was "I

Young Chuj woman at her home in San Mateo Ixtatán, 1985. Photography by Celia Williams.

know this is an inconvenience on a crowded bus and we'll let you get away with it" or if the patroller insisted, the passengers would grumble but say, "If it's the orders, OK."

ECONOMIC CHANGES

Land Tenure

While the violence of the counterinsurgency campaign in Huehuetenango did not disrupt traditional patterns of land tenure, it did provoke widespread change in ownership and usufruct.[101]

Because extended families were rarely wiped out entirely, even in villages that no longer exist, much of the land that belonged to the massacred is now being farmed by family members. It is often a different story for the abandoned land of people who are now in Mexico. In some cases, when members of a village fled and others stayed, the land is farmed by family members or neighbors. Where an entire village fled, the land may still be abandoned today. As in the Ixcán region, however, the army is now making a major effort to resettle some of this land with landless peasants from various parts of Huehuetenango.

Such activities help improve the army's relationship with those who benefit and discourage the former owners from returning. It is a highly divisive mechanism, encouraging poor peasants to identify their own interests with those of the army, instead of with those who have fled.

Some new residents believe the army will give them titles. With or without titles, however, many feel they have a right to the land through usufruct. The supply of municipal land which people can sometimes obtain for use has shrunk over the past few decades, and what remains is often unproductive. Thus, while some authorities downplayed the problems that might arise when refugees return from Mexico to find their lands taken over by others—saying that the refugees need only clear municipal lands—this is not a realistic alternative. While there is land available to rent in the San Mateo municipality (much belonging to the *ladinos* who fled), the price is high and the supply small. Thus, if people are unable to regain their lands, the possibilities of getting municipal lands or renting land are not good.[102]

Throughout Huehuetenango many express the fear that there will be trouble if the original owners return. In fact, refugees have encountered problems upon returning to their communities because others are now using their land. In most cases the rest of their property has been stolen or destroyed as well. While there are cases where people have returned to their original villages and are again farming their land, this is most common when only part of a family had fled. In other instances, however, family members have refused to relinquish land that belonged to returning relatives.[103] Everyone agreed that in many instances both the original and the new owners will be willing to fight for land. Many worry about violence if the refugees return, due to the large number of people armed through the civil patrol system. A civil patrol commander said:

> When the old owners return they are going to want their land back, and of course people will fight for their land. But, after being there for four years, the new people have usufruct. It is a big problem now that people are armed (through the civil patrol). It is a very hard situation.

A Protestant religious leader said, "Some of those who come back may only get part of their land back, if any. Some will have to go somewhere else." In Huehuetenango no substantiated cases exist of army personnel enriching themselves with the abandoned land, although rumors of such activities are heard. The isolation and poor quality of the land might account for this.

A series of brief reports follow, documenting the variety of situations at the village level in Northern Huehuetenango.[104]

Village Reports

Chacaj

Chacaj is a destroyed village. It's eighty families are reportedly living in refugee camps in Mexico. A model village is under construction next to the original Chacaj, designed with the initial goal of resettling 10,000 refugees from Mexico and largely funded by Taiwan. Between the two there is a military outpost. The first inhabitants settled there in 1983, after the planting season. An informant explained.

> The army forced people to work while they tried to educate them. They were given military training, marching. . . . The earth is unproductive, and people were so busy building and fixing roads and being reeducated, that they didn't have time to plant for two years. When construction was finished all the institutions just left, and the people had nothing because they'd been provided with everything for all that time.

Thus, as controls loosened, most of the families decided to leave. In December 1984, seventy people left, leaving only seventeen families. The makeup of the village population is in flux, rising and falling constantly. A year later there are still rows of empty houses in the village.

When a mass repatriation did not materialize and the model village lay waiting, the government began a recruitment campaign in the villages of the municipalities of Nentón and San Mateo, offering free land, housing and electricity to those who wished to settle in New Chacaj. The army continues to call Chacaj a model village for refugees, although few of the 120 families living there as of September 1985, are refugees or original inhabitants of Chacaj.

Many people from San Mateo villages decided to resettle there after the army's offer was announced by the auxiliary mayors, and today 50 percent of the residents are from San Mateo.

Chacaj is a grim arid place. Yields are low and the inhabitants have no money to buy fertilizer. Unlike other model villages where the population is from conflict areas, forced to settle by the military, Chacaj is made up of "landless volunteers." Since the model village is not in an active conflict zone nor are the settlers rounded up from conflict areas, they might be able to leave the model village without major difficulty as long as they assume their financial responsibilities.[105] Because of the population makeup, this ability to leave is different than other model villages.

At times the pass system has been quite strict. While the research team was in Chacaj, a government-employed nurse notified the military detachment about leaving for a few days vacation. He was questioned in our presence, having to give personal reasons and explanations about his leave.

Río Seco

In 1982 there was a massacre in Río Seco; the army burned everything except the Evangelical church. All of the surviving inhabitants fled to Mexico. The village and the lands around it were left entirely abandoned for some time. According to informants, in late 1984 and early 1985 the army invited the residents of Ixpajau, San Mateo to settle the lands. Through announcements on the area's Evangelical radio station Radio Maya, which broadcasts in the local languages (the majority of the residents of Ixpajau are Evangelicals), urgings from the mayor, and personal visits from the army, the military encouraged people to settle in Río Seco, saying that it was safe to live there and that good land was to be had. At the time of the field work some forty families had taken advantage of the offer, and were "looking forward to a good crop."

The government has reportedly promised to give these people title to the lands, but the new residents have yet to receive them. The mayor of the municipality claims that the resettlement is illegal, as there is no documentation that the owners of the land have died and left no heirs.

He and all other informants agreed that there will be problems if the original owners of the land return.

Yolcultac

This is a large village perched on a high and cold mountainside overlooking the huge valley of the river Nentón. In 1985, its population was about 1,100 people (224 families). In 1982 soldiers killed several people after prompting villagers to make denunciations. In the same year, two people were hung in the village, apparently by other villagers. At this time, many families fled to Mexico. Two single men returned in 1984 and had taken up residence when, according to several observers, they were pressured to leave by the local patrol commander. Presumably this had something to do with villagers' fear that their presence might "bring trouble." These two villagers then went to live in Chacaj.

In May 1984 a group of 30 crossed as unofficial returnees from Mexico through the border town of Gracias a Dios. Most were from Yolcultac. They were escorted to the town of San Mateo where the mayor and civil patrol commander sent word to the Huehuetenango military base to receive instructions. The Catholic priest provided housing in the parish while they awaited orders from the base. The priest prevailed upon the local officials to release them, as no official word to the contrary had arrived from the military after some weeks. The refugees were then permitted to return to their villages but as with all returnees, "are especially watched," according to the civil patrol commander. They have had no problems. Their land had been under cultivation by others during their absence, with the understanding that it was merely "borrowed," as one informant explained, "The people here are honorable. I've heard of places where people, even family, refuse to give land back, but not here."

Civil patrol service which had been every 14 days, was extended to every 24 days in 1985. Boys as young as 13 are participants in the patrol.

Yuxchén, Nentón.

Yuxchén lies close to the Mexican border and is higher and colder than neighboring villages. The inhabitants are Chuj agriculturalists who cultivate corn, beans and potatoes. Poor and insufficient land prompted them to secure land through INTA in the 1970's in the lower lands to the north. Yuxchén was completely abandoned in 1982 when the inhabitants fled to Mexico. The refugees stayed near the border at first, later settling in a Chiapas camp further in. A few returned to Guatemala shortly after the flight, most stayed in Mexico. Those who returned were permitted by the army to resettle in Yuxchén, but were closely monitored, and made to conform to strict patrol duties, though not provided with guns.

In late 1984 three families opted to leave Mexico and return to Yuxchén. They crossed at Gracias a Dios and arrived at their village welcomed by their relatives and neighbors. One of the men traveled to Gracias a Dios to retrieve some belongings. He made this trip within a day of a major guerilla ambush. Several soldiers were reportedly killed in what was apparently a well-planned attack. Army officials questioned residents in the neighboring settlement of Las Palmas who said the returned refugees had passed through the town. According to Yuxchén residents, the following day, "we were all working, we saw the helicopter come, it landed in the middle of the soccer field, and they took [the refugee] away. From that day, he never returned." Following the disappearance all the residents once again abandoned Yuxchén, and went to live in neighboring Aguacate. Eight months later they returned.

The families still do not feel secure in travelling to their more productive land parcels. In addition all their animals, belongings and housing were lost in 1982, aggravating their current economic situation. Currently there are only 14 men of patrol age, and thus a shift of two is responsible for patrolling every seven days.

Xoxlac, Barillas

This village is in the north of the municipality of Barillas, near the border with Mexico and the municipality of San Mateo Ixtatán. It is about eight hours walk to the nearest road.

When the village was abandoned in 1981 and 1982, some fled to Barillas and its surrounding villages, others fled to Mexico. Their fear was so great and flight so sudden, that some parents left behind their children who were studying in the municipal capital. Xoxlac remained abandoned until late 1984. In November 1984 one family returned officially from Mexico, yet they were detained and held in the military base for several days. The mother of the family became very ill and religious workers, alerted by her son awaiting the family's arrival, secured her release from the base. The head of the household was also eventually released. He was made to sign an amnesty document.

In mid 1985 several families returned and a group of 72 persons returned in April 1986. The army escorted this last group to the village "to provide for their safe arrival." Food assistance, promised to help them survive the first months, did not arrive until October of that year. The food was left in Barillas, and the refugees had to pay the cost and see to the transport to Xoxlac. They were allotted rations based on a "food for work" program monitored by the Barillas based DIGESA promoters.

Nubilá, Barillas

The village was colonized by Kanjobales from San Miguel who bought a *finca* that had been repossessed by BANDESA. They planted corn for subsistence and coffee and cardamom for the market. The village is in the eastern Huehuetenango lowlands about an hour walk from San Ramón and two hours from the Ixcán river. The 70 families lived in Nubilá for about 10 years, until 1982, when army sweeps drove them to safety in Mexico and Barillas. The abandoned village was destroyed, and the animals killed or lost. In late 1983 some internally displaced families asked for permission to return. According to army standards they needed to have an adequate number of families and thus recruited outsiders to join them. They reportedly arranged a written agreement whereby the newcomers could maintain the land and harvest the crops but could not claim the land of the villagers who took refuge in Mexico.

One of the original residents accrued substantial power, developed a close relationship with the military base in Barillas and was bestowed with the office of military commissioner. He made public on several occasions that he would not allow the return of the refugees.

In January 1985 the first family returned from Mexico. He harassed them, extorted large sums of money, but did allow them to stay. Three additional families returned in the summer of that year, after first passing through the military base where they were held for several days. Their relatives complained to the army about the harassment they were being subject to in the village. The army interceded on their behalf because they had been "properly processed."

The houses of the new Nubilá, unlike the original village, are concentrated in the center of the village. In addition to patrol service every five days, villagers are frequently forced to work on community projects as the patrol commander and military commissioner orders.

Yolanhuits

This village of San Mateo lies in the hot, fertile lowlands. During the violence all but eight to ten families fled to Mexico. A catechist appointed as civil patrol commander began taking over the abandoned land. He cut down the coffee trees and began to plant cardamom. He reportedly threatened to kill anyone who returns to reclaim their land. He has also taken over the lands of several people who left the village, disgusted with his policies, but afraid to complain. By the end of 1985, three or four families had returned to this village from internal exile. The commander has allowed them to resettle and farm new lands, but not to reclaim their old lands, which he replanted. After they were allowed to clear and cultivate municipal land, little unused land remained in the area. All informants felt that if others try to return, they will not get any additional land, much less their own back, and they might be killed.

Momunlach

Momunlach is a village of Barillas which was abandoned completely. New residents, reportedly with army encouragement, began to move in several years ago. When the original owners of the land returned, with army permission, there were serious disagreements. The new residents claimed usufruct rights, and the dispute apparently became violent. The case was finally taken before the governor in Huehuetenango, who settled in favor of the original owners.

Todos Santos Cuchumatán

In Todos Santos (the town) sixty to eighty people were killed in 1981–1982. The army also burned an estimated 150 or more houses. Many of these houses remain destroyed and abandoned. We were told that the land of people who were killed is generally being used by relatives and not outsiders.[106] Land does not appear to be available to buy, and this shortage may make it difficult for anyone returning from Mexico to obtain land.

La Victoria

This village in the north of the municipality of Barillas was settled by people from San Marcos several years before the violence. Formerly a plantation, the people joined together to buy the land. They were doing very well raising cardamom, sugar cane, and coffee, when they heard that the army was coming, burning out villages and killing people. All 32 families fled back to their home village. Many were landless and what land they did have was infertile. So when they heard that the violence had diminished, they sent scouts to confirm this. They found their houses still standing although most of their belongings and all of the animals were gone. Sixteen families decided to return; the rest said they were too frightened to go back. Those that have gone back live under tight army control. They had to rebuild their houses in a central location but many say they are happy just to have their land again.

San Antonio Ixcakchín

At the height of the violence everyone fled this village. When some returned at harvest season, the army, stationed in nearby Ixquisis, would not allow them to harvest cardamom in their own fields. But they were allowed to harvest the crops of others. When they were through, the army claimed the cardamom wasn't theirs and took the crop. It is unclear if they are now able to cultivate and harvest their previous land holdings.

Village Conditions in 1984

A survey (Programa, 1984) lists the following abandoned villages in northern Huehuetenango.

Abandoned Villages in Northern Huehuetenango

1. El Aguacate (farm)	24. Puente Quemado (hamlet)
2. El Campamento (hamlet)	25. El Quetzal (farm)
3. Campo Alegre (hamlet)	26. La Reforma el Carmen (farm)
4. Candelaria Siete Pinos	27. Salamay
5. Cantarrana (farm)	28. San Antonio (farm)
6. El Carmen (farm)	29. *San Francisco (farm)
7. La Ceiba (hacienda)	30. San Miguelito (hamlet)
8. El Ceibón (farm)	31. Santa Rosa (village)
9. Chacula Viejo (farm)	32. Santa Teresa (village)
10. La Ciénaga	33. Saquisbaj (farm)
11. Cipa (farm)	34. Siete Pinos (haciendos)
12. Las Delicias (farm)	35. Tintul Siete Pinos (hamlet)
13. La Libertad (farm)	36. Tunalito El Espino (farm)
14. La Libertad (hacienda)	37. Tzalá Grande (hamlet)
15. La Memelita (hamlet)	38. Tzalá Chiquito (hamlet)
16. Miramar (hacienda)	39. La Unión
17. Nueva Esperanza (hamlet)	40. Las Violetas (farm)
18. Ojo de Agua (village)	41. Yalambojoch (village)
19. Ojo de Agua (farm)	42. Yalcastán-Buena Vista
20. El Olvido (farm)	43. Yalisjau (farm)
21. Potrero del Morro (farm)	44. Yaltoyás
22. Pozo Hediondo (hacienda)	45. El Zapotal (hacienda)
23. Puente de Tierra (farm)	46. Santa Elena

*Number 29, above, San Francisco Farm, is the site of the military massacre of July 17, 1982 in which 302 men, women, and children were killed. In mid-1986 there were five families from Bulej living on the site.

OTHER ECONOMIC CHANGES

Violence and political changes have precipitated economic disruption throughout Huehuetenango. Coupled with the nationwide economic crisis, the situation for many residents of this area has become increasingly difficult. The time constraints of the civil patrol service decrease the time available for work in the fields or for doing day wage labor. Some villagers said their crops were suffering because they were unable to tend them and weed them as before. Partly in response to the one-month limit on travel, people migrate to the plantations in nearby Barillas to work.

Widows and single women appear to be migrating more frequently than in the past although this is not readily verifiable.

Credit is difficult to obtain. The agricultural bank, BANDESA, has few offices outside the department capital. Loans are not available to buy land, and often a land title is necessary to receive any money. In the past, coastal migration formed the basis of a local credit system whereby a *contratista* provided advances, later repaid by work on coastal plantations. The disruption of this system has created further problems for obtaining credit. People go to the local priest or religious workers in an emergency, or turn to relatives in times of need.

In the past few years many residents lost their animals, which the military slaughtered or commandeered for food or profit. The violence in the area of San Mateo led many *ladinos*, who in general were wealthier than most Indians, to relocate. With these went a source of income for women who would do washing and other chores.

Guatemala's general economic crisis has penetrated the most isolated communities of the highlands, and San Mateo is no exception. Markets seem well stocked; it is people's inability to buy that is the problem. Villagers complained about the price of beans, which increased substantially in 1985. They would also mention the rise in the price of thread used in weaving and embroidering of traditional clothing,[107] clothing in general, chemical fertilizer, and the exorbitant prices or unavailability of medicine. The solution for many families is to do without.[108] While the number of widows in the San Mateo area is not as overwhelming as in other areas of the country, their situation is precarious, as work is scarce. Some women migrate with their children either to the coast or to plantations in the nearby lowlands of Barillas. In general women who try to find employment in the cities as domestics receive low wages and are often the objects of sexual exploitation. The presence of the army in a town creates many problems, but at times also provides employment for local women who cook and do wash for the soldiers. This is not a dependable form of income, however, as the army is often on the move.

Physical Changes in the Countryside

Although on the surface the region appears little altered, there is ample physical evidence of the army's violence and occupation of the past six years throughout northeastern Huehuetenango. Most of the towns included in the fieldwork have suffered massacres during this period, and many of the houses of those murdered have been destroyed or remain empty. In Todos Santos the shells of destroyed houses have remained in the town center for almost four years. No one either has been allowed or is willing to reinhabit these sites. The same is true in San Mateo. While many live in small shacks or outlying houses, fine stone houses remain abandoned in the town centers, as the family members of those killed in the 1981 massacre prefer to live elsewhere.

Several villages in the municipality of San Mateo were completely destroyed by the army. In Petenac, for example, all of the inhabitants were killed, many of them burned to death, and all of the houses burned or leveled as were the crops. Now the only indications of the life that once existed are the remains of a few house foundations. Relatives of those murdered in Petenac, who live in nearby towns, have planted much of the area where the town once stood. Now, from the road, it is almost impossible to see any remains of the town. Informants describe the army's efforts to resettle such villages as an attempt to cover up their actions and erase the memories.

The area around San Mateo was transformed in 1982 when the army ordered the people to cut down the trees along the roadside. Where once a thick forest grew, the land is now cleared for hundreds of yards on either side of the road, littered with rotting tree trunks. For miles, up to and beyond the boundaries of Barillas and Santa Eulalia to the north and south, the roadside has been cleared.[109]

In the centers of many towns and villages the army also had the residents build kiosks and install loudspeakers. The public address systems are used to call men to civil patrol duty, to make announcements, or to call people together for sweeps or army educational meetings.

The army recently established semi-permanent military bases in many towns and villages throughout Huehuetenango. In Barillas, the main entrance to the town is surrounded by the base, with a check post, high wire fences and a host of buildings, many containing murals with army slogans and pictures of soldiers. The army is not currently in Barillas, but the base remains. A building in the center of San Mateo which once housed a library was taken over by the army for its quarters in late 1982 and painted in camouflage. The civil patrol now uses it as its central post, and the army bivouacs there when it takes up residency in the town.

OTHER CHANGES IN COMMUNITY LIFE

Witnessing spouses, children, and parents murdered is psychologically devastating. One informant grimly remarked that, "The after-effects of massacres, the terror, the nightmares, do not bother the victims. They are already dead. The survivors are the ones that suffer." The loss of family and neighbors who had to flee is also difficult to bear. Those who remain may not be sure if their loved ones are living in Mexico, or if they are dead. Moreover, there is constant terror that the massacres may begin again, or that a family member may disappear or be murdered at any time. Health workers report a great deal of trauma in their patients, especially among children, and say that tranquilizers are sought-after drugs.

The violence has affected women in subtle yet debilitating ways. While many women were murdered, the majority of the victims were men, leaving women to deal with the after-effects. In addition to personal trauma and loss, the women are often left as the sole providers for the family in situations where every member's contribution is vitally important for survival. While some widows try to cultivate their own land, often with the help of male relatives, the tasks are so demanding that at times they are compelled to leave the land fallow, sell it, or even abandon the plot until their sons grow old enough to farm. Some go to the cities to try earning a living, but this journey is precarious at best, and they are often brutally exploited.

Rape by army personnel and at times civil patrollers is an additional source of terror. Informants related that incidences of rape, relatively unknown among the Indians in the past, were increasing. They stated that this rise was due in part to greater outside influence from the *ladino* culture, and the presence of the military in isolated towns for long periods of time.

There are many war orphans in Huehuetenango (although the numbers do not approach those in El Quiché, especially in the Ixcán area). In general, relatives or neighbors take in these children. While taking in a child was often an act of mercy, assuring that the child would be raised in a family and as an Indian, there are reports of families mistreating children, expecting them to act as virtual slaves in return for room and board.

Some informants say that the onslaught of the past few years has called into question basic beliefs. "How can one explain all the massacres? What has happened to our protecting spirits?"

THE SITUATION OF REFUGEES IN HUEHUETENANGO

Few refugees have actually returned to Guatemala from Mexico,[110] and specific information about them is hard to come by. What follows is a summary of discussions with a variety of informants regarding the situation of returned refugees.

All refugees who return from Mexico must first pass through the nearest army base before being permitted to return to their places of origin. Officially this procedure enables the refugees to be counted or given medical care. Most informants agreed, however, that the primary reason they must spend days, weeks, even months in some cases in the army base, is to be investigated. It is a common belief, though not confirmed, that some do not survive their stay in the base. One informant said, "If you're on the army's "list" and they take you into the base, they will kill you. Many people die in the base." The civil patrol commander in a small village said he would not send returning refugees to the base because "they may not come out again." Another informant said: "Some refugees get killed before they even reach the base. If they want information then they take them there. When they're done they might send the refugees to one of the model villages."

Refugees have also been detained or killed just after leaving the base, and others have gone home and lived for weeks or months and then been killed, according to secondary informants. After leaving the Huehuetenango base in December 1982, a woman was murdered before reaching her house. In February 1983, Yolanda de Aguila was reportedly killed by the army after returning to her village. In April 1983, three refugees went back to Barillas after passing through the base in Huehuetenango and receiving a letter of amnesty. Three months later they were called to the base and disappeared. Their families asked the local priest to help them. He sent a telegram to the base reminding them of the amnesty and the next day the three men were released.[111]

Even those refugees who return safely to their homes often face an atmosphere of mistrust and control. A development worker said, "Refugees can apparently return without being killed, but they will have problems, especially if they come back with any ideas. People here don't want any more problems." The civil patrol commander in one town told of three refugees who had returned to the town and had no problems picking up their lives again. However, "they are always watched and carefully controlled. We let them patrol with everyone else but they are carefully controlled." A family was allowed to return to their village in Barillas and has faced no violence. But a young man from the village says "the control on them is very strong. The army is always aware of those who return."

The first refugees to return were settled in a camp near the military base in the department capital of Huehuetenango. Many of them lived for a year in abandoned houses and sheds before being allowed to go back to their villages. Now when refugees are released from the base, they often carry a special permission from the army.[112]

Refugees must also confront the army's unchanged convictions about them (despite the official "open door" policy). While some army personnel refused to discuss the refugees, claiming that such information was classified, the perspective generally expressed in official publications and by members of the armed forces is that the refugees were involved with the guerrillas, whether as willing participants or because they were deceived. As such they are "subversives," but the army wants them back anyway. As one officer explained, "The army has made the country peaceful again, and we want all Guatemalans to live together. We need the support of the people, so of course we won't kill them." The same officer said that all returning refugees must pass through the army base so that they can be "investigated". "They will have no problem if they return. If they want to they can go back to their own land, no problem. If not, they can go to Chacaj or any of the model villages." He did admit, however, that some of the refugees were a security problem. "Many of them want to infiltrate and sabotage. We must keep our eye on them."[113]

A *Kaibil* (member of the army's elite special forces) stationed in Huehuetenango said,

> The refugees are subversives. That makes them our enemy, just like inflation is your enemy in the U.S. You have to do whatever you can to get rid of it. For me, once I see a subversive, he's a dead subversive. I can spot one a mile away. You can see it in their faces. They are bad.

Returning refugees must also confront problems related to the continuing atmosphere of terror in the highlands, which generates considerable suspicion about them even among their fellow villagers. In numerous instances people expressed fears that the presence of suspected sympathizers in their villages might cause a return of the violence. In other cases, villagers more closely echoed the army line. A *ladino* informant explained, "The refugees are probably all Communists, and if they come back, they will have to be watched carefully."

Yet many other informants from the towns and villages of the highlands from where many of the refugees fled, expressed an understanding that the refugees had fled in terror of the army and stayed away for the same reason. Many showed compassion, the refugees often being their families and friends. A shopkeeper in Huehuetenango stated, "I would rather die than have to live away from Guatemala, but if they come back *they* might die."

To illustrate the complexity of the situation, a church worker explained that in Huehuetenango:

Returnees must stay on good terms with the army to survive. In some communities houses of refugees have been burned and their land taken because they are accused by their own people. If they denounce the violence or disappearances they too will suffer. That is why there is no information available. No one will admit it but a lot of denunciations occur for personal reasons: land, fear, etc.

Thus, in Huehuetenango, refugees who return from Mexico face considerable difficulties and danger. Often their land and property has been lost. While some of their old neighbors may regard them sympathetically, they must also face distrust and possible denunciation in their native village. Or they have the alternative of resettling in a development pole (see Ixil model villages) or some place other than their home. Most importantly, their right to life is not guaranteed. Recently the army asked the Catholic Church to encourage the refugees in Mexico to come back to Guatemala. The Bishop of Huehuetenango declined: "The army is in control of everything, and as long as they stay in control, the refugees may be killed if they return." Based on the fates of those who have returned and the attitudes of the army concerning refugees, the refugees in Mexico cannot be assured of safety upon their return to Huehuetenango.

4

The Case of the Ixil Triangle Development Pole

The three Ixil municipalities of El Quiché compose one of the regions most profoundly affected by the violent turmoil of recent years. Army scorched earth operations have totally or partially destroyed many villages and led to widespread deaths. A large part of the population, displaced from their home communities, took refuge in nearby towns, while others fled further into the mountains. Many remain displaced. Unlike the northern Huehuetenango area, the scars of the counterinsurgency campaign are visible throughout the region, and a direct military presence remains in many communities.

Thousands of survivors of army massacres now live in marginal housing surrounding the larger towns, or in model villages built as part of the counterinsurgency program. The presence of the army and the demands of the civil patrols dominate daily life. Moreover, army attempts to control the population through restrictions on land use and civil patrol service have exacerbated the traumas of the current economic crisis. Once a guerrilla stronghold, conflict still occurs in the area, and it is unlikely that the military will withdraw soon.

Since the government plans to relocate most of the refugees now in Mexico to model villages, the Ixil region provides insights into the situation refugees would face upon returning to Guatemala.

GENERAL BACKGROUND AND INTRODUCTION

The "Ixil Triangle" is a term used by the Guatemalan military to describe the three municipalities in northern Quiché that are predominantly inhabited by the Ixil people.[114] The area is mountainous, the altitude rising sharply from Sacapulas until it reaches over 2000 meters above sea level. The three municipalities are Santa María Nebaj (pop. 27,255), San Juan Cotzal (pop. 11,900), and San Gaspar Chajul (pop. 18,000). Chajul has by far the largest land area; Cotzal is the smallest and most densely populated.[115] The distance by road from Nebaj to Cotzal is approximately twenty kilometers, and to Chajul twenty-three kilometers. A road for vehicles has never existed directly between Chajul and Cotzal (although one is now under construction), and other roads in the area are new.

The Ixil Indians compose one of the smaller ethno-linguistic groups in Guatemala. Some 90 percent of the area's 60,000 people are Ixiles. Interspersed and surrounding the Ixil are villages of Quiché speakers.

Ladinos penetrated the town centers (Nebaj, Cotzal, and Chajul) in the late 1800s, but did not consolidate their local power until the 1930s. Aside from the region's large coffee plantations, *ladino* presence has generally been limited to the municipal towns, primarily Nebaj. Cotzal, known regionally as the town of the *comerciantes* or commercial vendors, was more resistant to *ladino* penetration than Nebaj, and Chajul retains a reputation as the town most closed to outsiders.

The municipalities and their corresponding outlying areas each have a slightly different Ixil dialect and various cultural differences. Most visible is the distinctive traditional dress of each area. Women almost universally wear the *traje*. Men also commonly wore traditional clothing only fifteen years earlier, but have begun wearing "ladino clothes." In Chajul, with its relative isolation, men wear traditional clothes more frequently, and throughout the region most men don special clothes for festival days.

The majority of Ixiles are agriculturalists, planting corn, beans, and other vegetables. Although land is generally more fertile than in the San Mateo area, the region forms part of the classic *minifundia-latifundia* system. Since the early part of this century, a few large coffee plantations have controlled large tracts of the area's most fertile land.[116] In the 1960s and 1970s, the military and large business interests began taking over large quantities of land in northern Quiché, ancestrally claimed by the Ixiles.

The shortage of land and the resulting marginal economic situation gave rise to large, seasonal migration to coffee, sugar, and cotton plantations on the south coast. During the harvest season entire towns would appear devoid of all men. *Contratistas*, locally-based labor contractors, filled their cattle trucks with people, taking them to prearranged plantations to work an average of one to three months each year. The *contratistas* also represented a ready source of credit, providing small loans at high interest rates that served to lock people into an endless cycle of debt. Wages were low, averaging about Q1 per day for men; women and children were often paid at half a man's rate, even for the same work. The estimated numbers of men that left the municipality of Nebaj per month ranged from 400 to 1000 in the 1960s.

Migration to the plantations is debilitating. The tropical heat is exhausting, working hours are from sunrise to sunset, and lowland diseases claim hundreds of victims each year. Living conditions are worse than in the home communities: open communal sheds, no sanitary facilities, no services, and an inadequate diet.

Traditional decision-making structures in the Ixil area have evolved through the years. The interrelated civil-religious structures, in which selected men rose to positions of authority either as *principales* or in the civil hierarchy, were still intact in the previolence period (mid-1970s). *Principales* and civil officials dealt with questions of land, family disputes, and local organization. *Cofradías* were also active, more so in Nebaj and Chajul than Cotzal, at that time. In addition, elders in the community were influential as resources of knowledge and advice.

The Catholic and Protestant Churches have conducted aggressive missionary work in the region. The Catholic Church expanded its work among the rural population following the 1954 coup. The Spanish priests in the Ixil region were at first isolated, but began to make a substantial impact in the following two decades. Cooperatives gained acceptance and popularity, and the Catholic Action movement became a vehicle for community participation. Christian study groups, consciousness raising activities and the development of "Christian base communities" led to the widespread grass roots organizing of the 1970s.

Evangelical Christian missionaries from the U.S. have also worked in the Ixil region for more than twenty years.[117] Under the Ríos Montt government,[118] the time of the worst violence in the Ixil region, Evangelical churches formed the relief organization FUNDAPI (Foundation for Aid to the Indian People). This organization served to support the government in the food relief, Food-for-Work, road construction, and model village aspects of the army's counterinsurgency plan. These efforts have touched many sectors of the community, both those who have converted to Evangelical Christianity and those who needed the resources that only the Evangelicals could offer.[119]

In 1980, the Catholic Church had to pull out of the department of El Quiche after three priests and dozens of lay catechists were killed. Catholic religious workers were able to return to the Ixil area in late 1984, but they have been met with military threats and continuing harassment despite their cautious and restrained work.

When the Guerrilla Army of the Poor (EGP) began to reach out from its initial bases in the Ixcán to the highland Indian population, increasingly desperate villagers in the Ixil area began to view the insurgents as allies. Ixiles joined the guerrillas in large numbers from the mid-1970s through 1981.

As insurgent strength grew and local support deepened, army repression intensified in an area considered to be EGP territory by 1978. The repression was unprecedented in both scale and cruelty. The army occupied the three towns in the region by the late 1970s, and by 1982, it had many outposts throughout the area, raiding and razing the region's villages and smaller hamlets. Chajul suffered a major massacre as early as 1978 and another in 1982. Government troops brutally murdered forty-six people in the Nebaj village of Acul on April 20 and 21, 1982.[120] Captured civilians were routinely tortured and executed on the assumption that "almost everyone in the villages is a collaborator."[121] Villages were routinely destroyed with grenades, and army planes and helicopters were called in for bombing missions.[122]

THE ARMY AND POWER

The "Ixil Triangle" is the region where the army has applied its counterinsurgency strategy with the greatest coherence. The army has carried out antiguerrilla activities and selective repression against civilians since 1975. The military required, however, eight years of increasingly brutal and widespread repression of the civilian population to establish itself as the dominant power. Even today, territory beyond tightly-controlled population centers is still actively contested by the guerrillas. Informants in the area made clear that despite the dearth of newspaper reports, clashes between the army and guerrillas occur two to three times a week, often with casualties.

Because of the insurgents' deep roots in the population and their continued ability to act militarily, the army still maintains a large presence in the Ixil area. Over 700 soldiers are constantly stationed in Nebaj, where the base is in the center of town. Major bases are also located in Cotzal and Chajul, and there are outposts and small garrisons throughout the area, including model villages. Due to major roadwork, carried out with the forced labor of the population, army vehicles can rapidly reach almost any of the model villages. There were soldiers present in many villages visited.[123]

Awareness of army presence, then, is unavoidable and adds to an underlying tension in villages and towns. In Nebaj, soldiers appear everywhere: lounging around, standing guard, training in groups, or chanting loudly as they run through the streets at dawn. In all of the towns, a few soldiers are always in the main square or wandering through the market. Troop movement is constant, as soldiers move from a village to the town and then to another village. Moreover, continual army sweeps through the mountains seek to combat guerrillas and to ferret out the "population in resistance", the internal refugees living above the "triangle" of Nebaj, Chajul and Cotzal in the zones uncontrolled by the military.

As elsewhere, the totality of military authority has undermined all other power structures. The army has turned over much less of its authority to civilian proxies, such as civil patrol commanders or military commissioners, because of the continued insurgent threat. While on occasion a commander may become tired of dealing with local problems and send disputes to the civilian mayor, the commander is still the court of last appeal.

As in northeastern Huehuetenango, the character and whims of the local military commander strongly influence community life. A commander in Cotzal surprised everyone by investigating a denunciation. Upon learning that the accuser was trying to get out of a debt with the man he had denounced, the commander found the accuser guilty of false denunciation and had him executed. Informants explained other commanders seldom look into denunciations; they "need hear only a whisper about someone to order them killed."

One new commander in Cotzal decided that he was tired of the potholes in the streets. He called a meeting of all of the men in town and informed them that they would be spending their Sunday filling in the holes. When asked about their work, the men said nothing more than "everyone must comply." Other army mandated community projects in Cotzal, built by unpaid, civilian work details, have included a *pila* (a communal sink with running water), a playground, and small lean-tos for a park near the river.

The local commander often decides if a certain region is secure enough for resettlement. If the answer is positive, the army oversees the work of rebuilding the community and defines the conditions of return. The army determines where the village will be built, its layout, the size of the houses and lots, and when and where cultivation can occur. Moreover, the commander evaluates if a refugee is "clean" and can go to a model village or move in with a family member. While the communities themselves often establish land distribution for returning relatives, the army commander is the final arbiter.

The army also imposes limitations on travel throughout the Ixil area. While passes are not always necessary, people generally carry them for travel between outlying villages. Military permission, for example, is needed to leave the village of La Pista, less than an hour's walk from Nebaj, for any purpose. This restriction complicates matters for the residents since there is no market in the town and they use the one in Nebaj.

The army keeps a record of all the inhabitants, developed initially through its own regional census. Thus, unlike Huehuetenango, almost everyone, including women, is registered and has documentation (the all-important *cédula*). Identification papers are checked frequently and carefully by both the civil patrol and the army. Cars as well as buses are stopped and checked at almost every checkpoint. And until recently, even the Catholic priest had to inform the army of his movements.

Informants maintained that denunciations are frequent, and emphasized the need to be careful. Monitoring of routine events is pervasive. The owners of the local boarding house in Nebaj, for example, must report information regarding each new arrival to the army, and a list of all guests is given to the base daily. In Nebaj, those who venture out after dark are routinely stopped by soldiers and questioned. One informant emphasized that all market places in the region are closely monitored by the military (although sometimes not by uniformed troops)[124] to detect if anyone was buying "excess" quantities of food that could be passed on to the guerrillas or to the population that continues to live in the mountains. More so than anywhere else in the study, save the Ixcán development pole, the atmosphere in the Ixil area is one of fear.

Interinstitutional Coordinators

While most relief development work is still carried out directly through the military, numerous state agencies are also involved, and church-related projects (both Evangelical and Catholic) are beginning to shoulder part of the activity. Through the Interinstitutional Coordinator, the army can control the work done in the region. Even the governmental development workers may not act without the knowledge and permission of the base commander. The IIC is more institutionalized throughout the Ixil region than in the rural areas of northeastern Huehuetenango. In Nebaj, where the IIC is strongest, all local institutions meet with the army commander to discuss and receive the go-ahead for their projects as well as petitioning for resources. Nonetheless, it was difficult to gain information on the IIC from civilian authorities, in part because of their limited participation and decision making in the overall process.[125]

Civil Patrols

The civil patrol has the same basic structure and functions as in northeastern Huehuetenango. Patrol duties keep the men occupied, limit their movements, and involve local residents in exerting control over their fellow villagers. Here, however, the army retains much of the actual control over the patrol, and consequently patrol commanders and squad leaders have less autonomy and less power than in other parts of the country where the army's presence is less direct.

In larger towns such as Nebaj there are ten civil patrol commanders. In Cotzal there are three. One of their primary duties is to sign travel passes for patrollers who need to leave town. Permission to travel is usually granted in cases such as travel to the south coast with a local contractor. It is usually necessary to provide a replacement. The fee most often quoted was two to three quetzales, although it varies. Because of the precarious economic situation, most people try to enlist family members or friends to take their place if they must travel. A civil patrol commander in Cotzal said that the replacement requirement is sometimes suspended if they know someone cannot pay. Merchants who travel frequently must pay for replacements, creating a new income source. Between patrol shift changes, around 4:00 PM, men begin to hang out in the Cotzal square where the patrollers report, hoping to find work as a replacement.

The civil patrol commanders also oversee the changing of the patrol shifts. Before the patrollers begin their duties, however, they first check in at the army base, where the squad leader presents a list of their names to the lieutenant in charge. "Twenty men reporting for civil patrol duty. Twenty rifles accounted for." After the list is taken inside the base, the lieutenant returns with the approval for them to begin patrolling. As in most of Huehuetenango, civil patrol shifts in the Ixil area are twenty-four hours long and range in frequency from every six to twenty days. During the migration season, when few men are left to act as replacements, the number of patrol groups is reduced. Thus, each remaining man must serve more often, sometimes patrolling twice as often as at other times of the year. In general, because of the smaller populations, residents of model villages patrol more frequently.

In the Ixil region, patrollers rotate through three distinct duties. They are generally not informed in advance of what they will be doing, for security reasons. When reporting for duty, they may be assigned to a *garita* (guardpost),[126] where everyone is checked for identification and passes; they may have to patrol the town streets all day checking in at each of these posts; or they may be sent on a twenty-four hour patrol into the surrounding mountains. These sweeps are meant to cover all of the surrounding area in the course of a week. Longer sweeps are also occasionally assigned, in which the patrol is sometimes accompanied by the army.[127]

Almost no one, except for the civil patrol commanders in Nebaj and Cotzal, maintained that the civil patrol was voluntary. One of the patrol commanders in Nebaj contended, "If someone misses a turn, we can't beat them or anything, because it is a voluntary service. But we go to their houses and try to convince them of how important the civil patrol is to protect them and their families from subversives." Others mentioned that missing the civil patrol would be looked on as subversive, and villagers believe that even a suspicion of subversion could bring retribution.

Civil Power

The pervasive military presence has undermined the power of traditional authorities such as *principales* and elected officials. Little mention was made in Nebaj of the imminent change in local government with the 1985 elections, perhaps because local power is so limited. In Cotzal, where the military-appointed mayor was believed to be involved in a shady land deal, a few people mentioned that they hoped the election would clear things up. However, most people stated that they did not think the election would make much of a difference.

PHYSICAL CHANGES IN THE COUNTRYSIDE

The physical effects of the upheavel of the past few years are apparent almost immediately. Until this decade, the population distribution was

Civil patrols on duty in Nebaj, 1983. Photography by Pat Goudvis.

characterized by small settlements, spread throughout a heavily wooded countryside, accessible only by small footpaths. This distribution was ideal for an irregular war, allowing the insurgents to move undetected among their popular base. Today the landscape is quite different. Virtually all the villages of the three municipalities were partially or completely destroyed, and relatively few have been rebuilt under the model village program. In the municipality of Nebaj, eleven villages (*aldeas*) and ninety-one hamlets (*caseríos*) have been reduced to approximately eight settlements.[128] Not only has the army created a vast, uninhabited no-man's land for improved surveillance, but the military has crowded the entire remaining population into a few, tightly-controlled centers.

The new roads throughout the region, products of forced labor and Food-for-Work programs of 1982–84, provided qualitative improvements in the army's capabilities for rapid ground movement. Previously, the trip to the village of Tzalbal, north of Nebaj, was a several hour hike on a difficult path. Now a jeep easily travels the thirteen kilometer distance in twenty minutes.[129] All of these roads are considerably better than the road from Nebaj to the department capital, Santa Cruz del Quiché, although the latter is a much more traveled route and a crucial commercial link to the rest of the department and the country. The army claims that the new roads are part of the improvements they are bringing to the local population, yet no new bus routes have been opened, and it is still a long walk to market. Moreover, mostly army and government vehicles are seen on the new roads.[130] For the military, the advantages of the new roads consist not only of quick access to the reconstructed villages and army outposts, but the increased capability to move and supply ground troops.

The heavily-wooded areas along the roadsides are also gone. The charred remains of the forests are now partially visible through the growing corn. The forest destruction (designed to impede guerrilla ambushes of moving troop convoys) was an unpopular task forced on the local population. The impact on daily life is significant: people must now walk several kilometers a day to find adequate firewood. In addition, overuse of available land, erosion and continued deforestation will lower agricultural production and speed environmental deterioration in general.

MODEL VILLAGES

The field study area is one of the major sites in the army's development pole program.[131] As conceived by the army, a development pole is a decentralized regional development zone, including model villages. The program represents the developmental and security part of the military's overall counterinsurgency strategy in two ways. First, model villages are intended to improve villagers' material conditions, undercutting a major part of the insurgent movement's appeal. Second, model villages concentrate the population into easily-controlled villages, making it difficult for guerrilla forces to establish an effective base of support in the area.

In this phase, model villages form the core of the development poles, and as such have received considerable attention from both the army and numerous government agencies. In the initial construction period, ground troops participated in the day-to-day supervision. Virtually every government agency that has anything to do with rural or community development is involved. These include: DESACOM (community development); BANDESA (agricultural development bank); INACOP (national association of cooperatives); INAFOR (national forestry agency); INTA (national land institute); ICTA (national agricultural research and extension agency); as well as health workers and teachers. All of their activities are coordinated through the civil affairs division of the army (S-5), which oversees the model village even after it is formally inaugurated.

Physical Description

Acul, Tzalbal, Pulay, Ojo de Agua, Salquil Grande, San Felipe Chenlá and Bichibalá all form part of the Ixil Triangle development pole and are among the model villages that the army considers completed. They represent the best of the army's development projects.

Villages, previously located on hillsides with each house surrounded by its own varied-sized, sometimes extensive lot, are now laid out in a concentrated, rectilinear grid pattern. The houses are built in pairs, generally separated from their neighbors by only a few meters, in lots 40 by 60 meters in size. Every house is identical, fashioned of wood slats and covered with corrugated metal roofing. Each displays an electricity meter, a number, and often government propaganda posters. Almost every street is named in Spanish and marked with signposts entitled: "Development Avenue", "Liberty Street", "Street of the Army", etc. Thus, while the populations of some of these rebuilt villages may actually be smaller than the original settlement, they live in a more urban form. It is still too early to know the ways in which this urbanization will affect the inhabitants' relationship to their home space and to their neighbors.

Most of these new villages have a prominent army garrison within or on the edge of the village boundary, and all have some type of guardposts such as those used by the on-duty civil patrollers. The new villages are equipped with or in the process of building a health post, a school, and both Evangelical and Catholic churches. Many of these facilities, however, are not currently staffed or supplied. In all cases, the army determines the design of the finished village, including the location and assignment of houses. In some villages the army distributed housing to each family by lottery. Families drew a number on the day of arrival and then had to occupy the corresponding house, eliminating the choice of living near kinsmen.

Reported Problems

The residents of these model villages face a multitude of problems, as local officials themselves admit. Informants' comments and field observations confirmed the following difficulties: land shortages combined with few alternative work opportunities; degraded living conditions, in some cases much worse than the original villages; inadequate services; and programs inappropriate to local conditions. Overall, traditional cultural and community life appeared undermined by the fusing of different ethnic and community groups into a single village, destroying autonomy and increasing material dependency.

The universal complaint in all the model villages was a shortage of land and a lack of compensatory income generating options. Residents of Ax'ctumbal (La Pista) said they had each received one *cuerda* for cultivation at a cost of Q30.00, but that it was "totally insufficient, so we must buy our corn most of the year." In Acul, local officials stated that the amount of land available to the resident population was much less than in the past. As one resident pointed out, "We can only farm up to these first hills [pointing to the nearby slopes], not any farther, not where we used to." Moreover, the army decides which land can be farmed and which is off limits, based on military criteria.

In many of these communities, the only option for residents who lack the land or the resources to support their families is to share with relatives. While the land is already extremely subdivided, many manage to borrow a small plot here or there. The 1985 mayor of Nebaj observed: "People are poor but they share what they have because they are aware of the need."

Work opportunities are few, and civil patrol obligations restrict the length of time villagers have to migrate to the coast. Publicly-funded roadwork employs a limited number of men and is only available for two weeks at a time. Marketing of agricultural or artisan production is limited, both because few people produce a surplus and travel restrictions are more tightly enforced for the model villages than throughout the rest of the area.

State and military institutions have initiated income-producing projects on a small and generally unsuccessful scale. An artisan production center was set up in Acul, but has found little market for its products and reportedly employs fewer than twenty men. One model village has a small bee project. A few exhibit some groundwork for fish ponds (including signs leading the way to nothing), but none were found to be completely built or functioning. The army projections of 1982, which outlined a new agro-export sector based in the development poles, have not materialized. A few "demonstration plots", set aside for experimentation with "high cash value" vegetables, have not yet provided any income for the population.

In every model village on which information was available, housing is insufficient. While many relatives are no longer neighbors (because of military housing assignment procedures), in other cases several families are made to share a single house. Whereas custom would dictate the construction of a new house as a solution for overcrowding, the army does not permit model village residents to construct houses that do not conform to the army-determined housing design and settlement plan. To conform to these regulations, residents must depend on the army to provide land for housing lots and approve materials for construction.

Although health clinics exist in most model villages, residents are quick to comment, "there are no medicines." A health worker in one village complained of being seriously handicapped without medicines. The main problems are malnutrition and worms due to an insufficient food supply and unsafe water, despite the supposed provisions of potable water.

The lack of land and work opportunities causes widespread dependence on international aid and government Food-for-Work programs. However, according to INACOP (National Institute of Cooperatives) officials, Food-for-Work programs end whenever a village is inaugurated. While much of the work involved in these projects continues, there are no longer the food rations that previously provided at least minimal compensation.

Without both land and sufficient food, credit is vital to enable peasants to improve their situation and to return to self-sufficiency. Yet, as a result of the economic crisis and the deterioration of the *contratista* system, the only available source of credit is BANDESA, the agricultural development bank, which gives credit only for the purchase of agricultural inputs, *not for land*. Since land is a prerequisite to receive a loan, those without land have virtually no access to substantial credit.

Basic agricultural inputs and technical assistance are not readily available to the population. While government officials maintained that some land and housing materials had been donated free of charge, in most model villages seed was never provided. Given the disruption in planting cycles, almost everyone resettled in the new villages had to purchase seeds for the initial plantings. An official in a government development agency felt the government should be investing money in providing land for self-sufficiency. He complained that there was plenty of land contiguous to some of the villages, which large landowners were willing to sell.

Many government projects seem superfluous. Effort and expense, for example, has gone into creating parks with picnic shelters and flower gardens, often near streams. In other cases, the order of the projects appears skewed. The army has equipped many model villages with electricity, one of the largest overall expenses in the model village construction plans, before fully meeting basic needs such as food and shelter. In Ojo de Agua, Cotzal, the electrification cost was Q92,480.00 (Ejercito de Guatemala, 1984:95–106). According to that figure the cost per family benefited would be almost Q1,000.00.

People not residing in model villages but in the municipal seats had varied opinions regarding these projects. One *ladino* contended "The government is helping the people after the guerrillas burned their homes." Others believed that "The army is doing its best to keep people under its control, and the model villages are the most obvious example of this." Interestingly, even those who spoke of people receiving free land and houses in the Ixil model villages admitted that they themselves had no interest in living in one.

The new settlements are generally mixtures of different villages and, at times, ethno-linguistic groups. Rather than promoting cooperation and support between these groups, the army, civil patrol, and informers create an overall environment of suspicion and control. Discussing the overall impact of these changes, a *ladino* working for a government agency in one of the villages explained:

> It's very difficult for the people to change their lifestyles, to have to live close together and be more urban. It's still us imposing our way on them, and that's not very good. It's really the government's idea of how they should be living [and not their own choice].

An indigenous government worker was concerned that traditional religious practices (*costumbres*) were endangered by the disruption and the nontraditional environment in the new villages. Some informants treated this as a deliberate army plan, while others saw it as coincidental.

VILLAGE REPORTS

Case Studies of Select Model Villages

The villages the military has programmed for reconstruction are: (Ejército, 1984:73)

Acul	Salquil Palop
Tzalbal	Atzumbal
Juil-Chacalté	Jua
Río Azul-Pulay	Ilom
Xolcuay	Chel
Ojo de Agua	Xemal-Xepatul
Santa Abelina	Amachel
Bichibalá	San Felipe Chenlá

The following model villages are considered completed: Ojo de Agua, Cotzal; Bichibalá, Cotzal; San Felipe Chenlá, Cotzal; Acul, Nebaj; Tzalbal, Nebaj; Salquil Grande, Nebaj; and Pulay, Nebaj.

Ojo de Agua

Ojo de Agua's Ixil name is K'anil. The remains of destroyed houses are visible only a few meters outside the rebuilt village. INACOP says there were 67 heads of family and 283 residents as of mid-1985. The army's cultural magazine and development pole publications state there are 100 housing units for 100 families for a total of 600 inhabitants. Construction was begun on September 1, 1984, and the village was inaugurated on December 21, 1984. Army documents maintain that 100 people worked on its construction under the Food-for-Work program.[132] The total cost of constructing the infrastructure and for technical assistance supplied by fourteen government agencies was Q344,251. The majority of the current residents apparently were from the original village and others nearby. Other former residents currently reside in the town of Cotzal and walk out to farm their land in the new village.

The town has two civil patrol posts; one was generally manned by eight patrol members. Because many men had recently received leave to work on the south coast, the army raised the required patrol service to twenty-four hours once a week. When everyone is in town, service is cut down to about once every two weeks.

Groups of ten or more men and some young boys do roadwork outside the village. Such labor is reportedly unpaid and required. Villagers said the frequency of this type of work would likely be raised with a new commander.

Some people in Ojo de Agua are renting land, reportedly for one *quetzal* per *cuerda* per year. One informant said land was for sale at Q25 per *cuerda*: "a very good price if one has the money."

Informants claim that, as in other such villages, homes were distributed by lottery, resulting in a random placement of families. Some houses were still empty and being held in reserve for future residents. The cost for new residents would be betwen Q30-60.

Services are limited and resources scarce. A mother with a sick child said there was a health clinic, but no staff and no medicine. She said she did not have the money to take her child to the clinic in nearby Cotzal.

The Catholic Church has a building, and at least one Catholic lay worker is in residence. But the nearest priest is in Nebaj and only comes to the village to say mass once or twice a year.[133] The Evangelical Assembly of God Church, based in Cotzal, also has a chapel in Ojo de Agua. A school building and municipal building were still under construction. An Ixil literacy worker trained by the Cotzal-based Wycliffe Bible Translators lives in Ojo de Agua. The teacher for the government school lives in Cotzal.

Several signs advertised the existence of a fish pond project, but there were no ponds. Another building was divided into two rooms, both empty, with one labelled a butcher shop and the other a corn mill. A few families seemed to be making string bags for sale, but no other income-generating activities were visible. Several residents complained about the lack of work, citing this as the reason why so many men had to leave to work on the coast and why so many children were sickly.

One striking aspect of the site visit to Ojo de Agua was the ubiquitous army propaganda. A painted sign near the civil patrol *garita* states: "Welcome to Ojo de Agua, Where We Have Said No to the Communist Subversion." At least two different posters promoting the army as friends of the people were liberally distributed throughout the town. Street signs carry nationalistic names. Buildings for public use are carefully labeled with wood placards.

Bichibalá, Cotzal

This village, inaugurated in February 1986 by Minister of Development René de León Schlotter, was largely constructed in 1985. It is built on land that was previously a private plantation, along with the neighboring village of Santa Abelina. The current residents, for the most part, were originally workers on this plantation. In 1985 there were 107 families. The houses are made of wood with metal roofing as in the other model villages. Bichibalá does not conform to the usual model village design of homes crowded together on a plain. Instead it is built on a steep hillside with stairs constructed to aid access in the rainy season. Erosion and the type of newly-constructed permanent housing could pose problems for the future.

San Felipe Chenlá, Cotzal

118 families and 474 persons lived in San Felipe Chenlá in late 1985, according to INACOP figures. The village had already been operational several months when it was inaugurated in June 1985, in a ceremony attended by then Chief of State, General Mejía Víctores.

The appearance of the village is distinctive; it is flat and bare, giving the rows of identical houses a particularly regimented look.

A municipal official related that San Felipe Chenlá had experienced various problems with local leaders. The army-appointed president of the local reconstruction committee (army-directed structure that works in conjunction with the Interinstitutional Coordinator system) had seriously abused his authority. This individual was not an original resident of the town, according to the informant, nor had he held any prior position in the community. He had tried to use his position to claim ownership of 100 *cuerdas* (about four hectares) of land that had belonged to people who were killed in the violence. While he had not been successful in taking over the land, he remained in office despite the residents' protests.

Acul, Nebaj

Acul officially hosts 450 families, with a total population of 2,700. Other sources reported close to 500 families in early 1985, with the number still growing.[134] The village was inaugurated in December 1983, the first model village of the army's Ixil Triangle development pole. Residents are primarily from the original villages of Acul and Chuataj and the approximately twelve hamlets associated with both. The army reports the current residents come from a total of seventeen communities. The majority are Ixiles, but many Quiché people live in Acul as well. Due to conflicts the structure of the local government was altered to include an equal number of each language group.

Area officials stated that survivors of the original Acul received their land back when the town was first resettled. If their particular land parcel was needed for housing sites, they were reportedly reimbursed. According to INACOP data, the government spent Q70,020 to buy land for 254 peasant farmers in Acul. Different officials reported various prices, (ranging from Q25–40 per *cuerda*) that were charged the Quiché and other outsiders for their lots.

Acul is the army's showcase model village. "When you go to Acul," one Nebaj resident commented to us, "just keep in mind that it is the nicest of all the model villages, the others are much worse off." Yet, housing, land, employment and basic services are far from adequate even there. Many in the community still rely on international food aid. Mothers with children can travel to Nebaj to request powdered milk and sometimes other foodstuffs from the government welfare office (*Bienestar Social*). Children, if they attend school, receive a cup of *Incaparina* every day (a soy-based, sweetened, high protein formula made with milk). The official policy is that they must both attend classes and participate in the afternoon community work projects (helping in the construction of the school, cooking, planting flowers, etc.) to receive the food. Teachers explained that for many, the one cup of formula constitutes the mainstay of their daily diet.

The problems of food, land, work, and resource shortages were explicitly and repeatedly described by the residents of Acul. There is a clinic, but insufficient medicine. A supply of medicine donated from the U.S. was a random mixture, labeled in English, and not necessarily corresponding to local needs.[135] And although the army-installed potable water system has received much fanfare, the original Acul had such a system since 1973.

The school has three teachers, but each class may have over fifty children, and the teaching conditions are difficult. Many problems arise because of the three different languages in use. Furthermore, some parents resist sending their children to school because they are needed at home to work or because they resent the imposition of an outside language and culture on their families. Extension workers from the community development agency (DESACOM), who do use Ixil translators, come to Acul once a week.

In the town center, Acul has a church, a flagpole, a civil patrol watchtower, and a municipal building which houses the health clinic. Construction continues on new buildings and housing units.

Civil patrol duties are twenty-four hours every twelve days. While Acul no longer receives Food-for-Work supplies, community service is expected. A workshop employs a small group of men to weave by loom the traditional *corte* (skirt) material of the area and other items. The major problem with the workshop, informants said, was difficulty in getting the goods to a profitable market. At times planes come and take away large loads of woven goods, perhaps to be sold in the U.S., but villagers complained that such sales were sporadic at best.

Tzalbal, Nebaj

Tzalbal was inaugurated April 30, 1984, just two months after construction officially began, with a total of 315 houses. Physically it follows the standard pattern or reconstructed villages of the area. Over 1,500 people currently live there in crowded living spaces and amidst poor general economic conditions. The two tiny stores in the village offer only candles, a few cans of juice and pieces of chewing gum. Otherwise the shelves are bare. There was an idle bread oven, because none of the residents have money to buy the bread.

Tzalbal lies quite close to territory still contested between the army and the guerrillas. Thus, control is strict. The fortified army garrison sits just above the village, in a location that makes for easy observation. Soldiers are posted at the garrison and often within the village as well.

Salquil Grande, Nebaj

The original village had a population of at least 1,100 people. Resettlement began in 1985, first with 123 families; by September there were over 400 families. Many Salquil residents were living in La Pista (see description of Ax'ctumbal) before the resettlement process began and some are still there.[136] Some of those who have resettled in Salquil were originally residents of nearby Palob, where they can farm but are not yet permitted to live.

In late 1985 the village was still being rebuilt and was an occasional recipient of the National Reconstruction Committee's Food-for-Work program. The food, when there is any, is delivered by INACOP.

Salquil Grande and the surrounding villages constitute the potato growing region of Nebaj, well known for both fertile land and the custom of making a fertilizer from the trees. Because of this, the deforestation of the area is a particular problem.

Salquil is several kilometers north of Tzalbal and near the newly-constructed army road. It is still, according to a government official, a "red zone" of guerrilla activity.

Pulay, Nebaj

Pulay was inaugurated September 30, 1984 with 138 houses. It is constructed in three sections along the road leading from Nebaj to Chajul and Cotzal, near the three-way fork linking the three towns. While most of the land area of the original Pulay lay within Nebaj, a few of the fourteen hamlets that belonged to it lay within the bounds of Cotzal. The original population (as of 1973) was over 800 people. In 1984 the surviving/resettled population was approximately 350 people according to INACOP data. One resident said that, in general, the occupants were all from the original Pulay and that many had taken refuge in Nebaj during the violence, living in a refugee camp until they could return.

According to one informant, returning residents received some land, sometimes their own, upon the initial resettlement. The government also provided some wheat seed for use on a trial basis, hoping that production could be used for home consumption and for sale. Land titles were promised, but had not yet materialized after a year. "Perhaps soon," speculated one resident, who expressed hope that his children would obtain enough education to one day be able to leave Pulay.

A vigilant civil patrol post stops every bus and passerby for thorough checks of papers and sometimes cursory searches of people and baggage. The main civil patrol post is in the middle of the village, staffed by about six people, with at least four guns between them. At times soldiers are also present, assisting in the monitoring.[137] Pulay residents had electricity in their houses but so far had not had to pay for it. Residents were not sure what would happen if the bill came due, and some expressed nervousness about the cost of a year's worth of electricity.

OTHER COMMUNITIES WITHIN THE DEVELOPMENT POLE

The three municipal seats, Nebaj, Cotzal and Chajul, are undisputed government territory.[138] Although never destroyed, they were marked by physical destruction and other acts of terror, and were repeatedly the stage for battles between the army and the insurgents. These towns suffered population dislocation and later had to absorb a sizeable overflow of internal refugees from the surrounding area. In 1986, the relatively new presence of large numbers of soldiers and new systems such as the IIC and the civil patrols exerted a significant influence.

There is also a group of villages serviced by army/government programs, but not described by officials as "model villages." Some of these are referred to at the local level as model villages, sometimes as "pre-model" villages, and sometimes with no specific categories at all. This group includes the settlements of La Pista and Las Violetas in Nebaj, that did not exist before 1982. It also includes Xix (Chajul) and villages such as Palop (Nebaj), which basically will be model villages, if enough funds become available to complete them in accordance with the army plan. A village such as Xolcuay (Chajul) might be considered a failed model village, although still involved in government programs. Finally, there are villages such as Asich, Chisis, and Cayxay (all of Cotzal), which are being informally resettled and may eventually resemble model villages, depending on army resources and strategy.

The municipal towns are well off compared to other area communities, which span a spectrum of unique situations, extremely poor in some cases, but left with more autonomy in others. All these villages are serviced and monitored by government institutions, participate in the civil patrol system, and operate under conditions similar to their model village neighbors. Similar problems affect them as well, especially the shortage of land and work.

Cotzal

San Juan Cotzal illustrates the difficulties that have arisen in larger municipal towns with a large displaced populaton. Many of the displaced widows and refugee families actually live outside the town center, on land owned by a man who had been allegedly involved with the guerrillas.[139] When the numbers of displaced in Cotzal began to overwhelm the existing resources, the refugees were settled on this parcel. Recently, a resident of Cotzal claimed the land, saying he was a relative of the original owner. He wanted to evict all the refugees, but was apparently persuaded by the local mayor that these people were in need and had no place to go. He settled for selling the land for twenty-five *quetzales* per *cuerda* (considered inexpensive). Several informants felt the man was lying and had perhaps falsified papers or paid bribes to claim the inheritance.

One source claimed that Cotzal's army base commander had permitted people to settle on abandoned land within Cotzal and claim it for their own. This act was portrayed as a measure benefitting poor and landless people, but actually some who were already quite well off were able to take the greatest advantage of the offer.

Neither the township of Cotzal nor the national government have been able to extend any aid to the displaced persons living within the jurisdiction. Consequently, refugees have had to rely on family, friends or private charitable organizations. For example, the WBT missionaries stationed in Cotzal, set up a project to build houses for widows, drawing money and volunteer work from the U.S. Some refugees were able to salvage enough resources to buy their own land and homes, but these were people who tended to be already financially secure before the violence. The majority of refugees in the municipal capitals are living on the floor of a family member's house or in other inadequate conditions.

Xix, Chajul

Xix is a Quiché village, although it lies nested above the town of Chajul in a primarily Ixil region. The original population reportedly collaborated as a community with the opposition and stayed in the mountains eluding army control until mid-1984. The majority of them surrendered to the army at that time, in hopes of regaining their land, which they eventually did. They were resettled, however, after the planting season, and the community was forced to rely on aid from international donors for at least the first year. The army occupied the town until March 1985 further straining scarce resources. During that time many of the corn rations meted out to each family reportedly were confiscated for use by the soldiers.

Conditions in the community remain impoverished. The army has promised housing materials and supplies and sent engineers to stake out the mandated grid configuration. Materials, however, have not been forthcoming. In the meantime, residents are not allowed to rebuild houses not meeting army specifications. Consequently, they were made to live in sheds throughout 1984 and much of 1985.

The population of Xix now numbers 274 people in about seventy families. There is a civil patrol, and since the army left in March 1985, a civilian governing structure has officially been in control. A literacy worker trained in Cotzal by the Summer Institute of Linguistics/Wycliffe Bible Translators (SIL/WBT) works in the community.

In August 1985, representatives of the EGP entered the town and held a political meeting that by one account lasted ninety minutes. The local civil patrol commander was not present, but other patrollers left Xix to inform the army of the occupation, as they are required to do. The meeting itself ended without confrontation or military action by either the civil patrol or the insurgents. By the time the army arrived, the guerrillas had left. There was a subsequent skirmish in the nearby mountains in which, it was reported, both sides lost combatants. Planes arrived from the capital shortly thereafter and bombed the surrounding countryside. One area resident claims that this is "done all the time."

While not reported nationally, people throughout the Ixil area knew of the incident and discussed it. Guerrilla activities in the area are frequent.

Xolcuay, Chajul

In Xolcuay there are approximately 189 families, 89 of which do not have permanent housing. They are *"familias colectivas"* (collective families), who, according to development officials, crowd together and share cramped living spaces.

The original site of the village was on a hillside near the newly-reconstructed Xolcuay; the ruins of the destroyed church are still visible. The present location is directly on the road from Chajul to the juncture leading to Nebaj and Cotzal. The army insisted on the new location but could not force the people to conform the village layout to the army model. Informants believed that the villagers paid for this defiance. They have received little from the army in the way of material and other assistance. Consequently, the village has a distinctive and less regimented look when compared to the other model villages in the area. The houses are not identical, nor laid out in a rectangular grid.

Xolcuay is one of the most problem-plagued villages in the region in terms of access to resources, health, and general standard of living according to development officials. Despite urgent need, in 1985 only forty-nine people received government support, and in 1986 a similarly small group is scheduled to receive aid. Additionally, displaced people originally from other villages (many of whom took refuge on the south coast) are being settled in Xolcuay. There is no available land for these people, and the cost of renting may be as high as eight *quetzales/ cuerda/*year. These people create additional pressure in an already dire situation.

Chisis and Cayxay, Cotzal

Both Chisis and Cayxay were destroyed. In Chisis, a brutal massacre took place, according to an informant, where "many, many people died — men, women and children." Surviving original inhabitants from both villages, living in Cotzal, walk together in groups of forty to fifty to work the fields. There are no houses in either village. In Chisis, some people not native to the village are planting, but most were relatives of former residents who were killed.

Asich, Cotzal

The original houses of this village were burned by the army, and during the most intense violence many members of the community died. In a single incident, the soldiers killed thirty-five men. Most of the survivors are in Cotzal and some are in Ojo de Agua. Currently, however, some 30 families have moved back to Asich where they have built temporary housing and are complying with civil patrol duties. They are supplying all of the labor, but have reportedly received supplies such as wood and nails from the National Reconstruction Committee (CRN). Some of those living elsewhere are beginning to return to Asich to plant their fields, but have yet to move back.

Ax'ctumbal or La Pista, Nebaj

Alternately referred to as a model village, a pre-model village and a refugee camp, this village lies north of Nebaj, adjacent to the military's air strip (from which it takes its name, La Pista). The translation of the Ixil name is New Life and this is sometimes used by English speakers.

Ax'ctumbal's history is unclear. One development official said that it was once a *finca*. Displaced people have lived there since 1982, and this population is constantly growing. Most of the current residents are from the destroyed village and hamlets of Salquil Grande, but several other villages are represented as well.[140] It was originally planned as a holding center for displaced people, who would stay until their original villages were brought under military control. It appears that some residents have now decided to stay permanently, despite the fact that they could return to their original area near Salquil Grande. Among those who are staying are many who had insufficient or no land in their place of origin. Even those who have no cultivable land in Ax'ctumbal feel that they "come out even" if they stay.

Residents of the village are now constructing more permanent housing to replace the makeshift huts which have been their homes during the past four years. Most say they have received little or no government help, although wood and corrugated metal roofing has been furnished. Many do not have housing and live in crowded conditions.

Officially everyone has been granted enough land to grow corn for their families. yet one resident explained that the land was totally insufficient, and he was forced to buy corn most of the year. Another resident, who was employed locally, claimed that his parcel of land was almost enough to feed his family. Most informants agreed that land was available locally but that no one had the money to buy it. They also said that fertilizer would increase their small yields, but at a cost of twenty-two *quetzales* per *quintal* (100 lbs.), it was impossible to procure.

Development officials claim that the land in Ax'ctumbal is loaned to the residents. Some people have bought land, paying thirty *quetzales* per *cuerda* and some rent for approximately three *quetzales/cuerda/*year. Officially, everyone has their 35x35 yard house lot, which cost them thirty *quetzales*.

The village of Ax'ctumbal has its own mayor, but the army is in charge of major decisions. A health clinic exists, but informants agreed that "there is no medicine". There is a school taught by Ixiles from Nebaj, and several families have joined to form a cooperative store and corn mill. The store's shelves, however, are almost empty except for a few bottles of Coca-Cola, bags of snack chips, aspirin, and batteries.

Everyone needs permission to leave town, even to go to Nebaj for market. They said that such permission is generally easy to obtain from the army, stationed at one end of the village by the airstrip. The army is thus always present. The civil patrol appeared rather lax; duty was required every ten or eleven days.

Economic Changes

General. In the Ixil area, the land of those who died has been generally claimed and is being farmed by relatives, *if* the army allows it. Because so much of the area is still in conflict, many only have access to part of their land or none at all. With the available land reduced and a large proportion of the population displaced, many Ixiles have less land than they did before the violence. The problems this causes are further compounded by the overall economic crisis and a much tighter control of movement.

When an area is declared "safe", according to the army, it is possible to regain one's own land on the basis of four witnesses. In some cases, the army mandated changes in land tenure to construct housing in the model villages. Throughout much of Quiché, the shortage of accessible land is acute, but even where the land is available for sale or rent (in areas of Nebaj for example), villagers often do not have the money to procure it.[141]

Throughout the Ixil area, the markets appear well-stocked, although informants claim the markets are still not as big as "before," when people came from all over to buy and sell. On the other hand, they have recovered fairly well from the days when shootings occurred in the streets and there were "no more than three women selling in the marketplace, prepared to run at the first sign of the soldiers." Merchants and townsfolk again travel between the three municipal capitals frequently.

International Aid/Government and Army Food Assistance

There is a greater presence of both private and government assistance programs in the Ixil, in marked contrast to the areas of Huehuetenango studied. Among private aid groups, most resources come through the Catholic or Evangelical churches, with the most extensive programs funded by the U.S.-based Summer Institute of Linguistics/Wycliffe Bible Translators (SIL/WBT). Particularly for SIL/WBT, the Ixil area has been a focus for overseas fund raising. Through SIL, food aid and home construction projects have been financed by U.S. church congregations and individuals. Both Catholic and Evangelical churches now economically aid residents of the model or reconstructed villages but are constrained by army control. And both profess an openness to provide aid regardless of religious affiliation, but those who choose to be a *practicing* Evangelical in Cotzal have a good chance of receiving housing materials and educational opportunities for their children. Because of the acute need, many people, especially in Nebaj and Cotzal, appear to be using church aid. In addition to the U.S. linked Evangelical Church aid, the Air Commando Association, reportedly has raised millions of dollars for the Ixil area.

International aid from the World Food Program and United States' P.O. 480 food program (channeled through USAID) is distributed by the National Reconstruction Committee, controlled by the local military. The model village of Acul, as described above, has been completely dependent on food aid for over two years, a sharp change from life in the original Acul.

These programs illustrate the fact that residents of the region have lost their small margin of economic independence, based on land and markets. Although people were accustomed to supplementing subsistence farming with seasonal migration, a measure of economic autonomy existed at the individual and community level. Now, residents are dependent on government handouts in a manner contrary to their traditions and preferences. Both churches argue against creating aid dependency, but are not running economic self-development programs. In fact, all institutions including the army and government are engaged basically in stop-gap, emergency aid measures.

Many of those most desperately in need of emergency assistance do not receive it. This shortfall is due both to insufficient overall supply and inefficient use of that which is available.[142]

Patterns of Work

As in Huehuetenango, the majority of the Ixiles have traditionally depended on subsistance agriculture supplemented by seasonal migration. As a consequence of the violence and militarization, villagers have come to more heavily rely on employment formerly considered an occasional supplement to family income.

Two traditional skills, women's backstrap weaving and men's foot-loom-weaving and crocheting, are now the livelihood of many. In both cases, children help by spinning the thread and marketing the goods. There is an obvious overabundance of weavings available and an inadequate market to absorb them. Women sometimes travel as far as Panajachel and Guatemala City to sell, but such long and expensive journeys may meet with little or no success. An intricately woven *huipil* (traditional blouse) from Nebaj or Cotzal, which takes several weeks to make, might sell for thirty-five to fifty-five *quetzales*, while the round trip alone to Guatemala City costs at least fifteen *quetzales* for one person. Even the raw materials for such crafts are scarce, and everyone complains about the sudden and steep increases in the price of thread.

The Ixil area is not well endowed with easily exploitable resources. Many villagers gather firewood to sell to townspeople and for their own use, but they must go far to find sufficient amounts. The depletion of high-quality nearby wood was a problem even before the years of intense violence. The army's "scorched earth" tactics exacerbated the shortage by destroying large forest tracts, and now military restrictions place important parts of the countryside "off-limits". Villagers' access to wood and other natural resources (such as wild greens and hunting opportunities) is further limited since they cannot work and travel beyond certain hours and risk harassment from soldiers or patrollers.

To the extent that agricultural day labor is available, informants stated that the daily wage ranges from Q1.50 to 2.0, slightly higher than in highland Huehuetenango. Trade and commercial ventures are options for some, but activities such as reselling oranges in the marketplace earn little, and there is no surplus agricultural production.

In Cotzal, many families spend everyday making *pita* or fiber cord from the *maguey* plant, which they harvest or buy locally. Women and children twist and string the rope with simple homemade winders, and men weave loose-knit sacks. These sacks are sold to out-of-town merchants. For a full day's work a family makes close to one *quetzal* (if they sell all they produce).

A few men work as regularly paid civil patrol replacements for merchants and local officials who do not want to patrol on their appointed turn. In a twenty-four hour period a man can earn from one to four *quetzales*.

There are few other sources of employment for indigenous people. *Ladinos* own all of the transport vehicles in the Ixil area, and held almost all of the jobs in this sector. While Indians sometimes hold positions of authority in the civil patrols, these positions involve heavy time commitments without pay. Government institutions employ some local people, particularly as translators, but most of the teachers and governmental authorities are from Santa Cruz del Quiché or other cities, and are non-Indian.

Roadwork has meant economic survival for many. Such jobs are so coveted that they are distributed by the transport administration (CAMINOS) and rotated every fifteen days. Sixty people are on the roadwork gang for each period, for which they earn thirty-five *quetzales*.

The army still forcibly drafts young men in the area, but the economic crisis has forced many to volunteer for the military. The pay is Q50 a month, with Q25 sent home "to the mother." The soldier is housed, fed, and clothed at army exense. Joining the army, however, weighs heavily in this area, where virtually every family has suffered at the hands of the military.

Three houses of prostitution have been opened in Nebaj since the establishment of a permanent army base. Previously there were none. An informant said the women are mostly from the eastern part of the country and from El Salvador and come "maybe because they have no choice and need money." The implication was that local women were not involved.

Migration patterns have changed significantly. The disruption of the *contratista* system and civil patrol obligations complicate arranging seasonal migratory labor, but with the need for work so acute, informants report that the same number of people are going as before. Instead of making arrangements through a local contractor, however, civil patrol commanders must be consulted regarding when, and for how long one may leave. Even with permission, there is the problem of finding a job once on the coast. A few civil patrol commanders have taken over some of the tasks once filled by contractors and may negotiate with a *finca* owner to send an entire civil patrol squad down for a month or so at a time. A local official commented that the obligation to pay replacement fees in Cotzal had even been suspended for the current migration season because the residents are in such dire straits. Wages on the coast are slightly higher than in the highlands, but are low after transportation, food, and medicine costs are subtracted. Villagers often return from the seasonal stint with little or no money.

Many widows find migration to the coast with their children their only economic option. The widows fear they may lose a child to illness or malnutrition, however, and do all they can to avoid the journey, according to social workers

RETURNING DISPLACED PEOPLE: THE INTERNAL REFUGEES

In the Ixil, the term refugee is used to refer to internally displaced people living in or recently returned from areas not under army control. Thus, those who are displaced in the towns, in the capital, or on the coast, are not included in this group. This population is variously described as those who actively collaborate and live with the guerrillas, people held captive by the guerrillas or, people seeking to avoid living in a model village. Many of the current residents in model villages and many within the local towns were once in the category of "refugees".

Throughout the past five years, people from the surrounding mountains have returned to army-controlled territory. Whether they were captured or came voluntarily, they arrived in great numbers for a period and are still trickling in. An army commander claimed that many came as a result of the Ríos Montt amnesty program, while others countered that military operations in that same period brought in large numbers. In 1984, incoming groups of refugees often numbered 200 or more, according to residents.

The pace has slowed considerably, but refugees still arrive. On the average, a group comes in every week or two, and some groups still number over fifty. Residents maintain that refugees arrive more frequently than nationally reported.[143] News reports in the country sometimes advertise the arrival of new refugees in headlines such as: "forty-six peasants, displaced by the subversion sought army protection" (Diario de Centroámerica, June 28, 1985).

The frequency with which people are killed after being discovered in the mountains by the civil patrol or the army is uncertain. Most brought to the Ixil military bases during the field study or reported in the press in that period were women and children, and sometimes the elderly. Whether young men had escaped, joined the guerrillas, been killed earlier, or were killed upon discovery is not clear.

Many turn themselves in because of lack of food, according to both officials and residents. To their sympathizers, who see them as civilians resisting army control, this is the result of a strategic army policy to starve them out. The army and the civil patrols regularly burn down crops found in territories not under army control, monitor possible supply routes, and try to keep the refugees continually on the run, sometimes with bombing attacks.[144]

The pattern in 1985 was fairly consistent. When a group was found, captured, or surrendered to the civil patrols, the people would be handed over to army authorities immediately. In general, the army base in each municipality handles cases within its area, although at times groups of refugees may be taken to Nebaj. Those captured come in terrified of their potential fate at the hands of the army, according to participants in civil patrol mountain sweeps. A civil patrol commander in the area stated that refugees were well treated during their stay in the base, and "now the patrollers have to treat them well *(hay que respetarlos.)* We can't kill them like before."

The refugees are generally held at the army base for about two weeks. Recently the time spent inside the base has been shortened. No one is absolutely sure what happens inside the base because most will not talk about it when they come out. In Nebaj there were rumors that people disappeared in the base, but data was not available on how many people had entered and how many had exited.[145] There is evidence, according to some informants, that torture has occurred inside the bases.

A large group of refugees (over fifty) brought into Nebaj in 1985 reportedly had only six men among them. These men were taken by soldiers to the mountains so they could "show where the guerrilla camps are." A week later those six had not returned and their families feared for their lives. An informant stated that refugees in general are under tremendous pressure to inform on others still in the mountains, and if they do not cooperate they reportedly may be killed.

After the stay in military bases, refugees enter a transition phase. In Cotzal, they may go to live with relatives until they are assigned a place in

After his house was burnt and his crops were destroyed, he and his family were taken away and placed in Las Violetas displaced persons camp, Nebaj, El Quiché, 1985. Photography by Jerry Berndt.

a model village. Some have to fend for themselves or are placed directly in a model village if they have no family or friends who will take them in. In Nebaj, they are generally placed in Las Violetas for "anywhere from a few days to several months." In Las Violetas the refugees reside in crowded *galeras*, open barn-like structures with dirt-packed floors, and receive insufficient food and clothing (seldom is anything brought down from the mountains). The army claims to be generous in supplying food and basic materials to the refugees, but other government and religious workers disagree. Some goods are provided by the army if they happen to have anything in stock, but survival has often depended on private aid. In Cotzal, the Evangelical network has made a point of assisting newly arrived refugees, and in Nebaj, the Catholic Church has provided food, material for clothes, and straw mats to as many refugees in Las Violetas as possible.

In most cases a family will choose where they want to go permanently and must then seek permission from the appropriate army officials. Generally people go where they have relatives or lived originally and seldom seem to encounter opposition from the army. Their cases, however, are duly recorded and their whereabouts monitored. When a family cannot return to its original village (because it has not been reconstructed) and does not have relatives who can take them in, they have limited options for where to settle. Refugees have built more permanent shelters around Las Violetas, and a new *barrio* has been created. Also near Nebaj, La Pista remains a fluid and growing village where those without other homes seek at least to share a crowded house, even if no land is available. In Cotzal, many refugees have settled just outside the main town on land that is currently privately claimed.

One informant said that in addition to material problems, returning refugees also face discrimination. Much of the distrust and fear instilled by the violence and the suspicion of army informers is turned against those recently arrived from the mountains. Refugee children are taunted in the streets and schoolyards, and landlords may be unwilling to rent to people who might be "*tendenciosos*" (sympathetic to the guerrillas) for fear of bringing suspicion onto themselves.

For those who have made the initial transition, conditions remain difficult. Often they are dependent for food on the government agency *Bienestar* (Social Welfare), one of the churches, or neighbors or relatives who somehow manage to pass on a few tortillas. Moreover, there can be considerable problems reclaiming land.

The majority of the internal refugees are women and children. Women must care for their children while earning enough to support the family, a nearly impossible task. Many try to produce and sell woven goods but face a saturated market. Sometimes widows cannot claim their land because the title was in the man's name. Without male relatives, and often with little command of Spanish, they are easily exploited. In the less frequent cases of widowers and their children, the problems remain. The men, according to an informant, "go and work, leaving the children uncared for. But they have no choice."

War orphans in the area present a serious problem. Some have been taken in by kinsmen or sympathetic neighbors, some given to local church workers for care (sometimes children found in the mountains are taken to churches by the army), others are sent to orphanages in Santa Cruz del Quiché or the capital. As in other parts of the country, rumors of abuses exist.[146] There have also been several reported cases of soldiers taking in war orphans and raising them for a time inside the base. In one case a child was later given to an orphanage in another department, where the social worker found him in a traumatized state.

Upon their "reintegration", refugees confront a range of attitudes from their neighbors. While some informants said that communities are open and welcoming to former residents, they look with suspicion on those unknown to them. Most officials, both army and municipal, emphasized that recent returnees are watched carefully for indications of allegiance. A community member stated: "They watch to see if you start acting badly or if you are involved (*metido*) [with the guerrillas]; if you are, then [the army] punishes you." The army informer network and the civil patrol structure is charged with watching the newcomers.

5

The Case of Ixcán

In the 1970s thousands of highland Indians successfully colonized the Ixcán, an impenetrable,
isolated, and unpopulated rain forest. During this
period, the area became the stronghold of the largest
guerrilla organization, the *Ejército Guerrillero de los
Pobres* (EGP). The military conflict between the army
and the guerrillas escalated, leading to a fierce
counterinsurgency campaign in which entire communities were massacred, most villages were abandoned or destroyed, and thousands fled. Ixcán today
is a development pole. The military tightly controls
the villages, while the EGP remains in the outlying
areas. Armed clashes occur regularly. There are also
thousands of villagers living in the jungle beyond
military control.

GENERAL BACKGROUND AND INTRODUCTION

No region in Guatemala has experienced the destruction and dislocation
of the Ixcán, giving it the grim distinction of having produced more
refugees than any other single area.[147] The Ixcán is composed of two
main areas. The western part between the Ixcán and the Xalbal Rivers,
known as Ixcán Grande, was settled in the late 1960s aided by Maryknoll
priests based in Huehuetenango. The eastern part between the Xalbal
River and the Chixoy River, known as Ixcán Chiquito or Zona Reyna,
became settled in the early 1970s with the help of Spanish priests from
the Diocese of Santa Cruz del Quiché.

Two key *aldeas* were selected as primary research sites, one in each
Ixcán subsection.[148] In addition, about a dozen surrounding *aldeas* were
visited briefly. Engaging in research here is perhaps more difficult than
anywhere else in Guatemala. Since the remote area is under tight military

control, neither the military nor the villagers are accustomed to seeing outsiders not linked to the government. The importance of the area is such, however, that any data that can be gathered is valuable for understanding the aftermath of the counterinsurgency war and the issue of repatriation.

The municipality of Ixcán, created on August 21, 1985 with its capital in Cantabal, is in the northern most section of the department of El Quiché. This area was previously part of three municipalities — Chajul, Uspantán, and Barillas — and two departments — El Quiché and Huehuetenango. It borders to the east with the departments of Alta Verapaz and El Petén, separated by the Chixoy River; to the west, the Ixcán River and the department of Huehuetenango; to the north the vast Lacandón Forest of the Mexican state of Chiapas; to the south are the massive 3,000 meter high Cuchumatán-Chamá mountains. Until the late 1970s there were no roads into the Ixcán.

The villages of Ixcán are part of the Playa Grande development pole and military Zone 22. Given the geography of the area, these villages are particularly closed-in by the military. The main way out of the area is through the new east/west unpaved road of the *Franja Transversal del Norte* (FTN), begun in the mid 1970s and still under construction. To reach the FTN road, the villagers might have to hike for hours on jungle trails, after which Playa Grande might be another day or two and several army checkpoints away.

Playa Grande, located in the eastern most part of Ixcán is a frontier outpost, not a town. On both sides of the Chixoy river there are buildings of virtually every rural-related governmental agency, two *comedores* (diners), and several rustic supply stores. The massive Zone 22 military base, reportedly housing between 2,000 and 3,000 soldiers, is by far the most imposing presence. In December 1985 unpaid work crews drafted from villages were building a large concrete wall around the base as well as engaged in military-directed work tasks. A few miles away is Cantabal, a new model village designated the municipal capital of the new municipality of Ixcán. Cantabal will become the civic and trading center, while Playa Grande will be mainly a military base.

IXCAN GRANDE: COLONIZATION BACKGROUND

The Ixcán Grande was colonized in two phases (1966–69 and 1969–76). The first stage, led by Maryknoll Father Eduardo Doheny, began in 1966. Father Eduardo entered the Ixcán in April 1966 with fourteen Mam-speaking Indian men from the highland municipality of Todos Santos and an INTA (Institute of Agrarian Transformation) surveyor.

The rain forest was uninhabited except for several small settlements of Todos Santeros, who supplied the new settlers with food when they set up a base camp along the Ixcán River. The original group was soon joined by a second group made up of Mam Indians from Ixtahuacán. The first two settlements, Primer Centro and Segundo Centro, were thus established.

James Morrissey, an anthropologist, did field work in the colonization projects in Ixcán Grande in the early 1970s. His study provides rich insights into the dynamics involved in colonizing.[149] Morrissey describes the elaborate process for the selection of colonizers and the preparation for the journey. Courses were set up to acquaint potential settlers with agricultural techniques such as soil conservation, use of compost and fertilizers, and grafting and crop diversification, as well as with social issues for their future settlements. The original preparatory course consisted of 140 men from sixteen different municipalities and three different language areas in Huehuetenango. At the end, the Indians themselves decided who among them qualified and would lead the colonization efforts. Priests such as Eduardo played a significant role, but ultimately the colonizers themselves made decisions based on consensus. While self-determination, social responsibility, community cohesion, and leadership qualities were paramount in the original settlements, the opposite is more likely to be the case today.[150]

Father Eduardo worked closely with INTA. The physical layout of the original settlements followed an Israeli moshavim design. Each *parcelario* (parcel-holder) was to receive an individual title to about twelve hectares (thirty-one acres); twenty-four parcels made up a center. By 1969 the colonization project had a band radio and a Piper Cherokee single engine plane, obtained from donations in the United States. The plane helped integrate the distant colonizers with the rest of the country, allowing them to transport cash crops out of the jungle and reducing the isolation in case of an emergency.

Despite excessive haste in the later phases of the colonization and the diversity of Maya languages spoken, the social mechanisms for cooperation and harmony were in place when needed. Most importantly, settlers had no reason to fear a neighbor's actions would endanger their lives.

Father Guillermo Woods, an American, took over the project in 1969 and the colonization of the Ixcán accelerated under his leadership. By the early 1970s, land-starved Indian peasants from Huehuetenango flooded the area. To speed the settlement of thousands of new arrivals, land tenure became collective, the settlements became rectangular rather than pie-shaped, and the social composition no longer followed strictly ethnic lines.

ZONA REYNA: COLONIZATION BACKGROUND

In 1972, a group of highland Quiché Indians accompanied by Father Luis Gurriarán, a Spanish priest based in Santa Cruz del Quiché, penetrated the area east of the Xalbal River.[151] The complex colonization process began in the provincial capital of Santa Cruz del Quiché with the formation of cooperatives. Although these cooperatives were successful, the peasants realized that insufficient land lay at the core of their problems. Given the adamant governmental opposition to land reform, the only hope appeared to be colonizing unclaimed national lands in the inhospitable jungles to the north. The Indians prepared for this difficult and path-breaking undertaking for months, expanding their knowledge of cooperativism and receiving instruction in tropical agriculture and health. Inspired by the teachings of the Bible, they also discussed fundamental civic and human rights as well as the economic and political history of the country. Starting with a common vision and philosophy, this intense process contributed to their confidence, determination, and *esprit de corps*. The collective hardships endured in opening the jungle would further strengthen their bonds.

In January 1970, an initial group of forty men and one woman began the two week journey on foot from the cool highlands down to the hot and humid forest. They encountered seven Kekchi families in the practically uninhabited area who were hospitable and invaluable in those crucial early months. The colonizers often went hungry, were overcome by debilitating tropical diseases, and suffered overwhelming fatigue after clearing the dense rain forest. By the end of the year, utilizing only machetes and axes, they had opened a site for settlement. With enough land cleared to plant the first maize, they sent word to the highlands that additional settlers could begin arriving. In two years, a close community of over 100 families produced enough to meet their needs, something they initially thought impossible. After dietery requirements were met, the cooperative members began to plant cash crops, such as coffee and cardamom.[152]

Organizing a cooperative enabled the settlers to buy and sell products more efficiently. Tasks were rotated and resources pooled and, in fact, the economic, social, and political activity of the community revolved around the cooperative. Utilizing their own ingenuity, self-determination, and cooperation to prosper, the settlers managed to break their plantation wage-dependency, and to gain a measure of independent power, first through their own cooperative and later through the federation of cooperatives. That combination of economic success and political unity provided a new vision of their own potential. These same factors, however, were unsettling to the national authorities.

Quiché woman, early colonizer in Ixcán, 1973. Photography by author.

Political Violence

Within five years, military repression began, in part due to the presence of the EGP and the population's support of the insurgents. Between 1976 and 1982, numerous community leaders were murdered. Father Guillermo Woods, involved in the Ixcán Grande colonization project, died in a plane crash in 1976 which most believed the military perpetrated, and the second priest, Luis Gurriarán, fled after the army threats. A third priest, Karl Stetter, from Germany, was able to replace Woods for only a few months before the military expelled him from the country.[153] Teachers, health promoters, committee leaders, directors of the cooperatives, catechists, and petty traders were killed in community after community.

Army soldier looking out of helicopter over the Ixcán, 1983. Photography by Pat Goudvis.

As the EGP gained combat strength as well as a social base, the area became a focus of the counterinsurgency campaign. The military finally assumed total control over populated areas following the iron-fisted sweeps of early 1982. Soldiers penetrated the villages in the Zona Reyna first and then swept westbound toward the villages near the Xalbal and Ixcán Rivers, leaving broken bodies and razed settlements in their wake. Between February and April 1982, the area became practically depopulated. Typically, about 300 soldiers would enter a village, staying from three days to a week. In places such as Trinitaria or Cuarto Pueblo, where the people had the misfortune of being in the *aldea* when the army arrived, everyone was massacred. In most cases, the inhabitants fled the approaching army, leaving abandoned villages to be torched.[154]

Those that fled remained in hiding in the jungle, waiting for the soldiers to leave. But as the occupation became permanent, thousands, including hundreds of orphans, began streaming into Mexico in late 1982. These refugees formed the camps of Puerto Rico, Chajul, and Ixcán, which were to become the largest camps in Mexico, housing from 3000 to over 5000 people.

As part of this flight more than 500 Guatemalan Indians from the Ixcán staggered into the Lacandón Forest camp of Puerto Rico in November 1982, which already had a population of over 5,000 (Manz, 1983). The new arrivals were visibly hungry, bewildered, and frightened. After hiding in the jungle for nearly a year, they had walked for weeks, pursued by troops along the way. En route they encountered two lost and naked children. Totally traumatized, the children would not say where they were from, what had happened to their parents, nor what happened to them. Even after arrival in the refugee camp they would not speak, gazing without expression, day after day.

IXCÁN TODAY

Many villages remained uninhabited for about two years, until the military decided to resettle the area in early 1984. The Ixcán now has 116 villages with a population of about 35,000, a combination of old-timers and new settlers, according to the latest census.[155]

The first year of resettlement was arduous, although physically less demanding than the hardships endured by the original settlers who confronted a dense forest with machetes and axes. But in 1984, the new settlers in addition to harsh living conditions had to endure a new affliction: the boundless power of the military.

The army's priorities were first to clear the center of the village, then the overgrown trails, and, finally, to work on the outpost and airstrip.

The villagers had to work from dawn to dusk on minimal diets and without pay—if they wished to remain and eventually obtain land. Permission to leave the area had to be obtained from the officer in charge and was not always granted. Leaving without permission was dangerous, because those caught could be targeted as "subversives". The villagers lived in near isolation, since few agencies penetrated the area and no Catholic priest or medical personnel were present. Informants remembered the hardships: stern security measures, onerous civil patrol service, and brutal punishments. Moreover, bitter hunger and devastating health problems were rampant, especially parasites, malaria, and malnutrition. Thousands of children remain critically malnourished according to widespread newspaper reports, and there are thousands of war orphans.[156]

Resettlement of a Village in Ixcán Grande

One destroyed *aldea* near the Xalbal river in Ixcán Grande, originally composed of 256 family parcels, was resettled in 1984. At the time of the research in mid-1985, there were 220 families, including thirty of the original settlers. INTA assigned land parcels belonging to the initial colonizers to new settlers. These villagers began to rebuild the *aldea*, but with a new military-imposed design. Instead of the old dispersed layout, the homes are now clustered and the village is surrounded by *garitas*, staffed by civil patrollers. Overlooking the *aldea* is the military outpost, reportedly housing 300 soldiers. The civil patrol service, initially a twenty-four hour shift every two days, was extended to a turn every eight days at the end of 1985. One informant recalled the resettlement:

> In January 1984, the military chose a man from Barillas to select people to settle the area. He took charge of getting the people together. Anyone that wanted land had to go to this person. He had the support of the army. The army said that we could have land and work. That there was still coffee and cardamom there. They also said that we had to go and fight the subversives. The army said they would no longer accept those kinds of people, the kind of *parcelistas* that had been there before.

The resettlement procedure appears to follow similar lines. The military tells radio stations in particular rural areas to announce both the availability of lands and where villagers should go it they want to qualify. The military then selects people to organize the repopulation of an abandoned area. A new settler commented:

> The military from Barillas went with us. We were about 135 *parcelistas*, all new ones. We walked through the mountains, ten soldiers, then

twenty *parcelistas*, and so on. We walked for three days, with little food and no ponchos. Along the way there were traps. We found five traps. Two soldiers were hurt. The first day we got to Piedras Blancas. Things went OK that day. The second day was harder; we had to climb. We left Piedras Blancas at 6:00 AM and arrived in San Luis Ixcán at 4:00 PM. The journey was especailly difficult for the two pregnant women because we had to climb and go under branches along the path. The children four and over had to carry their own things.

About 150 soldiers from the military outpost by Xalbal met the group in San Luis Ixcán. The soldiers from Barillas then headed back.

The muddy overgrown jungle trail and the heat made the journey exhausting. When finally arriving at their destination, the group found a burned village and no houses to stay in. An informant recalls the way a lieutenant greeted the exhausted arrivals:

> He said to us "why have you come here?" The man from Barillas answered that we had come for land. It was about 3:00 PM when we arrived, so the lieutenant said, 'OK, leave your things there, there is no food here, there is nothing. You can have water, leave your things, grab your machetes and get to work.

The new arrivals were made to chop vines and clear the land. They had to line up every morning before beginning work at 6:00 AM and every evening when they were done at about 6:00 PM. They were counted.

> We were constantly watched by the military to see who wasn't working. If we didn't work we were punished. The punishment could be to carry heavy stones. The lieutenant was like our *caporal*. He supervised the work crews. Everyone was afraid of him, so everyone worked. He yelled a lot. The food was so meager we couldn't take it any more. The jungle was full of mosquitoes and so many were suffering from malaria and stomach problems. Everything we did was for the military, their housing, the airstrip, everything.

Informants recall slave-like conditions during the first months. No leaves were granted, whatever the reason. Many did escape, knowing they risked death if caught. Ironically, the military confidant also left the village without authorization to complain to the higher military authorities at the base in Playa Grande about the unbearable conditions, particularly regarding food. When he returned to the village, no one anticipated major problems, given he was the military confidant, except for the fact that he had left the village without permission. The man reportedly told the lieutenant: "we are human beings, we feel pain, we feel fatigue, we feel hunger, and for our work we do not get a cent". Nonetheless, he was beaten and put in a pit. The lieutenant called everyone together to ask if anyone else had been involved with his trip to Playa Grande. The people immediately said no. They were particularly frightened of being considered accomplices and also of the implication that forbidden meetings might have taken place. After five days of punishment, the man secretly left the village, heading for Barillas, leaving behind his daughter, son-in-law, and their small daughter. The soldiers did not notice his escape that night, but the lieutenant flew into a rage when it was discovered the following day. He ordered a soldier into the house to shoot and kill the man's son-in-law. This incident was devastating to the settlers, particularly given the stature of the person involved. The people felt the military would accept nothing less than total submission, and they had little alternative but to obey. They silently buried the man.

After completing the main military tasks, the villagers were allowed to build their homes, made of cane walls and thatched roof, and then to begin cultivating the fields and harvesting the coffee and cardamom planted by the original settlers.

Resettlement of a Village in Zona Reyna

During the February 1982 sweeps through the Zona Reyna, the southern colonization projects near the Tzejá River were particularly hard hit. A 1984 Texas Tech University report (Dennis, et al, 1984) evaluates the general conditions in the area:

> The average number of families per settlement and the total number of settlements would have been higher had it not been for military action in the area during 1982. People were killed selectively in some communities, and others fled to Mexico to escape the army. Three entire settlements were also completely exterminated: Trinitaria, Santa Clara, and El Quetzal. It is estimated that army action in 1982 accounted for 1,000–1,500 settler deaths . . . . [In Trinitaria] promised services were not provided for these families. The Trinitaria colonists were understandably unhappy . . . the community became a trouble spot for the project. It may well be this reputation that led the Guatemalan military to kill everyone in the ill-fated settlement in March, 1982.

Trinitaria today is inhabited again with new settlers brought by the military from Cobán. These landless Kekchí Indians are happy to have land and to settle what now is called "New" Trinitaria. Villages are still being resettled throughout the Ixcán, usually with a majority of new settlers.

In one village south of Trinitaria the army found a deserted community when they arrived in February 1982. Having had two hours notice that the army was coming along the jungle trail, the villagers quickly fled into the jungle. The soldiers found empty huts, thousands of domesticated animals, a church, a social hall, a large cooperative building full of merchandise, machinery, a safe with Q12,000, a building with an electric generator, a small tractor, a motor for the river launches, a band radio, and other possessions. The villagers hid in the nearby forest while the army spent the night in the village.

For the next five days the soldiers moved from house to house looting everything they wished, helping themselves to the painstaking accumulation of eleven years of hard labor. The *parcelarios* could hear their cattle being slaughtered with gunfire as well as the subsequent feasts each day.[157] Over the next three days as the army burned every home and building, including the school, the co-op, and the church, the villagers witnessed the flames and black smoke from a distance. The destruction had a profoundly personal meaning to the villagers. The maize meant life and freedom from the coastal plantations; dreams were built around the cattle; the chickens meant a special meal or cash; the pig was an even bigger feast, or perhaps a source of cash for an emergency.

Despite a two hour warning of the approaching soldiers, the escape was hurried, and random events determined much of what followed. Families became separated, and lost track of each other. A small group, overcome by hunger and sickness, turned themselves over to the military. The army killed some, and took others to the military base in Playa Grande, where they were kept for about three months. The majority of the villagers held out in the jungle but, unable to survive after a year, journeyed to Mexico where they are now in refugee camps.

In 1983 the army took the *parcelarios* under their control back to the site of the destroyed village and brought in new settlers from various departments, comprising a total of four language groups. The new settlers were given the land of the refugees and the dead. The military set up an outpost with about seventy soldiers, directed the resettlement, and organized the civil patrols while still bivouacked in the village. Once the village functioned according to the army's mandates, the soldiers left and now check in about once a month. The civil patrol commanders report to the military base once a week.

The army concentrated the village layout in what formerly had been the communal area. A military confidant explained the logic behind the new layout:

> I can see better from here who enters and who leaves [the village]. If we went back to our lots, it would be better. Here we are mounted one on top of the other. We can't raise animals. But, in the lots, how can one

see who enters a house and who leaves? How does one know then what's going on?

But, interestingly, not even the military confidant is satisfied with the arrangement or prospects for the future:

> We have nowhere to turn (*no tenemos para donde agarrar*). We are very demoralized. We lost everything. We came back with our arms crossed, we had nothing. The army offered roofing, but hasn't given us any. The economic situation is terrible. Everything is going up. The prices of the necessities are three times the prices of before. . . .Yet, cardamom is only Q75 or Q80 per hundred pounds.

Little room exists for individual initiative and even less for community-based decisions. An original settler complained: "There is no cooperation, there is no trust among us. We don't know each other now." Another old-timer added, "We would like the refugees in Mexico to come back so we can be a community again." The social unit is the individual and his or her relation to state authorities, therefore, there is no

Typical village in the Ixcán, 1987. Photography by author.

unity or ethnic cohesion. As a consequence, fear of the authorities and mistrust among villagers are pervasive.

In addition to the divisiveness, two other changes have taken place, one economic and one political. First, individuals are now allocating their own resources rather than pooling the resources of the community. Given the scarcity of economic resources, this individual approach clearly limits the potential for economic improvements. Second, military-imposed constraints limit the area of decision making. A local elected mayor and a representative to Congress have not fundamentally altered the village's relations to outside power structures or increased the villagers' rights and autonomy.

Ixcán residents expressed support for and hope that the election of Vinicio Cerezo would bring about changes. One informant stated with a mixture of expectation and apprehension: "We can't go on like this. . . . Lets not even think about it. We have nowhere to go. If it doesn't work now with the new government, then I don't know. It's the last hope we have." While the villagers anxiously await changes, daily life continues as usual:

> A note came yesterday from the [military] zone that everyone had to be present to work. Half today, the other half tomorrow. The *jefes* are a bit mean, they have a black list of whoever doesn't go. We are punished and threatened. So, even if one doesn't feel like going one is obliged to go.

The villagers dread the continued military domination, particularly the forced labor for the base and the civil patrol duties, which restrict their freedom of movement. When asked if they are paid for this labor, a group of men laughed at the question. They joked that it was done on the basis of custom (*costumbre*). One villager elaborated:

> The worst is that after you do forced labor you still have to do your patrol shift the next day. So, you lose a day working for them, then you lose a day in your shift. If they call you again you have to go, because if you don't show interest, they say you are against them.

A third villager added that the army has become accustomed to think that they can do what they want with the civilian population. Another said:

> This is slavery. They tell you to go work for the base, then to do your shift, then that they saw some men somewhere so you have to go look for them and if you don't do as you are told they punish you. The

soldiers do nothing. If there is something going on they say the civil patrols should go and check it out.

The civil patrols are often ordered to go on sweeps, with patrollers and soldiers alternating in the column to provide the soldiers better protection against guerrilla ambush.

The army has a detachment present in some villages, and visits others about once a month, staying for a few days. The military's power is so embedded at the village level that the army no longer requires a direct presence to insure full compliance. As the sun begins to break, for example, the village males congregate near the flagpole for a civic act, with or without the army present. Moreover, even in virtually inaccessible villages (without roads), the civil patrol shift will spend the whole day and night at their post. The villagers complain about military demands and restrictions, but fear challenging the army. They internalize feelings of guilt and as a result unconsciously self-censure themselves, assuming they have no rights.

The brutality was virtually inconceivable to the people of Ixcán. What they held most sacred, the army intentionally desecrated. Soldiers killed children with machetes before a stunned population, publicly raped and killed pregnant women, viciously murdered elders. Rumors and horror stories were exchanged among villages, as information about the terror spread.

The army's profanity has left a deep impression on the once self-assured people who witnessed or were close to it. Even today when someone recounts an incident, even if well known to the listeners, everyone attentively follows the recollection. One informant in Ixcán, after listening to another villager recount the massacre of a neighboring village, commented:

> The people in the capital [GAM] can demand to know the whereabouts of their disappeared relatives, but here who is going to lay claim to the people from Trinitaria, Santo Tomás, El Quetzal, and all the other villages that were massacred? Who is going to raise the voice? Those souls don't count (*esas almas no las tienen en cuenta*), those souls were swallowed by the earth (*esas almas se las tragó la tierra*.) And the military, they are proud because they could do it.

The new and old settlers each followed a completely different path to the Ixcán. The original colonizers shared an identity, the experience of forming the cooperatives and a philosophy of autonomy and self-determination. The new settlers were given land by the army, but the condition was compliance with the military. Moreover, the new settlers had to assume the financial obligations of those that fled. Now villages are characterized by divisiveness, fragmentation, mistrust—not the elements of a well-functioning rural community. Thus, the villages are unable to pursue independent initiatives, develop networks, or establish the necessary contacts with cities and organizations of their choosing.

Modus Vivendi

The daily treatment Indians receive is discriminatory and contemptuous. Though this treatment is not new in Guatemala, it has particularly unpleasant overtones, given their dependence on the military today. Indians are shouted at, ignored, and summoned for errands and labor at whim. If they don't line up according to military standards, they are subjected to abusive language and shoving. A once independent and self-assured people, they now encounter constant humiliation.

After two years, a certain routine has set into village life. Some villages have a resident military officer, the S-5 or civilian liaison officer, who conducts daily civic programs.[158] He also presides over evening meetings which might last one hour and are largely lectures on nationalistic and authoritarian themes. In these meetings a good citizen is portrayed as one who respects, honors, and complies with the army. Morality and village matters are also brought up.

Little room exists for personal decisions regarding matters of time, movement, association, and even commercial activities. A person needs permission, for example, to leave for Guatemala City or other centers of possible employment or to sell or buy products.[159] Moreover, there are few options for selling cardamom, the main cash crop. If the village has a functioning airstrip, a company plane comes in to buy the product. Otherwise the people must cart the cardamom out to Playa Grande. In either case, the buyers determine the price. Previously, when villagers were organized in independent cooperatives, they had some bargaining power. They could plan and organize the sale in a commercially effective way, often selling cardamom directly in Guatemala City, and thereby bypassing a layer of intermediaries.

Most of the villages in Ixcán still lack roads. The FTN road connects the eastern part of Ixcán with the Xalbal River, but villages located to the south of the FTN or north toward Mexico have no roads.[160] Some of the airstrips built during the 1970s are once again in operation. Others are still not functional. In the past the Zona Reyna and Ixcán Grande cooperatives had their own ham radios and planes. Now they have no radio communication and the planes belong to the military or to private companies.

The civil patrol service has particularly onerous dimensions. The service compounds the already considerable difficulties in providing food and other essentials for the family, because the rotations are more frequent and the tasks patrollers have to perform are more time-consuming. Moreover, patrols are often required to carry out sweeps in the jungle, where regular clashes occur between members of the EGP and the military. During the period of fieldwork, confrontations were frequent, especially in the Ixcán Grande area. The surveillance function of the civil patrol creates tensions and mistrust, fostering social breakdown. The population in general is supposed to report any unusual observations to the military. If there is extensive guerrilla activity in the area, the civil patrol leaves are likely to be cancelled. Under these circumstances, to leave without permission is tantamount to being labeled a guerrilla. And, the military's appointment of confidants as patrol commanders and informers tilts local political power in favor of selected men in the community, representing an outside force.

Civilian Structure

In addition to the civil patrol service, villagers have to perform one day of community work such as clearing brush. Also, the military at any moment "can call and give you work to do."

The civilian structure at the village level is largely responsible for carrying out military orders, not making decisions. In one village the structure was composed of a president, vice president, secretary and treasurer, and six "delegates." Each delegate is assigned to one area: purchasing, education, social work, agriculture, housing, and health. The village also had a women's committee. The army S-5 officer tightly monitors all village activities. It is not up to the villagers what programs will be organized. The education delegate, for example, cannot promote an adult education program similar to a late 1970s program that included subjects such as political and social history of Guatemala; Indian movements; leadership training; human rights; legal rights; agrarian structure, etc. The purchasing person cannot decide to institute an independent way to buy and sell products, such as forming a regional federation of cooperatives, as was previously done. The housing person cannot implement the wishes of the villagers to locate the houses on their individual parcels, rather than crowding them into the center of the village. The military set up the village, and it is the military ultimately who decides when and what changes will take place in village life.

While villagers have outwardly adjusted to losing their rights, they have not accepted this status quo. In fact, interviews indicate deep resentment of the army. Military leaders seem to be aware that while they physically dominate the village, they have not won the allegiance of the villagers.

REFUGEE LANDS GIVEN TO NEW SETTLERS

The military has imported peasants from throughout the country into the Ixcán, assigning land parcels belonging to the refugees. Ingeniero Búcaro González, head of INTA, commented about the refugee lands:

> During the years of violence entire communities abandoned their lands. There is a clause that states that if lands are abandoned the state will take those lands. That's what happened. Two or three years went by and the refugees would not appear. So the land was given to new people. For the time being there have been no problems because the refugees have not returned, and those that have returned have been put in 'development poles.' Living conditions are better in the development poles.[161]

Ing. Búcaro further elaborated that if a refugee returns and wants his land back "if his parcel is already occupied, we will have to tell him that he will have to get land somewhere else. He will have to find other land and start all over again." He clarified that this loss of refugee lands is not generalized throughout the country, but "is specific to the Playa Grande area." In May 1986 a Guatemalan newspaper carried a headline reading "The Refugees No Longer Have Lands, They Lost 215 *Caballerías* [23,000 acres]" (La Palabra, May 6, 1986). The article quoted Ing. Búcaro as saying that one thousand peasants who are currently in the Ixcán would be given, in the first week of June, lands previously held by the refugees now in Mexico. Licenciada Raquel Blandón de Cerezo has taken a special interest in the issue of repatriation. In an interview in June 1986 she stated that it would take at least a year before the refugees could return. She thought one solution to the land and security problem would be to resettle the refugees in or near municipal capitals.[162]

Refugee Rights to Land

One study details the land tenure situation of Xalbal prior to the exodus. Xalbal was the most important cooperative center of Ixcán Grande (La Contrainsurgencia y la Tierra, 1985). The INTA collaborated on the colonizing project from the initial stages. According to this study, on May 30, 1974, one month prior to the end of the Arana administration, the government gave property titles to the Cooperativa Agrícola de Servicios Varios "Ixcán Grande" for three peasant-occupied land areas.[163] The total area was 8,098 hectares; one area was national land, and the Catholic diocese of Huehuetenango had purchased two others.[164] The government had repeatedly recognized the valid legal standing of land property of the Cooperativa Ixcán Grande, and the cooperative still formally exists today.[165] This recognition is cited because it confirms the legal property rights of these cooperative members, now refugees in Mexico or living outside military control.

As the army crossed the Xalbal River on March 14, 1982, thousands of cooperative members fled, fearful of being killed. The army massacred more than 300 people in Cuarto Pueblo, and from there moved to the other cooperative centers, according to refugees. The peasants temporarily left behind their fields, homes, and domesticated animals while they sought safety. Xalbal was burned to the ground on March 31 and April 1. The settlers could not predict how long they would be away from their parcels, but no one thought it would be for years. Although they did not abandon the land voluntarily, the government is citing decree 1551, articles 114 and 115, which defines reasons for forfeiting land rights. A clause states that land rights may be lost for voluntary abandonment of the land or an indefinite absence from the home without justifiable cause and/or bad conduct which may put in jeopardy the peaceful life of other cooperative members.

According to the new constitution, the right to indemnity is inherent in the right of private property, even in the case of war (art. 40); it recognizes the right of cooperative land-ownership (art.67); and states the right of private property cannot be limited in any way due to political activity or *delito político*.[166]

Refugee Background

FEW CHOICES

The Guatemalan refugee exodus in the 1980s is unprecedented: previous economic, political, or natural catastrophes have not driven tens of thousands of Indians to abandon their communities, depopulating entire regions. While the military onslaught affected all levels of Guatemalan society by the early 1980s, the nature of the persecution varied depending on ethnic background, class, and region. Students, professors, lawyers, doctors, and most *ladinos* were generally hounded as individuals. In contrast, the Indians in the highlands and northern lowlands were persecuted as communities or groups.

The reaction to the repression also ranged from the individual to the collective. *Ladinos* and urban populations, including the middle classes and professionals, reacted as individuals or perhaps as families. Although adjustment to exile can be traumatic for anyone, it is probably easier for urban *ladinos*. In contrast, Indian cooperatives fled en mass. Falling between the individual and collective flight are Indians from highland communities, such as Huehuetenango, who fled both as groups of families and at times as total communities. A typical rural pattern was first escaping to nearby mountains or forests, expecting to return home after the army had passed. When the scale of the destruction and the continued military presence became clear, Indians basically responded in three ways: 1) leaving the country for safety in Mexico; 2) turning themselves over to the military to become part of the "model village" population; and 3) remaining in the country either in urban areas or in regions not controlled by the army.[167]

THE EXODUS

In response to Central Americans who fled to Mexico, the Comisión Mexicana de Ayuda a Refugiados (COMAR) was created by presidential decree in 1980. The first large-scale arrival of Guatemalan refugees took place in May and June 1981.[168] These people came from cooperatives in El Petén founded in the 1960s along the Usumacinta and La Pasión rivers[169], which were attacked by soldiers from the military base at Poptún. Villagers sought refuge in Chiapas, and found warm hospitality.[170]

The exodus of Guatemalans was more dramatic than previous exiles arriving in Mexico, prompting extensive coverage in the Mexican press.[171] Unlike Spanish Civil War exiles, or more recently Brazilians, Uruguayans, Argentines or Chileans, entire indigenous and impoverished communitites flowed over the border. These refugees related shocking stories of gruesome killings, unheard-of tortures, and the destruction of entire villages. The Mexican government was unprepared. Its first response was large-scale deportation of the Guatemalan refugees,[172] tarnishing Mexico's worldwide reputation for generosity in granting political asylum.

The refugees posed a considerable problem for the Mexican government. Federal and local officials were fearful that the overflow would draw Chiapas into political, economic, social, and military chaos. Yet, the Guatemalans were arriving in increasing numbers — little could realistically be done to stop the flow — and the policy of forced repatriation was drawing criticism. At first, intense disagreement among officials and agencies led to paralysis and confusion. At the local level, Chiapas state officials and federal border authorities lacked a clear understanding of the central government's plans. Many assumed, or at least hoped, the situation would be temporary. Amidst orders and counterorders, the only certainty was the refugees meant problems and therefore were not welcome. In this context, there were incidents of corruption and abuses among the multitude of border authorities, who often acted with considerable autonomy. Hostility flared between the Chiapas authorities on one side, and the refugees and their local protectors on the other.

In August 1981, following escalating numbers of arrivals, the United Nations High Commissioner for Refugees (UNHCR) sent a representative to Mexico to discuss the agency's role and possible assistance. Although troublesome, the refugee situation remained manageable, particularly compared to what was to follow. The total number of refugees did not surpass 2,000 in 1981, and the UNCHR opened an office in Mexico City in March 1982.

Following the military counterinsurgency drive in the Ixcán, the refugee flow surged in 1982. At first, tens of thousands of refugees hid near their communities in the Ixcán, hoping the military would withdraw. After a year of starvation, and weakened by disease and malnutrition, many entered Mexico. According to Pierre Jambor, then head of the UNHCR office in Mexico City, a ten-fold increase in refugees occurred in 1982.[173] In December 1982 COMAR reported 56 camps with 36,000 Guatemalan refugees spread along the border from Ciudad Cuauhtémoc to the edge of the Lacantún River in the isolated Marquez de Comillas rain forest. The figure rose to 46,000 refugees in about 90 camps in 1983. Oscar González, director of COMAR, estimates that in total there are 200,000 Guatemalan refugees in Mexico.[174] In the Motozintla-Tapachula area alone there are about 50,000.

The size of the camps ranged from 50 to more than 5,000 inhabitants. The largest camps were those in the Lacandón Forest; Puerto Rico had a population of over 5,000 and Ixcán and Chajul had about 3,000 each.[175] The large-scale exodus of entire villages and the absence of many Mexican communities in that inaccessible area accounts for the size of the camps and the concentration of refugees. In more accessible and populated areas, such as Tapachula, refugees would more likely enter as families and could find work, relief, or in general fend for themselves.

The refugee camps are located in what many perceive as the most socially active Diocese of Mexico—San Cristóbal de las Casas. The popular and charismatic Bishop of San Cristóbal, Don Samuel Ruiz García, worked tirelessly and without compromise to aid the refugees. In the initial period, a total debacle was avoided by the refugee's own tenacity and spirit of survival, combined with church efforts as well as government aid. Two factors allowed relief to be quickly organized: many refugees came as communities with organizational structures intact, and the church had an existing network of village organization throughout the Diocese. The effort required a high degree of commitment, volunteerism, and a strong sense of solidarity with the refugees, qualities the Diocese could quickly mobilize.[176]

Once the refugees had met basic needs such as shelter, food and medicine, they organized the construction of the camps. In fact, the outstanding feature of the refugee camps in Chiapas was their self-organization. Shelters that initially consisted of a plastic sheet or branches became regular huts made of thatched roofs with walls of wooden poles. Soon the camps had pathways, central communal buildings, and a plaza with a kiosk. Even roads and airstrips were constructed in the virtually impenetrable Lacandón Forest. If the camp was large, such as the Puerto Rico camp, it was divided into sections or pueblos. Eight such subdivisions existed in Puerto Rico. The work was done communally. When hundreds of people arrived at a camp, for example, everyone would become involved cutting down trees to build a shelter. Each camp division had a representative, who would oversee the organization of general tasks. There were refugees responsible for food distribution; medical assistance; food collection in the forest; running workshops; and communal constructions, such as warehouses, clinics, schools, churches, and social buildings. Soon refugees were productively involved in weaving, and children were attending classes and contributing to communal errands. Concerned about their relations with the Mexican communities, the refugees concentrated on making contact with nearby villages. To whatever extent possible, the Guatemalan newcomers took matters into their own hands and made the best of a difficult situation.

But not all was positive. The previous hardships took their toll, particularly on those who had spent an extended amount of time hiding in Guatemala. The physical reserves of many were exhausted. The head of the Comitán hospital has referred to this as the "pathology of poverty". Additionally, the sheer number of arrivals was overwhelming. Four thousand refugees arrived in the Puerto Rico camp in October and November 1982 (Centro de Estudios Económicos, 1982:62). During a field visit to this camp in 1982, two deaths were occurring daily, mainly children and elders. Ninety refugees died in a three month period at the end of 1982, according to the Comitán hospital.[177]

In the isolated Lacandón Forest, security was a particular concern since some camps were just meters away from the border. The Guatemalan army frequently crossed over into Mexican territory and could easily enter a camp and remain for days without the outside world becoming aware. Some incursions resulted in assassinations and kidnappings. Several early ones were carried out openly, such as overflights and helicopter landings in Mexican territory, the kidnapping of refugees by uniformed troops, and raids by soldiers in broad daylight.

Although these actions initially appeared to be excesses by local military officials, the Guatemalan army was clearly troubled at its highest levels by the presence of a large antimilitary population close to the border, yet outside its control. In addition, although the Guatemalan regime was not overly concerned about its international image, the refugees were a clear indictment of the appalling human rights situation in the country. Throughout this period the Guatemalan military maintained two contradictory positions: the army accused the refugees of being guerrillas and their camps guerrilla bases, while simultaneously seeking to convince the refugees to return to Guatemala.

The Guatemalan high command viewed the refugee camps as a factor in winning or losing the counterinsurgency war. A senior official is quoted as saying "we have gained an advantage over the guerrillas. Our next problem is to get the refugees back. As long as that problem exists, we cannot win the war" (New York Times, June 12, 1983). The Guatemalan military has made it clear that it wanted the refugees either back home where it could control them, or away from the border. The refugee situation was important enough to the Guatemalan government for it to make the country's participation in Contadora conditional on Mexico's actions in this matter.

Newly arrived refugees in the Puerto Rico, Lacandón Forest camp, 1982.
Photography by author.

CHANGE IN POLICY

The Mexican government, assessing political conditions in Guatemala, concluded that the refugee situation was likely to be a long-term problem. Oscar González, the director of COMAR, maintains that the Mexican and Guatemalan governments, with the concurrence of the UNHCR, began exploring a major change in refugee policy in mid-1983. COMAR and the UNHCR were both concerned about ensuring the refugees' safety. Three options emerged: 1) repatriation of the refugees; 2) relocation of the refugees to a third country or countries; and 3) relocation of the refugees outside Chiapas. The first option, repatriation, was discarded. (The Mexican government held a strong position against involuntary repatriation because the safety of the refugees could not be guaranteed.) The second option appeared unfeasible, given the ethnic and occupational character of the majority of the refugees, Indians and peasants. The Mexican government decided that the only realistic option was relocation outside Chiapas.[178]

The Mexican government had further domestic reasons for removing the refugees from Chiapas. On one level, Mexico wanted to stop the flow of refugees into its territory, and the relocation to distant and controlled camps would facilitate that. On another level, Chiapas is the poorest and in many ways the most neglected state in Mexico — therefore one of the most politically volatile.[179] The government perceived that self-organized and politically conscious Guatemalan Indian peasant groups could provide an unwanted example of resistance to Chiapanecos.[180] Moreover, the ruling party was not anxious to make the most troublesome Diocese even stronger. The presence of refugees would inevitably bring social, political, and economic issues to the forefront among the parishoners and would mobilize Catholic grass roots organization. The efforts of the Diocese on behalf of the refugees had already brought international recognition, volunteers, and money into the area.[181] But ultimately, aside from the protest by the San Cristóbal Diocese, the refugees did not have a powerful ally or lobby, and therefore Mexico felt no political pressure against relocation.

There were also external pressures on Mexico concerning the location of the camps. The Mexican government did not want to be drawn into the Central American conflict, particularly when it was trying to promote peace in the region as a member of the Contadora group. Moreover, the United States has favored repatriation or at least their relocation from the border for several reasons. First, the presence of a large refugee population along the border undermined the Reagan administration's assertion that human rights were improving and therefore military and economic aid should be given to the Guatemalan government (Avebury, Manz and Fauriol, 1985). Second, the State Department felt the camps needed to be better controlled. Relocation would solve that problem.[182] Third, the United States shared the Guatemalan military view of the refugees as pro-guerrilla or at least as antigovernment and of the camps along the border as aiding subversion.[183] Easy communication with the refugees could foster resistance by other Guatemalans; moving the camps would sever these links. Finally, the U.S. feared the camps could become a magnet for more Guatemalans who ultimately might drift northward toward the United States.

The Guatemalan guerrilla organizations basically supported the Mexican decision on relocation, at least publicly. (They were hardly in a position to oppose it.) Opposition to the move varied among the three main guerrilla organizations. The EGP and FAR were most opposed to the move, ORPA somewhat less so. On June 18, 1985 a unified statement was issued about the refugee situation outlining some of the following points, *vis-a-vis* the Mexican position: the refugees have to abide by the laws and the interests of Mexico; the URNG recognizes and respects the Mexican decisions on the refugees; the URNG has no objections to the relocation of those refugees that voluntarily choose to do so; and it also recognizes the efforts by the Mexican government to improve the conditions for the refugees in Campeche and Quintana Roo (Unidad Revolucionaria Nacional Guatemalteca, 1985.)

THE RELOCATION

The Mexican decision to relocate the camps was announced on April 30, 1984. On that very day, some 200 Guatemalan soldiers made another incursion into Mexican territory, raiding the Chupadero camp about six kilometers from the border. Seven refugees were killed. The raid took place at night, but most refugeees had enough warning to escape. They fled to Las Delicias, and later to La Gloria de San Caralampio.[184]

Ironically, these refugees in La Gloria resisted relocation most fervently, even though they had been repeatedly attacked by the Guatemalan army and had already relocated several times as a result of army incursions. This camp became known as the most determined dissident camp. While COMAR cut off food supplies and medicine and made clear there was no choice, the refugees — through their own organization, the support they had among the population, and the San Cristóbal Diocese — were able to resist the move. Other camps, particularly those in the Lacandón Forest, which resisted for up to a year, eventually faced three choices: return to Guatemala; fend for themselves in the Lacandón Forest; or go along with the move. Most eventually gave in to relocation.

The reasons refugees gave for opposing relocation centered around geographic and cultural concerns. For them, proximity to the border meant being close to their home communities, which kept alive the dream of returning and helped maintain kinship and communal ties. Moreover, the refugees felt close cultural ties with the local population in Chiapas, with whom they had social and even kinship relations and had now established even closer bonds.[185] Thirty-seven percent of the refugees have relatives in Chiapas, according to a census carried out by the San Cristóbal Diocese.[186] The border is a political division, not a geographical or cultural divide. In fact, Chiapas was once part of Guatemala. By 1984, the refugees also had a considerable social and material investment in the Chiapas camps. In Las Cieneguitas, for example, the refugees had planted 3,000 mango and citrus trees. All the camps had stable and permanent constructions. The Guatemalans became well known for their hard work and skills. They did carpentry, weaving, and field labor. Many young Guatemalans married Chiapanecos. The refugees were also appehensive about a long journey, since they had lost so many children and elders crossing into Mexico. The Yucatán was unknown, distant, and uncertain.

Refugee woman in Chiapas showing *huipil* stored in a box until her return to Guatemala, 1985. Photography by Christian Garcia.

The response from the La Gloria refugees made the Mexican government speed up the relocation process in the Lacandón area. During July and August, over 10,000 people were moved, mostly from the forest camps. Since the infrastructure was not ready, refugees spent months in large, hot grain warehouses in Chiná and Hecelchacán and in a large gymnasium in Palenque, a midway point.

We observed the relocation from the Lacandón Forest in early August 1984. The refugees were taken by motor launch on the Lacantún River to Boca de Lacantún, which became a reception center for those in transit to Campeche. Five barrack-style buildings housed the refugees while they waited to be taken by buses or trucks to Palenque, site of the classic Maya ruins, 200 kilometers away (Manz, 1984).

Mexican officials, including COMAR, sought to make outside communication with the refugees impossible, even for the Mexican communities and the Diocese. The Mexican authorities became defensive and suspicious. They exerted considerable and varied pressure on the refugees in the forest to force them to relocate: threats of repatriation to Guatemala; aggressive and abusive language; cutting off food and medical supplies; and burning an entire camp—the Puerto Rico camp, with close to one-thousand homes, food warehouses, and a clinic stocked with medicines.[187] The Mexican government also successfully prevented the national and international press from entering the area, thus avoiding public criticism of human rights violations. In addition, the government prevented human rights organizations from visiting the refugee camps,[188] and prevented the Catholic Church representatives from the San Cristóbal de las Casas Diocese from entering the area. The refugees were thus cut off from the outside world. At this point, they were solely dependent on governmental institutions and psychologically felt isolated and without support.

The UNHCR was prevented from visiting the camps on five crucial days but did not publicly protest this. During this period, the UNHCR's Mexico office was criticized for whitewashing Mexico's mistreatment of the refugees and for not acting as an advocate in their defense and protection. Human rights monitoring organizations and journalists had difficulty observing and reporting on the refugee's conditions as a result of the many impediments.[189]

The relocation which burst forth with lightning speed stalled less than twelve months later, with fewer than half of the 46,000 refugees moved out of Chiapas (see below). At the end of 1985 the relocation and repatriation were at an impasse. As one refugee said in resignation, "our future is out of our hands."

Author (center) with refugees who had crossed the Lacantún river in 1984 trying to avoid being relocated.

Relocated Camps (as of April 1985)

	Population	Percentage	Ethno-Linguistic Groups
Campeche	12,490		
Maya Tecún	7,653	61%	Kanjobal, Mam, Chuj, Quiché, Kekchí
Quetzal Edzná	4,837	39%	Mam, Kekchí, Quiché, Ixil
Quintana Roo	5,450		
Rancho I	3,842	64%	Mam, Kanjobal, Quiché
Los Lirios	1,968	36%	Quiché, Mam, Kekchí, Kanjobal
Total relocated	17,940		

According to the UNHCR, the number of Guatemalans repatriated as of March 31, 1986 is as follows:[190]

1984	715
1985	204
1986	123
Total	1042

The Relocated Camps in Campeche and Quintana Roo

GENERAL DESCRIPTION

The camps in Campeche and Quintana Roo are located on the hot plains of the Yucatán peninsula, isolated from the Mexican population (Quetzal Edzná is closest to a Mexican town at three kilometers from Pich). Campeche is particularly arid. The camps are essentially urban communities housing from 2,000 to 7,000 inhabitants each, with streets laid out along a grid, closely packed house lots of uniform size (somewhat less so in Quintana Roo), and a central square containing school rooms, a meeting hall, a church and other community buildings. Each camp also has a market area, a health clinic, workshops for community projects (sewing, carpentry, etc.) and a large two-story house where two or three COMAR camp coordinators live.

Most camp buildings are made of poles sunk into the ground and lashed together with wire. Houses are roofed with creosote-impregnated, corrugated cardboard, with dirt floors, and many are surrounded by four to five foot pole fences. While all houses are the same size, people have divided the interior space in a variety of ways (although usually into two rooms), sometimes with a kitchen shed separate from the house, sometimes with the kitchen as part of the interior space. In Quetzal Edzná, latrines were constructed at one end of the camp, so some people have to walk a quarter of a mile to use a sanitary facility. The hand-made wooden furniture is sparse, perhaps a table, a few stools or chairs, a couple of slab cots and maybe a shelf or two. Families often have chickens running about the house and yard; hogs are kept in pens away from the living area.

There is almost no shade in the Campeche and Quintana Roo camps; streets are glaring white limestone. Generally there is one family per house, although these may be extended families, and it is not uncom-

Los Lirios, Quintana Roo, refugee camp, 1985. Photography by Pat Goudvis.

mon for eight to twelve people to be living in two rooms. In Campeche, people complain about small house lots, saying that one family is piled on top of another, that the neighbors chickens are always running into their houses, etc.[191] In Quintana Roo, lots are somewhat larger, the streets wider, and the vegetation taller and greener. Water is not a problem as in Campeche (see below), and little ponds were opened so that people would have some place to wash clothes.

In general, the environment in Quintana Roo is more like Guatemala than Campeche is. Any refugees still being relocated (very few in 1985) are taken to Quintana Roo, where efforts have been made to correct earlier problems, and where water is more abundant.

The camps are broken down into "modules," with a maximum of 600 families per module. These are then subdivided into "groups," the basic organizational units in the camps. Families usually live on the same street (or *linea*) or on adjacent streets. Groups were usually established (at the refugees' request) according to their prior Chiapas camp, although a few groups were set up according to their last Guatemalan community; groups then bear the name of that camp or community. They may vary from about 30 families to more than 100 families. Each group chooses its representative, who serves until he asks to be relieved or people decide to replace him (all are men). They participate in daily organizational meetings of all group representatives, general camp representatives, and the COMAR camp coordinators. The distribution of food, water, land, and tasks is done by group and coordinated by the group representatives.

Most camps also have general representatives (usually three) who are chosen by an assembly of all men in the camp. They also serve an indeterminate term. The general representatives are among the most respected refugees and generally have an excellent grasp on the overall dynamics and difficulties of camp life. One camp, Rancho Uno, in Quintana Roo, chose not to have general representatives. Informants there explained the decision was made due to previous experiences, in which they felt COMAR had manipulated the general representatives of some Chiapas camps in the period immediately prior to the relocation. They felt manipulating the main body of group representatives would be more difficult than just two or three men.

CONDITIONS IN THE CAMPS

The new camps unquestionably meet fundamental needs in the refugees' lives: They are no longer at risk from the Guatemalan army, they have a roof over their heads, and they have food. In meeting these needs, credit must be given to the Mexican government, the United Nations and the specific agencies involved.[192] Compared to most countries receiving displaced people (see Appendix A), the Mexican government can certainly be complimented for its treatment of the refugees. What follows are the perspectives of refugees interviewed in the relocated Campeche and Quintana Roo camps concerning the relocation and their life in the camps. As such, this section focuses on their perceived problems.

Virtually everyone interviewed said they had been better off in Chiapas. They cited both material and emotional factors, including a more varied diet and better land, friendships with Mexican neighbors, rivers and the familiar landscape, greater freedom and less dependence on COMAR, and most importantly being closer to their home communities in Guatemala. One positive feature, the refugees consistently stressed regarding the new camps, is that they feel more secure knowing they won't be attacked by the Guatemalan army, nor made to move again. Yet, despite the peace of mind, most said they would go back to Chiapas if they could.

Refugees repeatedly explained they had not wanted to leave Chiapas, but had finally given in to pressures from COMAR. As one man put it, "We finally gave in because we didn't know how to resist anymore." Some were worried if they refused relocation, they would be sent back to Guatemala, as some COMAR agents had warned. A number of people expressed resentment regarding the way the move was carried out, claiming promises were made and then not kept. These promises included: abundant and fertile land; better rations; documentation that would allow them to travel freely; skills training; production workshops; and access to transportation. Instead, permission is required to leave the camp for *any* reason, and permits for travel outside Campeche or Quintana Roo (even to see relatives who stayed behind in Chiapas) are almost impossible to obtain. The land needs capital inputs to make it productive, and food rations have been cut back.

A camp representative summed-up the following:

> We were a thousand times better off in Chiapas. It was very similar to where we lived in Guatemala . . . We went through hard times in the beginning in Chiapas because we had left everything behind. But the Mexicans lent us land, and then we were fine. Everyone says the same thing.

Another refugee elaborated:

> Materially things were better for us in Chiapas. We are more secure here, but the food and money were better in Chiapas. Things were

cheaper, we had friends and relatives who helped us find land and work. There's less land for us here, and everything is more complicated. We'll never be able to get ahead here.

A third observed:

> In Chiapas I felt like I was in my country; I even sold corn. But here the land isn't very good, and, while COMAR helps some, we can't plant vegetables, there are no greens and there's no river to fish from. Here, even basic necessities are scarce.

A woman concurred, "We were better off in Chiapas. We never lacked water and we never lacked food. There we wasted the *minsa* because we have corn. But now, *minsa* is a great thing."[193] Another complained:

> Here we'd like to have fish and more chicken. But they cut the chicken [from the rations]; we don't know why. And they cut other things, like milk . . . That's why you can get desperate here. At times I think about going back to Chiapas, to happiness. We could plant as much corn as we liked, with the help of the Mexicans there.[194]

People emphasized two aspects of the eroded material conditions. On the one hand, COMAR has cut many food rations and eliminated some products that it used to provide, as part of their plans to generate self-sufficiency and fully integrate the refugees into the region. On the other hand, the land is poor, dry, and they have less access to it than in Chiapas.

COMAR officials insist that refugees are still being provided with enough food to meet the minimal dietary guidelines established by the UNHCR. Nonetheless, refugees contend they must seek employment to complete their diet and to give it some diversity. Generally, they receive sufficient corn and beans, but the only fruits supplied are two bananas per person per week, and the only vegetables are one or two carrots, two potatoes and a medium-sized cabbage per person per week. At the time of the visit, they no longer received milk (even if they had small children), canned fish had been eliminated, and canned chicken had been cut back to less than half of what was provided during the first eight months in the new camps. In addition, they received about 6 oz. of rice, 6 oz. of sugar, 4 oz. of cooking oil, 1/2 Tbsp. of salt, 2 eggs and a third of a bar of soap per person per week. They received no coffee and no clothing.[195] Corn and bean rations were totally eliminated in the camps for the six month period after the first harvest. COMAR states that all groups should have harvested enough to meet their member's needs for that time. For a number of reasons, however, that estimate is probably not realistic, and many people will either have to buy grains or go without during the last two months of that period.

COMAR maintains that rations have only been cut as the refugees become more productive and better "integrated" into Campeche and Quintana Roo, that if the same amount of food is provided to people, they will be fostering dependence. Thus, to meet their basic needs, the refugees must leave the camps to work as agricultural day laborers on sugar cane and cotton plantations or clearing scrub vegetation for ranch pastures.

The refugees stated that the area is very dry, the land is poor and needs fertilizer, and one must work hard to make it produce at all. An educator in one of the camps explained:

> It really makes us sad because the land is so dry; only with irrigation can we get vegetables to grow. . . .Here the land isn't apt for production, it really doesn't help us.

He continued:

> They say that we are going to become self-sufficient, but we still doubt it. The land only produces with fertilizer. This year COMAR gave us the fertilizer. But what will happen when COMAR pulls out (as they say they are going to); how are we going to be able to buy fertilizer?

A source of discontent as well as an economic hindrance is the refugee's loss of freedom of movement. They frequently cite restrictions on travel (none of those interviewed could remember a case in which permission was granted for a trip to Chiapas) and the need to get permission to leave the camp for any reason. One informant explained that it often requires three permits for even the shortest of trips; one from a group representative, another from COMAR, and a third from local immigration authorities. Several men stated that if they are caught outside the camp without a permit, they may be sent to jail.[196] Their ties to Guatemala are limited by these restrictions, as well as by distance (many of the camps in Chiapas had traditional commercial and family ties to Guatemala, and the flow of people back and forth between the two countries was a constant source of information for the refugees). Moreover, outside work may only be contracted through COMAR, making refugees less independent than they were in Chiapas.

In Chiapas most refugees were freer to take initiative in matters of camp organization, such as the structure of the camps, where to put their houses and latrines, where they could work, and how to work their fields.[197] This margin of independence is valuable for people who have had traditional lifestyles disrupted, and especially those who have undergone traumatizing experiences. Furthermore, most Indians in the camps were independent peasants—"pioneers" from colonizing projects in Guatemala—whose lives depended on their initiative, self-determination, and self-reliance. The stifling of those qualities, as well as the restrictions on their movement and their right to seek work contribute to the resignation and demoralization, the lack of deep community spirit, and the insecurity, described by informants in Campeche and Quintana Roo.[198]

Thus, while many of the concepts developed by COMAR and the UNHCR regarding "integration" and "self-sufficiency" create possibilities for people to reconstruct their lives and overcome their dependency, access to work, education, and the neighboring population, is obviously important. The conditions under which they are applied—the methods, options, and refugee involvement in decision making regarding their integration—will certainly affect the results.

PROBLEMS IN THE NEW CAMPS

Despite the fact that the refugees state their concerns within a general context of gratitude for the refuge granted them in Mexico, it is obvious that the relationship with COMAR is strained. Informants expressed concerns that their skills and experience are often ignored and that their points of view are not sufficiently taken into account. They stated they are "scolded" when raising serious camp problems to COMAR officials. These stories were consistent enough from camp to camp and informant to informant to make them credible.[199]

In some areas, COMAR effectively utilizes the skills of the refugees, especially in education. They have instituted a bicultural program sensitive to the refugees cultural integrity. They also have well-run carpentry and sewing workshops. In other areas, however, COMAR ignores skills available in the refugee community or makes it difficult for people with special training to practice in their areas, preferring instead to centralize the activity. The situation is especially pronounced in regards to health care. Among the refugees, there are numerous certified health promoters and midwives who received training while still in Guatemala, yet are effectively excluded from responsibilities in health related activities in the new camps. One man, a health promoter in the Ixcán for years, finally decided to get retrained as an educational promoter because the doctors at the camp clinic in Campeche wouldn't let him "even touch a patient." A number of midwives who had practiced for years in Guatemala decided to stop pressing for permission to attend pregnant women in the

Campeche camps because they "don't want any problems with COMAR."[200] COMAR explains that if they allowed the midwives to work, then pregnant women wouldn't go to the clinic, and they would not be able to assure quality attention to the women. There were similar stories of unutilized skills regarding production projects, such as home vegetable gardens and beekeeping.

By all accounts, water is the most pressing problem in Quetzal Edzná and a limiting factor on productivity in Maya Tecún as well. At the time of the field study (approximately one and a half years after refugees were relocated to the new camp sites), the single pump in Quetzal Edzná, meant to serve 5,000 people, still did not function 50 percent of the time.[201] Since rainfall is limited to just three or four months of the year and there are no rivers and few streams on the limestone plain that makes up the Yucatán peninsula, if the well isn't working, refugees simply have no water at hand.

When the pump breaks down, water is trucked in from Alfredo Bonfil, an *ejido* with a good well system, about fourteen kilometers from the camp.[202] While all informants agreed that the trucks usually come at least once a day now (they are supposed to come twice a day), in the first months refugees often went forty-eight hours without water being brought in. Even now the trucks rarely follow a schedule, and people often do not know when the trucks will arrive or how much water they will be allotted that day. In the very best of cases, the amount will barely cover a family's minimum needs for cooking, drinking, and washing.

The water shortage creates serious difficulties regarding sanitation and agricultural production; in Quetzal Edzná, distribution problems occasionally cause friction among the refugees, and life seems to revolve around the water trucks.[203] Although multiple harvests each year are possible, the short rainy season and the lack of resources for irrigation limit people to a single crop annually. Horticultural projects such as home vegetable gardens and fruit tree plantings have been largely abandoned because of the extremely limited water supply, particularly in Quetzal Edzná. Several informants cited this problem as a key factor in the lack of dietary diversity, as well as in their feeling that they will never get ahead.

Refugees in the new camps (as well as in Chiapas) face a number of problems in finding adequate employment. In addition to basic household tasks, such as cooking, cleaning, gathering wood, finishing and maintaining houses and yards, and tending chickens and pigs, refugees engage in three main kinds of productive labor: work outside the camps, work in the camps, and community agricultural production.

Most employment for refugees outside the camps is contracted through COMAR, ostensibly to protect refugees from potential abuses or inequities by Mexican employers.²⁰⁴ Nonetheless, refugees claimed such problems exist anyway, and they viewed the system as limiting their ability to find work freely. Generally, COMAR would arrange to have trucks come to the camps to pick up groups of refugees and take them to sugar cane or cotton plantations at harvest time, cattle ranches in Campeche, Quintana Roo and Tabasco, and oil fields in Tabasco. Other jobs, such as planting, weeding, and clearing land may also be available. According to one camp representative in Campeche, typically a plantation owner will make a request to COMAR for up to 100 men. COMAR then notifies the group representatives, who together divide up the jobs and then distribute them to the men in their groups. Minimal shelter, but no food, is provided.

Jobs vary from a few days to two or three weeks, depending on the task and the distance from the camp (usually jobs farther away are for longer periods). In peak employment periods, up to one-third of the men may be gone from the camps at any one time; at other times of the year, weeks may pass without a single truck coming for workers. Generally, men do not get more than the equivalent of several months work each year. This kind of seasonal labor is the most important source of cash income for a large majority of refugee families.

Wages also vary somewhat. In early fall 1985, refugees in Quintana Roo generally received 860 pesos for a day's agricultural labor (about $1.70 U.S.). In early 1986 in Campeche, according to one informant, refugees were receiving 400 pesos per unit of sugar cane harvested. On the average, a man might cut three to five units a day, making 1200 to 2000 pesos ($2.40 to $4.00 U.S.). Clearing ranch land paid 12–14000 pesos/hectare, requiring eight to ten days of work (thus ranging from $2.40 to $3.50 U.S. per day).²⁰⁵ Several informants considered 1500 pesos ($3.00) to be a better than average daily wage.

In general, informants agreed that refugees are paid at about the same rate as Mexicans; however, almost everyone told of experiencing some kind of discrimination or problem on the job. At times, for example, the Guatemalans are put in the worst parts of the fields, where the sugar cane is thinnest, making it more difficult to accumulate weight quickly. There were numerous reports of underweighing or paying for only a portion of the work done.²⁰⁶

People engage in remunerative labor in the camps as well. Men may work as tailors or make simple furniture for other refugees.²⁰⁷ In Campeche where the refugees themselves run the schools, close to 100 people work as educational promoters (teachers with nonprofessional training). In all of the camps, there are small, refugee-owned stores and market stands, selling sodas, clothing, fruits and vegetables, candles, soap, and other household necessities. Women occasionally make candies or breads for sale, but returns on the investment and labor are minimal.

Educational promoters receive a salary for two weeks of every month they teach; the other two weeks are considered to be their contribution to the community and exempts them from community agricultural work. Educational promoters are paid through COMAR. In early 1986 they were receiving 12,000 pesos for their two weeks paid work each month. In addition to private jobs, tailors and carpenters may also be involved in community production projects, making school uniforms for the children (the fabric for the first year was donated through COMAR), benches for the schools and furniture for other community buildings. This work is unpaid and also counts as part of their contribution to the community.

The third type of work, community agricultural production, involves almost all of the men in the camps and some women. The women are most often widows who work as cooks for the men when they go to the fields for several days at a time. This work makes up for the fact that their families do not have men working to produce food for the group (part of the camp organizational structure). At least in Campeche, problems associated with community agricultural work are often cited as among the most serious work-related problems confronting the refugees.[208]

As part of the program to promote refugee self-sufficiency, COMAR acquired land for the production of basic grains and assigned a small tract to each group. Although it worked out to about one hectare per person, COMAR required that each group work the land collectively, insisting that was the only way it could provide technical assistance and other support. There was considerable refugee opposition.[209]

One camp representative explained:

> One of our greatest problems is the individualism we brought with us from Guatemala. Here we must work in a communitarian way . . . And while we have worked to promote a strong collective spirit, many people still want to work alone.

While the majority of refugees were from Ixcán and Petén colonization projects, where most belonged to cooperatives that played an essential role in their economic betterment, the co-ops were for marketing and storage and not for production. Each family had its own parcel, took pride in that fact, and worked and invested in the land as they pleased. There had been no significant prior experience in collective production ventures.

Working collectively meant that all able-bodied men worked the land, scheduling more or less the same number of hours per man. The production was distributed according to the needs of the entire group, including widows, the elderly and infirm, as well as those who serve the communities in other capacities. Scheduling decisions, assigning responsibilities, defining work and distribution procedures were done at group meetings. Many hours were spent in meetings seeking to make things run smoothly, especially in the larger groups with dozens of families.

Production difficulties arose when men didn't work as scheduled or didn't work as hard as they might, had the land been for their family alone. Men were often confronted with the decision of maintaining a commitment to collective production or taking a job that would bring in cash to meet their family's needs. In some cases, men simply refused to participate, on principle, and went off on their own. While there were not many of these occurrences, they did create a sense of divisiveness.

Production in those groups in which people were committed to the idea of working together was actually quite good, about one ton of corn per hectare.[210] Production was considerably lower in groups with more difficulties. In the best cases, enough corn and beans were produced to meet group needs for about six months, prompting COMAR's decision to eliminate corn and bean rations entirely for the first six months after the harvest. Families in groups that produced less, either because of difficulties with the collective model or because there were many widows and elderly in the group, will have to find some way to buy grain when the supplies they produced run out.[211] There have been other problems related to distribution and the shares various groups should receive.

As a result of these kinds of problems, COMAR has decided that refugees can make their own decisions about how they will work their fields for the upcoming growing season, and that it will provide assistance to all, independent of their decision. At the time of the field investigation, some groups remained firmly committed to collective work, some were wavering, and others had decided to abandon the collective model.

While the impact of this more flexible stance is not yet clear, some feel it may help smooth over frictions and divisions. The exhaustion and disillusionment that comes after having created communities so many times before only to see them destroyed or being forced to abandon them, has obviously taken its toll. Moreover, the fact the model was implemented from above further complicates the situation.

8

Conclusion

The legacy of the counterinsurgency and the continuing military repression have left deep scars in the rural communities. In the primary research areas — the highland municipality of San Mateo Ixtatán, the Ixil speaking region of El Quiché, and the northern lowland area of Ixcán — the evidence suggests three broad conclusions: The military has embedded itself in the countryside in new and far-reaching ways, forcing major cultural adaptations; political constraints continue to prevent fundamental economic and social reform; and the essential guarantees of life and safety are absent.

I make the argument that the Guatemalan military in the counterinsurgency campaigns of the 1980s, particularly the period of mass terror, lashed out with unprecedented ferocity to eliminate any potential challenge to the status quo. The immediate trigger for the onslaught was an armed insurgency. The response, however, went far beyond what was militarily necessary to confront the rebels. Instead, the military's assault was aimed at broad sectors of the civilian population where the military perceived a threat. The army feared not simply several thousand armed guerrillas but an increasingly disaffected and mobilized population. Though that threat was real, the actions taken violated universally accepted rules of war let alone the most elemental concepts of human decency. In this dual war, against combatants and civilians, no prisoners were taken. The silence of the United States and its support of Guatemalan governments through this period is reprehensible and particularly ironic given the increased U.S. pronouncements about freedom and democracy in the region.

With the civilian population subjugated and the guerrillas driven back to more remote areas, the army has embarked on a program of rebuilding and consolidation. To fully understand the nature and effects of this program, the similarities and differences of the regions prior to the counterinsurgency are important. On one level, San Mateo Ixtatán and the Ixil shared a central characteristic: both are ancestral highland regions. In contrast, the Ixcán is a new lowland colonization site. On another level, the extent of guerrilla support differed: the insurgents had an especially strong following in the Ixil and the Ixcán. In San Mateo, the guerrillas were not as strong, but the EGP was nonetheless a formidable force throughout the municipality for a good part of the time between 1979 and 1982. Reflecting the differences in support, the counterinsurgency was especially intense and vicious in the Ixil and Ixcán, leaving more extensive physical destruction, larger numbers of widows and orphans, and greater social dislocation.

MILITARIZATION OF THE COUNTRYSIDE

Today San Mateo represents in many ways a "typical" highland community while the Ixil and Ixcán development poles are areas of more concerted military involvement. Despite this difference, important similarities span these areas. The most central is the extent to which the army has penetrated and sunk institutional roots in rural communities. As a result, military and paramilitary organizations have become a dominant force in the daily life in the countryside irrespective of whether troops are directly present or political change takes place in the capital.

The period of mass terror delivered a traumatic shock to the society. Tens of thousands of lives were lost and hundreds of thousands were driven from their home communities in the most large-scale population displacement in the country's history. Less visibly, the trauma produced severe cultural disorientation. The strong community networks vital for survival under normally precarious peasant existence were torn apart. Cultural norms such as local patterns of authority, bonds of trust, decision making, kinship ties, and patron/client and *compadrazgo* relationships, essential in Indian communities, were disrupted. What has been interjected is a widespread climate of caution, fear, mistrust, and divisiveness.

In a country well known for the longevity of the indigenous cultures, the quick adaptation of Indians to the dramatic new demands on their lives was surprising, though understandable given the viciousness of the terror. In some places in a matter of only a few weeks, the stunned population received and carried out the orders concerning their new obligations from singing the national anthem to mobilizing in the civil patrols. The new behavior has become integrated into daily life. The flag is raised and lowered and allegiance is pledged with or without the presence of soldiers.

While this behavior is rather uniformly observed throughout the Indian areas, these new concepts are not necessarily believed nor has allegiance been won. The fact that new behavior is not deeply rooted but is a manifestation of raw power and practical fear does not make it less important or easily shaken off. Reestablishing damaged networks today is complicated, given the absence of freedom and trust to develop new relationships. The military has created a network of informers and proxies whose activities breed mistrust and are extremely unsettling. However, the potential for self-organization has been crippled, not permanently paralyzed. Deep resentment and dissent still exist but are now more latent, although occasionally flaring into open acts of resistance.

Rebuilding devastated areas provides an important lever for the extension of military authority. In San Mateo, the area least damaged by the counterinsurgency, the physical scars are substantial. The military is playing a major role, establishing new forms of dependence with the food and building materials it distributes. In addition, the civil patrols and *orejas* allow the military to maintain its authority by proxy.

The fact that the military has this generalized new presence, however, does not mean that the differences in levels or methods of exerting authority are unimportant. In the context of the broad similarities of the three areas, the research data points to significant differences. Since the development poles were initially guerrilla strongholds, the original population is viewed as subversive and thus the military presence is more direct and all-encompassing. The military has physically reshaped village settlement patterns and altered traditional land tenancy arrangements. The necessity for travel passes is more likely, more checkpoints exist, civilian and religious authority are more undermined, the villages are more atomized, scars from the scorched earth campaign are more visible, more widows and orphans are present, and there is a very aggressive penetration by evangelical churches. The guerillas remain strong and territory is still contested. Because of the direct presence of the military and constant troop movements, the population is more tense.

Although there is an overall ideological blue print to the development pole/model village conception, no two development poles are exactly alike. One obvious difference between the Ixil and the Ixcán, for example, concerns the makeup of the population. The Ixcán, as a colonization site, is experiencing a rapid population increase. The army is resettling land-starved peasants, recruited from throughout the country, on land formerly farmed by the refugees who fled. This recruitment has resulted in an extremely diverse population mix, and sows bitter discord.

The rural population in all three areas remains under externally imposed conditions that stifle individual freedom and community autonomy. A climate of fear and mistrust effectively inhibits or eliminates the freedom of speech and association, and other personal freedoms such as the freedom of movement are severely restricted.

POLITICAL CONSTRAINTS AND SOCIAL REFORM

Much attention has focused on the presidential election and the return to civilian government. What has received far less attention is that this electoral change has occured in a society in which the oligarchy and the military have blocked any social or economic reform. The foundation of this state of affairs is a confident, disdainful, ruthless, and fully autonomous military, an unyielding and intolerant plantation and business class, and their expectation of political passivity on the part of the overwhelmingly poor majority of the country. Under these circumstances, "harmonizing" merely seeks to appease the ruling elites and thus reinforce the status quo.

In the absence of even minimal reform, land tenancy, a longstanding problem in Guatemala, has reached critical proportions. Hundreds of thousands of peasants are in need of adequate land for subsistence. Yet, the civilian government is unable to propose let alone introduce a comprehensive land reform. To make matters worse, some lands remain off-limits for cultivation in Indian areas by military orders. Instead of dealing realistically with these problems, the military and the new civilian government have distributed lands belonging to the refugees to land starved peasants. While this strategy might solve the problem of a handful of landless peasants and perhaps even win their allegiance in the short run, it dramatically increases divisiveness and complicates repatriation.

Guatemala is locked in its worst economic crisis since the depression, aggravating the social tensions created by the militarization of the countryside. As in the case of land, reforms addressing the extraordinary and growing disparities of wealth and social polarization are ruled out. As data from the three regional studies indicate, traditional patterns of employment such as migrating to the coastal plantations and peasant market initiatives have been constrained, making an economically precarious situation even more difficult. With large numbers of the population pushed to the level of subsistence or even below, the roots of future conflict are ever present and growing.

HUMAN RIGHTS

The new civilian administration's credibility, both nationally and internationally, depends on its ability to curb human rights abuses. Improving the human rights situation is essential for the population to feel a basic sense of security, without which all other social and political changes will be impaired. Guatemala's history of human rights violations, however, has often been short-term improvement followed by worse levels of repression. A central question, therefore, is whether an improvement represents a temporary ebb or a basic shift in direction. Two measures of fundamental change are whether those responsible for atrocities have been brought to justice and whether institutions capable of preventing these crimes in the future are in place. The reality in Guatemala today is that neither of these conditions have been met nor do they appear likely soon. Not only hasn't a single military officer been tried for human rights abuses, but many of those suspected of the worst atrocities have been promoted to positions of greater responsibility. This is one indication of the severe constraints and the government's lack of substantive power. Under these circumstances, the occurrence of human rights abuses in any given day or month depends on the judgement of the same individuals who have perpetrated years of the most heinous crimes rather than on the values of the elected civilian administration.

Until the civilian administration is able to demonstrate real control over the military, indicated by actions such as bringing human rights violators to justice, and investigating the whereabouts of the disappeared, there will be no trust that the right to life and safety can be guaranteed.

While human rights violations plague all Guatemalans the refugees are particularly vulnerable. The military associates their flight with complicity or even direct involvement with the insurgents. The Chief of Staff of the armed forces, General Héctor Alejandro Gramajo, even after the elections and the well-publicized campaign for repatriation, continues to assert the refugee camps in Chiapas are guerrilla sanctuaries, and by implication, that the refugees are either guerrillas or collaborators. He claims "we know where these bands that infiltrate [into Guatemala] originate from . . . [and they carry] material donated expressly for the refugees" (La Jornada, July 1, 1986). The refugees, therefore, fear army reprisals, and villagers in the home communities are apprehensive that the refugees' return could bring a military response. In spite of these dangers, there is support for the refugees' return.

CONDITIONS FOR REPATRIATION

A number of basic steps are necessary for the process of repatriation to be successful. Given the nature of the exodus and the make-up of the refugee population — primarily Indian peasants — an international presence is needed to protect and guarantee those rights beyond the immediate time of resettlement. Repatriation should be only individual and voluntary. Even though the refugees by and large fled in groups and as entire communities, the repatriation should not be collective if that means some individuals returning against their will. Moreover, the input of the refugees should be exercised at all levels of the process and their own conditions for returning should be a central consideration in any repatriation plan. Refugee representatives have expressed in detailed terms their central concerns and conditions for returning. Some of these conditions were outlined in two letters addressed to President Cerezo (see Appendix E).

For any repatriation to be successful, the refugees need to regain their economic means of survival, which means regaining their land and reintegration into the local economies. They will need economic aid to farm that land and assistance must be guaranteed until the refugees have achieved self sufficiency. In addition, as a point of justice, the refugees should receive compensation for the material losses they sustained.

A concerted and valid effort at all levels of Guatemalan society to prepare the population and create the climate for a positive return and reintegration into society is essential. This effort should include a clear, unambiguous public commitment from the civilian and military authorities, otherwise local officials will have no guidance as to their expected role. Under these circumstances, local authorities could easily feel confident to apply abusive measures and treat returnees in an exploitative or repressive manner. In this regard it is essential to have a prior assessment of the specific village conditions and prepare the village for the refugee's arrival. Another element is not to side step the injustice done to the thousands of citizens who were forced to abandon their country. A related issue to facilitate reintegration is finding alternative lands for those resettled on the refugees land.

Ultimately, the basic conditions for the refugees' return are those that would make Guatemala a safe place for those living in the country now. These would include the right to life and basic freedoms such as free exercise of movement, association, and speech. One central guarantee of these rights is military cessation of interference in rural community life, and in general, civilian control over military activities.

The refugees fled a war that was largely hidden from the outside world. The veil of silence still hangs over Guatemala.

World Refugee Crisis

In seeking to understand the Guatemalan refugee situation it would be useful to place it in a broader context by examining the difficulties, successes, and scope of the world refugee problem.

The flight of the refugees and their eventual repatriation, together with the closely related problems of their protection, care, and resettlement in a host country, are not new phenomena.[212] In recent history, however, the dimensions of the problem have intensified. The economic crisis and long-term conflicts throughout the Third World have both swelled the international refugee population and forced refugees to remain in foreign territory for unusually long periods of time. Not only is that situation destructive for the welfare and cultural survival of the refugees, it also challenges the resources and often the security of the host nation. Despite the many international resolutions, dialogues, and conferences dealing with the protection of refugees, serious problems have arisen: refugees have encountered difficulties in obtaining any haven at all, received harsh treatment once admitted, and been subject to premature and involuntary repatriation. In other cases, however, new approaches have met with good results.

A review of the statistics compiled by the United States Committee for Refugees (1984) provides a good starting point for the analysis of these issues. The data shows the number of refugees in need of protection and assistance in various host nations, as well as the ratio of such refugees to the local population. The small African nation of Djibouti, for example, has some 23,000 Ethiopians in need of such assistance, giving it a refugee to local population ratio of 1 to 13. Somalia has about 700,000 Ethiopians requiring such assistance, and a 1 to 8 ratio. Pakistan shelters some 2,925,000 Afghan refugees within its territories, giving it a ratio of 1 to 33. Thailand has approximately 126,000 Southeast Asians in need of protection and assistance, not including persons at the Thai/Cambodian border. Mexico, according to this data, has a total of 170,000 in need of protection and assistance.[213] The survey documents the refugees who have entered and been resettled in host nations between

1975–1983. Nicaragua has resettled some 26,000 Salvadorans and Guatemalans, giving it a ratio of resettled persons to local population of 1 to 108. The per capita GNP is $874. Somalia has resettled 61,000 for a ratio of 1 to 87, with a per capita GNP of $282. The United States has resettled the largest number, 895,000, but has a ratio of 1 to 261, with a per capita GNP of $12,530.

Finally, the data demonstrate that, although the United States was by far the largest overall contributor to international refugee aid agencies, it lags behind Norway, Sweden, Denmark, Switzerland, and Canada in terms of per capita contributions. Norway gave a per capita contribution of $5.73 in comparison to $1.15 for the United States.

As is clear from these figures, many of the smaller and more economically fragile Third World countries are absorbing an enormous number of refugees for their population size and per capita GNP. Given that the present refugees may be unable, for a long period of time, to repatriate, and that new refugees continue to arrive, the strains placed on these countries is even more severe than these numbers might at first suggest. The burden on the larger, wealthier nations is also far from insignificant. When the problem of a national security threat is added to this overall picture, it is easily understood why the present day refugee situation has been deemed a crisis.

The world response to refugees, given the problems described above, has in many instances been harsh. Some of the worst examples have occurred at the earliest phase of the refugee experience, *i.e.*, that of seeking entry into a safe territory. Perhaps the best known and most tragic illustration is the plight of the Vietnamese and Cambodian refugees.[214] Roger Winter notes that Thailand was accused of several incidents in which authorities actually pushed off boatloads of Vietnamese and Cambodian refugees, resulting in significant loss of life (USCR, 1984:3). Moreover, violent attacks by marauding pirates in the Bay of Thailand reflected in that year, a "qualitative augmentation in the level of violence," according to the UNHCR (Ibid:4). During the spring of 1984, over 100 persons were killed by pirates in a two month period alone. Some were tied and thrown into the sea and in one case pirates poured gasoline on their victims and set them ablaze (Winter and Cerquone, 1984). In 1984, 56 percent of the arriving boats had suffered attacks. Despite the violent and frequent nature of the attacks, official efforts to protect these refugees were both inadequate and inefficient, a fact for which the government of Thailand has been criticized:

> Perhaps the grimmest explanation for Thailand's lack of concerted effort is racial animosity. Burdened with thousands of Vietnamese as well as thousands more from Laos and Cambodia and experiencing incur-

sions by Vietnamese at their eastern border, many Thai maintain an antagonistic attitude towards the Vietnamese which dates back from hundreds of years ago. Many individual Thai fisherman help boat people in distress, nevertheless, piracy may be a perverse way of discouraging still more Vietnamese boat people from trying to reach their shores. Even if this is not so, it is the case that Thai officials repeatedly suggest that boat people exaggerate the severity of the pirate problem, despite the detailed checks by UNHCR field staff of accounts of attacks (Cerquone, 1984:11).

Southeast Asian refugees have also been suffering from the so-called "humane deterrence" policies recently adopted by the neighboring nations to which they seek to flee. Such measures have been adopted in both Thailand and Hong Kong. In response to the dropping level of resettlement by Western nations, Hong Kong, a stopping off place for refugees en route to such places as Australia, the U.S., or Europe, took drastic steps to deter new arrivals. Closed camps were announced in 1982. According to Patrick Sabatier, the Hei Ling Chan and Ching Ma Wan camps were run by the penitentiary department of Hong Kong. The refugees could not leave the camps without a permit, were subject to search and mail censorship, and lived regulated lives (Sabatier, 1984:37). A spokesperson for the Hong Kong government admitted that the principle aim was to discourage the Vietnamese from leaving their country (Ibid). In 1981, a humane deterrence policy was announced in Thailand. According to a USCR report, new arrivals from Laos and Vietnam were incarcerated under austere conditions, while Cambodians were sent to border encampments (Hamilton, 1985:12). UN agencies provided food and shelter, but the newcomers were prevented from registering as formal refugees, or being presented for interviews with potential settlement countries, for an indefinite period of time. According to this report, the humane deterrence policy was instituted with the concurrence of U.S. refugee officials. Again, declining assistance in accepting and resettling these persons from larger Western nations doubtless played a role in this situation. Burden sharing is a critical factor in the current refugee crisis. Furthermore, the USCR report states that 15,000 of the 20,000 persons already in the Khao I Dang refugee processing center have already been rejected for resettlement to the U.S., evidently on a finding by INS officials that the individual stories lacked overall credibility. U.S. procedures in this regard have evoked criticism.

Thailand and Hong Kong are not alone in their harsh treatment of persons seeking asylum. Certainly the United States' interdiction of Haitians on the high seas is in this category. Moreover, despite the well-documented and widespread human rights violations in Central America throughout the last five years, the United States has denied asylum to the vast majority of Central American applicants. In 1983, 1.5 percent of the Guatemalans applying for asylum and 2.4 percent of the persons applying from El Salvador were granted such status. In 1984, .4 percent of the Guatemalans and 2.5 percent of the Salvadorans were accepted. In 1985, these Central Americans fared little better – 1.2 percent of the Guatemalans and 3.1 percent of the Salvadorans were granted asylum (National Immigration Project, 1986, Attachment C). These denials, as in the case of the Southeast Asians in Thailand, are usually formally based on rejecting the credibility of the refugees' stories, requiring the refugees to present proof of persecution, which is difficult, if not impossible, to obtain. Moreover, application for refugee status while still outside the U.S. is extremely difficult. A 67,000 ceiling has been set for the year 1986, smaller than ever. Of these slots, 37,000 will go to the resettlement of Southeast Asians and 500 to the orderly departure program. Only 3,000 will go to all of Latin America. The same number of spaces was allotted for 1985 but was adjusted down to 1,000. There were 138 actual arrivals. The same situation occurred in 1984, with 160 actual arrivals. The contrast with the actions of Belize, Mexico, Nicaragua, and Honduras, is noteworthy. As one commentator has noted:

> It might even be suggested that the U.S. has something to learn from these Central American countries if it hopes to regain its moral leadership in the area of refugee treatment and assistance. Rather than conferring refugee status or even safe haven to Central Americans on a group basis, the U.S. continues to make case by case asylum determinations while stressing stricter border enforcement, incarceration, and deportation. UNHCR has raised the possibility that U.S. policy regarding Salvadorans who reach the U.S. may be in violation of the U.S. obligations under the International Protocol Relating to the Status of Refugees. Meanwhile, the Honduran government, which is not a signatory to Protocol, permits UNHCR to decide who, among the asylum seekers arriving in Honduras, should receive refugee status (Sharry, 1984:24).

Even once a group of refugees gains entry into a country, their status is far from secure. As support from the wealthier countries dwindles, and large influxes of refugees continue to arrive, inevitable instances of backlash occur. In Djibouti, for example, a number of asylum seekers were involuntarily repatriated in 1982 (Rubin, 1983:7). Dijibouti gained independence in 1977 and was almost immediately faced with a large inundation of Ethiopian refugees. Some 31,600 were registered as of March 1983, reflecting a 15 percent increase in the population of Djibouti. Although some sources have stated that the 1982 incident involved the unintentional capture of registered refugees during operations aimed at expelling undocumented people, other reports have been far more grim, and include allegations of violence and brutality. In Thailand, in 1979, it was announced that Cambodians would be forcibly repatriated, as they created an intolerable security threat:

> In one widely-publicized incident, Thai soldiers rounded up more than 44,000 refugees, pushing them back into Cambodia through a mountainous border region, trapping them on the edge of a Vietnamese minefield.

Journalist Gail Sheehy described this event in early June 1979 in a Washington Post article:

> Those who panicked at the edge and tried to run back were shot. Over the course of several days, 44,000 Cambodians were forced at gunpoint over the precipice. . . .Thousands died, many from the fall, and others as they tried to cross the minefield at the bottom of the cliff (Hamilton, 1985:10).

The question of border security has also caused outbursts of abuse in other countries. Both Mexico and Honduras, faced with armed incursions against the refugees from neighboring states, and resistance from the refugees to proposed inland relocations, have reportedly used violent methods to "encourage" the moves. As discussed above, Mexican authorities actually burned camps and cut food supplies (Americas Watch 1984). Similarly, the brutal attack on Colomoncagua by Honduran authorities received much publicity.

Even without these occasional incidents of abuse, the refugees often face an existence filled with restrictions. This low quality of life, on a daily basis, proves extremely difficult over extended periods. In West Germany, for example, applicants for asylum could work and receive social benefits until recently. In 1982, the government decreed that applicants should remain in camps or centers, pending final determination of their status. Depending on state law, persons would receive social benefits only if they remained in the centers; movement in and out of the center was to be strictly confined. Employment was curtailed. Only a minority of asylum applicants were actually placed in these centers. Nonetheless, the new laws drew sharp criticism, including charges that conditions in the centers were inhumane, and that denial of work opportunities and choice of residence make life in West Germany little better than life in the original oppressor state (Rubin, 1984).

As discussed above, similar criticisms may be raised with respect to the treatment of Central Americans within the United States. Persons entering illegally face potentially lengthy detentions if unable to obtain proper release on bond. Moreover, those persons being processed have had difficulty in obtaining work authorizations. Most importantly, because the vast majority of requests for asylum eventually result in orders of deportation, persons are inhibited from exercising their right to seek asylum. As a result, they remain part of a vast underclass of undocumented persons, barred from working legally, or from receiving most forms of federal assistance. Working illegally to survive, they receive the worst jobs, under unsafe conditions, and at substandard wages. Many also live in inadequate housing. Abused by landlords, officials, and employers, they cannot complain for fear of being reported to the Immigration and Naturalization Service.

In Honduras, the government has reportedly insisted that the Guatemalan and Salvadoran refugees remain in closed camps (Torres Rivas 1985:70). As in Mexico, persons found outside the camps are considered illegal and risk deportation. They may not work. (Interestingly, some Nicaraguan refugees are not restricted in the same way, reflecting a clear political bias on the part of the Honduran authorities.) A group of 500 Guatemalans living in a Honduran camp could not leave without permission and were permitted little, if any, outside contact. Nor could they participate in local markets (*Refugee* Magazine, May 1985).

In Costa Rica, the standards set forth in the UN Convention and Protocol are generally complied with. Persons recognized as refugees are granted freedom of movement, the option of resettlement, free medical care, and educational opportunities. Work permits are also given, though limited to occupations which will cause little competition with the local labor force. Self-sufficiency projects have begun. The real problems arise with respect to undocumented persons, who are not entitled to protection or assistance. As requirements become more complex and stringent, this unprotected class continues to grow (Torres Rivas 1985:71).

Nicaragua and Belize provide useful examples to examine. In February 1980, Nicaragua acceded to the UN Convention and Protocol on Refugees. Refugees reportedly are granted resident status as well as freedom of movement and the right to work under the same conditions as nationals. This was confirmed by Jose Mendiluce, UNHCR representative in Nicaragua in 1984 (Chichini 1984). Mendiluce also describes the continuation of Nicaraguan projects for the integration of refugees into agricultural cooperatives along with the Nicaraguan nationals themselves:

> In the Nicaraguan Ministry of Agriculture there is a department responsible for agrarian reform which has distributed good agricultural land to the refugees; 6000 hectares have been made available to them. They

work in mixed cooperatives — 50 percent refugees and 50 percent Nicaraguan citizens — and receive technical assistance from the government. This has seemed to be the best solution, not only because it allows for assistance to the local population living in the areas where the refugees are being settled, but also because cooperatives conceived in this fashion encourage the social integration of the refugees.

These cooperative efforts appear to be successful to date (*Refugee*, February 1985).

Belize has maintained a generous policy toward refugees, although it has a population of only 150,000 persons, and a fragile economy. Nevertheless, a general amnesty was declared in 1984 so that all aliens could regularize their status. Some 8,860 were registered (Torres Rivas 1985:80). Despite potential cultural and racial conflicts, Belize has made efforts to provide for these refugees. The UNHCR has been invited to work in the country, and a joint UNHCR and Mennonite agricultural project has been developed. According to Piers Johannessen the largest group of refugees live in the central and northern part of the country, working on rented land and sugar cane plantations (Johannessen 1985:28). A poor nation, Belize is nevertheless experimenting with ways to make the refugees self-reliant. The Valley of Peace project, a multicultural settlement is described by Johannessen as near complete, and reasonably self-sufficient.

A central question concerns the treatment of refugees once they are admitted to a new country and it becomes evident that they cannot return to their homelands in the near future. Harsh conditions and restrictions which might be tolerable on a short-term basis become intolerable when applied over an extended period. At the same time, the economic and administrative strains caused by these newcomers can be increasingly burdensome to the host country. Recently, there has been considerable discussion of ways in which large refugee groups can be constructively integrated into the host society.

According to Poul Hartling (1984:17), the only alternative to keeping refugees endlessly inactive and dependent is the establishment of income-generating projects. He suggests that ending refugee isolation is necessary, and that projects should be planned with an eye to creating jobs and benefits for both refugees and local populations. The goal should be to contribute to the overall development of the area, hopefully fostering integration and lowering local resentment. Accordingly, Hartling reports that a meeting of experts was held in 1983 to discuss such ideas. There it was urged that the UNHCR, together with the interested governments, should take the initiative in formulating projects combining refugee and development aid. It was also recommended that the UNHCR help secure needed financing. These concepts were again discussed in 1984.

A good illustration of such an effort is Pakistan, which now houses close to three million Afghans, giving it a refugee to local population ratio of 1 to 33, despite a per capita GNP of only $349. The refugees have been arriving since 1978, with no end in sight to the conflict in their homeland. Pakistan has regularly received praise for its generous policy toward these refugees, despite the obvious strains, including security problems. Arriving refugees are interviewed, registered, and provided with clothing, food, cooking utensils, tents, and a cash stipend. They are encouraged to remain in established camps, and can only receive material aid if they do so, but the Pakistanis permit them to make the choice. The refugees are free to move about, find work (though permissible categories of work are restricted), or go to the cities. Due to the shortage of arable land, agricultural efforts are not available to the refugees (Jones 1985:4). Most importantly, emphasis is shifted from care and maintenance to self reliance. Poul Hartling describes a joint pilot project being developed by the Pakistani government, the World Bank, and the UNHCR. The presence of large numbers of refugees and their flocks had caused ecological damage to certain regions in Pakistan, including loss of water and deforestation. The pilot project includes efforts at watershed management, irrigation control, flood protection, and road improvement. All efforts are labor intensive. The goals are to repair the environment and to give the refugees as well as local needy people an opportunity to work and to secure an income.

In addition to Pakistan, some fourteen African nations met to consider projects to lighten the socioeconomic burdens of refugee flows on that continent. One commentator noted that care and maintenance of refugees can often come at the expense of national progress (USCR 1984:17). At the Second International Conference on Assistance to Refugees in Africa (ICARA II, July 1984), some 127 projects were discussed and presented, and sources of international assistance sought. These were designed to aid both refugee as well as local populations. Unfortunately, the famine crisis later overshadowed these projects, but they remained part of the UNHCR program (Hutchison, 1985).

Although these projects are of great significance, the critical questions for all parties remain those concerning when and how the refugees may return to their homelands. Clearly no refugee should be involuntarily returned to a nation where he or she still faces persecution. Instances of obviously premature repatriation, such as those involving Thailand and Djibouti, have been described.

Unfortunately, there are few examples of planned repatriation. Most repatriation efforts appear to involve little more than the provisions of transportation to the home country and some effort at registration. One planned effort, however, occurred when in 1983 Djibouti and

Ethiopia, with the official sanction and financing of the UNHCR, began to plan and implement an $8 million dollar program to return Ethiopian refugees to their homelands (Atchison, 1984). Under the plan, the refugees were to be sent to Ethiopian centers, where they would receive food and supplies for four months. Later tools and seeds in self-sufficiency packages would be distributed. Plans were made for work on irrigated agricultural projects. Also, part of the budget was allocated to building support systems, such as irrigation, within Ethiopia for the returnees. UNHCR staff were to supervise and oversee the repatriation efforts. Some 5,900 persons registered and were repatriated between 1983 and 1984; another 6000 later appeared at the sites.

The program has been criticized on several grounds, however, including failure to properly assess the situation of the strife that caused the refugees to flee in the first place (Ibid.). Moreover, insufficient information has been collected to properly assess the results. Nonetheless, the example indicates an effort to organize and supervise the repatriation of refugees and to provide them with long-term resettlement assistance in their homelands. The difficulties in returning to homes and farms that have been abandoned for years, if not destroyed, is significant. As one Ethiopian returning from Somalia said, "What we had before was destroyed and we will need help to rebuild" (*Refugee*, December 1985).

Guatemalan Refugees and International Laws

International pacts and pronouncements lay out a network of basic human rights, which if protected and enforced, would greatly alleviate the difficulties encountered by Guatemalans in both Mexico and the United States. The refugees, however, have benefitted little from these treaties. In some cases, the host country has failed to sign or ratify the relevant pacts; in others, a critical eligibility definition is narrowly applied or ignored, so as to avoid responsibility. Moreover, open-ended clauses providing for the rights of nations to protect their security interests are read so broadly as to extinguish the very human rights protections that the treaty or convention was striving to establish. Perhaps most importantly, enforcement mechanisms either do not exist or have been ineffectively utilized.

This appendix contains a brief description of the key treaties and covenants dealing with human rights and refugee issues. The major dilemmas facing the refugees in the United States and Mexico are discussed in light of the protections provided by these documents. Finally, the deficiencies of these treaties and their interpretations and applications are discussed.

Convention Relating to the Status of Refugees: 1951

One of the most widely recognized documents is the Convention Relating to the Status of Refugees of July 28, 1951, which must be read together with the Protocol Relating to the Status of Refugees of January 31, 1967. Both Canada and the United States are bound by the terms of these documents. Mexico is not.

The terms of the Convention, as supplemented by the Protocol, define a refugee as a person who:

owing to a well-founded fear of being persecuted for reasons of race, nationality, membership in a particular social group or political opinion, is outside the country of his nationality and is unable, or owing to such fear is unwilling, to avail himself of the protection of that country . . . (Art. IA(2)).

The Covenant then sets forth a number of protections for such persons, including freedom of religion equal to that accorded nationals (Art.4); treatment no less favorable than that afforded other aliens in the same circumstances with respect to movable and immovable property and other rights pertaining thereto (Art. 13); free access to the courts (Art. 16); for refugees lawfully in the country, the most favorable treatment accorded nationals of a foreign country in the same circumstances, regarding the right to work (Art. 17); equal treatment to that afforded nationals with respect to education (Art. 22); for those lawfully in the country, the same treatment afforded nationals with respect to labor regulations and social security (Art. 24); for those lawfully in the country, the right to choose a place of residence and to move freely (Art. 26); for those persons who entered illegally, a prohibition against any punishment for such improper entry, so long as the persons present themselves promptly to the authorities; and against unnecessary restrictions on their freedom of movement (Art. 31); for all refugees, a prohibition against returning such persons to the frontiers of territories where their life or freedom would be endangered (Art. 33); and, for host nations, the duty to facilitate the nationalization and assimilation of such refugees (Art. 34).

The American Convention on Human Rights

The American Convention on Human Rights (or the Pact of San Jose, November 22, 1969) has been signed and ratified by Honduras and Mexico. The United States has signed the document but has not yet ratified it, and is therefore not bound by its terms. Nevertheless, as a signatory it should refrain from acts which would defeat the object of the Convention (despite its failure to ratify).[215]

The Convention sets forth numerous protections similar to those provided specifically to refugees in the 1951 Convention discussed above. It requires respect for the right to life, and humane treatment of all persons. It also provides for the rights of free association and assembly, freedom of speech, and freedom from arbitrary arrest and imprisonment. Article 22 provides for freedom of movement and choice of residence, subject only to national security interests and the need to protect morality, public order, public health, and the public interest. Article

22 (7,8) provides that every person has the right to seek and be granted asylum in a foreign country, and that in no case may an alien be deported or returned to a country if his or her right to life or personal freedom is in danger of being violated because of race, nationality, religion, social status, or political opinions. Article 27 permits derogation of some rights in case of war or other public danger, but not on the basis of race, religion, etc.

Universal Declaration of Human Rights

The Universal Declaration of Human Rights was adopted and proclaimed by the General Assembly in 1948 and can be viewed as an authoritative interpretation of the United Nation's Charter, which is binding on all member states. UN declarations may also be read as authoritative statements of the international community, and may be binding customary law.

Like the American Convention, discussed above, the Universal Declaration concerns persons in general, not refugees in particular. It provides for the rights to life, liberty and the security of the person, prohibits torture, slavery, and discrimination, and provides for freedom to travel, the right to own property and to receive an education, freedom of thought and assembly, and the right to work. It also provides for the right to seek asylum from persecution (Art. 23).

International Covenant on Civil and Political Rights

Like the Universal Declaration, the International Covenant on Civil and Political Rights has been described as an authoritative interpretation of the UN Charter. The United States has signed, but not ratified this document, and is therefore not bound by the terms, yet should not defeat the purpose of the Covenant (*Vienna Convention*, Art. 18). Mexico has acceeded to the Covenant.

The Covenant provides for all persons the right to life and physical integrity, the right to travel freely and choose one's place of residence, the right to freedom of thought, conscience, religion, and association, and the right to freedom from discrimination. Article 13 provides that an alien lawfully in the country may not be expelled without a proper hearing.

Convention on the Status of Aliens

The Convention on the Status of Aliens (Sixth International Conference of American States, Havana, February 20, 1928) was ratified by both the United States and Mexico, although both filed reservations. The first article states that all states have the right to establish by means of law the conditions under which foreigners may enter and reside in the country. Article 5 states that nations should extend to foreigners within their territories "all individual guarantees extended to their own nationals, and the enjoyment of essential civil rights without detriment."

Convention on Territorial Asylum

The Convention on Territorial Asylum (Tenth Inter-American Conference, Caracas, 1954) was ratified *with reservations* by Mexico in 1981 (the United States is not a signatory). This Convention established the right of every state, in the exercise of its sovereignty, to grant asylum without giving rise to a complaint by another state (Art. 1). No state is under the obligation to expel or surrender persons within its territory who are persecuted for political reasons (Art. 3). The fact that the person has entered the country surreptitiously or irregularly does not affect the provisions of the Convention (Art. V). Article IX provides that a state may be requested to intern at a reasonable distance from its borders those political refugees or asylees who are notorious leaders of a subversive movement. Interestingly, Mexico filed a reservation to this article, on the grounds that it was contrary to the constitutional guarantees enjoyed by all inhabitants of the Republic.

Statute of the Office of the United Nations High Commissioner for Refugees

The Statute of the Office of the United Nations High Commissioner for Refugees was adopted by the General Assembly on December 14, 1950 as Annex to resolutions 428 (V). The Commissioner is to provide protection to refugees by promoting the conclusion and ratification of international conventions for the protection of refugees, assisting governmental or private efforts to promote voluntary repatriation or assimilation within new national communities, and promoting the admission of refugees, even the most destitute, to the territories of States (Ch.II-8). The Commissioner is also to engage in additional activities, including repatriation and resettlement, as the General Assembly may determine, within the limits of the resources placed at the commissioner's disposal (Ch. II-9); and shall administer funds among public and private agencies which the Commissioner deems best qualified to administer refugee assistance.

The language of the General Assembly's Resolution calls upon all the governments to cooperate with the High Commissioner for Refugees in several ways, including entering into appropriate treaties, admitting refugees to their territories, not excluding those in the most destitute categories, and promoting voluntary repatriation and, alternatively assimilation, especially by facilitating their naturalization.

ANALYSIS OF PROBLEMS OF REFUGEES IN THE UNITED STATES AND MEXICO

Refusal to Recognize Refugee Status: USA

There are no reliable figures of the number of Guatemalan refugees currently in the United States. Some 26,480 have been apprehended by immigration authorities from 1980-1985 (Natonal Immigration Project, 1986: attachment C). Most refugees are in the southwest (Los Angeles is estimated to have the largest concentration), although Guatemalans are also found in Florida, Boston, and New York. The Sanctuary movement has provided support, but most refugees are outside that network. The state of New Mexico has declared itself a sanctuary state, the New York State Assembly passed a resolution declaring the region a sanctuary, as have 22 cities, and 290 religious dominations (see below).

City Councils

Berkeley, California	Santa Fe, New Mexico
St. Paul, Minnesota	Seattle, Washington
Duluth, Minnesota	San Francisco, California
Cambridge, Massachusetts	Burlington, Vermont
Ithaca, New York	Sacramento, California
Tacona Park, Maryland	East Lansing, Michigan
Olympia, Washington	Davis, California
West Hollywood, California	Swarthmore, Pennsylvania
Brookline, Massachusetts	Minneapolis, Minnesota
Madison, Wisconsin	Santa Cruz, California
Santa Barbara, California	Rochester, New York

Denominational Breakdown of Sanctuaries

Catholic	49	Seminaries	1
Friends	50	Episcopal	4
Unitarian	47	Disciples of Christ	3
Presbyterian	29	Jewish	18
United Church of Christ	14	New Jewish Agenda	5
Lutheran	9	Other Protestants	30
Methodist	12	Universities	22
Mennonite	12	States	2
Brethren	7	City Coucils	22
Baptist	5	National Bodies	28

A key problem facing Guatemalan refugees arriving in the United States has been the U.S. refusal to grant them asylum, or to otherwise normalize their immigration status. Although the recent history of Guatemala has been well documented, from 1983 through 1985 less than 0.7 percent of the Guatemalans seeking asylum were granted such status. In instances where asylum is denied, cases are often appealed; however, between 1980 and 1985, some 11,042 Guatemalans were deported or returned through "Voluntary Departure" procedures (National Immigration Project, 1986). Given the current statistics, it is likely that the great majority of those cases now on appeal will also terminate in orders of deportation. As a result, refugees still arriving in the United States are intimidated from exercising their right to seek and enjoy asylum. Their inability to normalize their status leads, in turn, to abuses of their civil rights, their labor rights, and their general health and welfare within the United States.

The Universal Declaration of Human Rights provides that "every person has the right to seek and to enjoy in other countries asylum from persecution" (Art. 14). Grahl Madsen argues that, in making this declaration, the states did not intend to assume a moral obligation to actually grant asylum (Grahl-Madsen, 1972:101). Rather, the Declaration stipulates a right to request asylum, without an absolute guarantee that it will be granted. The right to "enjoy" asylum thus means the right of the host state to offer refuge and to resist demands for extradition, as opposed to an actual obligation to grant asylum.

The Convention of 1951 is binding upon the United States. Article 33 prohibits the expulsion or return of a refugee to any territory where the refugees' life or freedom would be endangered. The term refugee is not limited in this clause to persons lawfully within the country. Article 34 states that all contracting parties shall as far as possible facilitate the assimilation and naturalization of refugees (this clause is also not limited to persons who initially entered the country legally). Although asylum is not specifically referred to, these articles indicate the United States should grant bona fide refugees, otherwise ineligible for entry into the U.S., legal acceptance and recognition.

Some commentators suggest that this is not the case. Guy Goodwin-Gill (1982:219-337) refers to "glaring ommissions" in the Covenant and Protocol, specifically the failure to provide for the refugee's right to be admitted, temporarily or permanently, into a country, and for the right not to be returned to the country of origin. Neither document, according to Goodwin-Gill, guarantees a right of entry or imposes a duty to admit. Refugees may thus find themselves in "limbo: their status unregularized by the country of immediate refuge, resettlement denied by other countries, and return to their country of origin barred by the rule of non-refoulement." This interpretation accords with that of other commentators as well (Rubin, 1983:21). Similarly, Grahl-Madsen (1982:72) notes that refugees have the right to have their claim examined and must be told if they may remain in the country or if they must seek admission to another country, but writes:

> the rule of refoulement . . . may be considered the modern version of Vattel's old dictum that a refugee has a right to abode somewhere on the face of the earth, even if this right is imperfect with regard to any particular country.

Goodwin-Gill also writes that the absence of an obligation to grant asylum, in the sense of secure residence and protection, together with the prohibition against refoulement, suggests that the concept of "temporary refuge" should be developed as a needed corollary. He further recommends careful development on this idea to avoid the assumption that a state's humanitarian obligations are fulfilled by providing temporary refuge, in the place of durable asylum.

This "limbo" situation, as described by Goodwin-Gill, is reflected in United States law. The Refugee Act of 1980 makes the granting of asylum discretionary [*8 U.S.C. 1158(a)*; but the withholding of deportation mandatory [*8 U.S.C. 1253 (h)(1)*]; even though both are based on similar definitions.

Given the issues discussed above, it seems that no individual refugee is currently entitled to asylum from a particular nation. Thus, the United States, as a sovereign nation, may place certain limits and qualifications upon the admissions of aliens, including refugees. Even the 1951 Convention, for example, permits the deportation of an otherwise eligible refugee where the presence of such person poses a threat to national security (Art. 33-2). Similarly, the definition of the term refugee excludes persons who have committed crimes against humanity (Art. 1-F). Various federal regulations also provide for the exclusion of certain types of persons based on traits considered undesirable and harmful to the American community at large. However, refugees who are not ineligible for any of these reasons should be entitled to receive asylum or at least suspension of deportation. The exercise of discretion by the U.S. government should not be unlimited. It should not be permissible, for example, to deny asylum on grounds of the protection of security or the interests of public order, where in fact no risks are posed. The concept of arbitrary decision making as an abuse of discretion is well grounded in American jurisprudence. Discretion should be exercised within the framework established by the federal laws and regulations promulgated by the U.S. legislature.

With respect to the Guatemalans entering the United States, an important question concerns asylum eligibility. In the U.S., the relevant document is the Refugee Act of 1980, (8 U.S.C. 1101), which echoes the language of the UN Convention by defining a refugee as:

> any person who is outside the country of the person's nationality, or . . . outside the country in which such person last habitually resided, and who is unable or unwilling to return to . . . that country because of the persecution, or well founded fear of persecution, on account of race, religion, nationality, membership in a particular social group or political opinion.

The Attorney General is charged with establishing a procedure for aliens to apply for asylum (8 U.S.C. 1158).

Given this definition, large numbers of eligible Guatemalans continue to be improperly denied asylum. The recent history of Guatemala provides reasonable grounds to fear persecution of catechists, union members, cooperative leaders, students, and Indians from areas subjected to massacres and current strict military scrutiny and control. Yet the standard of proof in U.S. immigration proceedings has, in many cases, been set so high as to be nearly impossible to achieve. Defense attorneys often claim that built-in procedural restrictions, such as those in the preliminary fact-finding stage of the proceedings, greatly hamper the preparation of a case. Fact-finders are often harsh in their findings of credibility, and it appears that the required State Department's advisory opinion letter is often given undue weight by the immigration courts. The great majority of the applicants, in the end, are found to be either economic refugees, or persons merely fleeing the effects of war. The discriminatory nature of this treatment, when compared to the speedy granting of asylum to important personages from the Soviet bloc, is self-evident. Moreover, such a stringent interpretation runs counter to the comments set forth in the UNHCR handbook (discussed below) with respect to the issue of repatriation.[216]

Given the large numbers of Guatemalans in the United States at this time, Congress could grant extended voluntary departure to these persons as a class, in other words, prohibit deportation of all such persons pending proper changes in their home situation. This was done in the case of the Ethiopian refugees, but has been refused with respect to Salvadorans. No efforts have been made on the part of the Guatemalans.

Some commentators suggest that the U.S. is in violation of its obligations under the 1967 UN Protocol, with respect to its treatment of the Salvadoran refugees arriving in its territory.[217] The same criticism would apply to U.S. policy toward arriving Guatemalans. Many of the Guatemalans within the United States should be entitled to be recognized as refugees, and to receive formal asylum status, under the applicable international treaties, but are not.

Welfare of Refugees within the United States

The denial of formal recognition of refugee status to Guatemalans living within the United States has lead to violations of their basic rights which would otherwise be prohibited. As members of a class of undocumented persons, these refugees cannot seek lawful employment and when out of necessity work is obtained anyway, it is often accompanied by illegal health and safety conditions, as well as illegally low wages and other labor abuses. Article 17 of the 1951 Convention requires that refugees lawfully within a country receive the most favorable treatment afforded nationals of a foreign country in the same circumstances, with respect to the right to engage in wage-earning employment. Clearly, if the refugees could have their status legalized, they would be able to obtain a number of protections and benefits with respect to the right to work which they do not now enjoy. Given the threat of deportation, however, many are intimidated from attempting to normalize their status.

Their illegal status has caused other problems as well, including the deprivations of various forms of federal assistance and other programs and benefits to which they might otherwise have been entitled. It is noteworthy that it was only in 1982 that the United States Supreme Court ruled in Plyler v. Doe [57 U.S. 202 (1982)], that undocumented school children should have equal access to the public schools.

Moreover, refugees unable to make their bond requirements, as established by the local immigration authorities, may suffer lengthy detentions while their cases are heard and appealed. Were the principles of asylum more readily recognized, this problem could be alleviated, if not avoided.

Prohibition against Repatriation

The treaties and conventions described above stress that refugees may not be returned to countries where they would face persecution. The 1951 Convention states that expulsion of refugees or the return of such refugees to the frontiers of any territory where their life or freedom would be threatened is prohibited, unless such refugee poses a threat to the community, or to the interests of national security. The Universal Declaration of Human Rights provides that all persons have the right to seek and enjoy asylum from persecution. The UN Declaration on Territorial Asylum (1967) prohibits rejection of refugees at a frontier, or expulsion or compulsory return to any state where they may be subjected to persecution (with the exception of cases involving national security, or to safeguard the population, if facing a mass influx). The American Convention on Human Rights states that:

> In no case may an alien be deported or returned to a country . . . if in that country his right to life or personal freedom is in danger because of his race, religion, social status, or political opinions [Art. 22(8)].

Arguments have also been made that the Geneva Conventions would prohibit the return of refugees (Sklar, Hing and Silverman, 1985). In addition, the OAU convention governing the specific aspects of refugee problems in Africa prohibits the repatriation of any refugee against his or her will. Goodwin-Gill (1982:304) argues that these documents, taken together with the various pronouncements of the United Nations, establish the principle of non-refoulement as a matter of customary international law. Accordingly, it is binding on all states, regardless of assent to particular treaties. It is clear then that no nation, either by virtue of binding treaties applicable to it or by virtue of general principles recognized by nations, can forcibly repatriate Guatemalan refugees if it is determined they would face persecution.

The critical matter here becomes the definition of persecution. In this regard, a number of the commentaries to be found in the Handbook of the UN High Commissioner on Refugees are particularly helpful. In Art. 51, it is noted that a threat to life or freedom on account of race, religion, nationality, political opinion, or membership in a social group is always persecution, but that other serious violations of human rights, for the same reasons, would also constitute persecution. Article 54 states that while discrimination is not, in itself, persecution, it may amount to persecution if it leads to consequences "of a substantially prejudicial nature for the person concerned, *e.g.* serious restrictions on his right to earn a livelihood, his right to practice his religion, or his access to normally available educational facilities." Similarly, Art. 63 explains that although economic migrants are not generally refugees, the distinction should be carefully examined:

> Behind economic measures affecting a person's livelihood there may be racial, religious, or political aims or intentions directed against a particular group. Where the economic measures destroy the economic existence of a particular segment of the population, (*e.g.* withdrawing trading rights from, or discriminatory or excessive taxation of, a special ethnic or religious group) the victims, may according to the circumstances, become refugees on leaving the country.

General economic measures applied equally to all are not, in general, grounds for a claim of persecution. Goodwin-Gill makes similar comments in his discussion of the Convention and Protocol, noting that less overt measures, such as the imposition of serious economic disadvantages, denial of access to employment, and restrictions of free speech, association, and assembly would also be included (Ibid:298). The U.S., as a party to the Protocol, should be influenced by these guidelines. Moreover, though Mexico and Honduras are not signatories, they are working closely with the UNHCR in providing for the refugees within their territories, and should also give careful consideration to these principles.

A refugee should not need to prove that he or she faces imminent death or imprisonment upon the return to the home country. Persecution encompasses violation of other human rights as well, including in some cases, the destruction of the means of survival. This concept is critical with respect to the matter of denial of asylum and subsequent deportation from the United States. It will likely become increasingly important in Mexico and other countries as consideration is given to the possibility of mass repatriation of the refugees (American Convention, 1969. Art. 22(9)). In considering this issue, careful scrutiny must be given to the conditions to which the refugees would be returned. As the analysis in this report of life in rural Guatemala makes clear, most refugees face continuing, albeit changing, threats of persecutions. They would be returning to continued violations of basic human rights.

Again, the OAU Convention offers an excellent model with respect to the repatriation issue. Not only does this document prohibit nonvoluntary repatriation, but it requires the receiving home country to "facilitate" this resettlement, and urges "all possible assistance" from voluntary agencies and international organizations (Art. V). The UNHCR is also required by statute to assist government and private efforts to promote voluntary repatriation. The governments involved should be working with the UNHCR offices to plan development projects that would facilitate such repatriation efforts.

Forced Resettlement and Travel Restrictions

Important questions are raised by the overall treatment of the refugees in Mexico and Honduras. In both nations, the refugees were, at various stages, subjected to personal restrictions. People were at times virtually confined to their camps, not permitted to travel or integrate locally and, at certain points, were forcibly relocated. While there is little doubt that these nations, neither of which are signatories to the 1951 Convention or its Protocol, have the power to protect their national security and public order, including the interests of the local labor market, it is less clear that the measures actually taken were appropriate (Ibid., Art. 22(1),(3)). It can be argued that the refugees, as "persons" also have certain rights, though subject to lawful governmental restrictions, and that such rights were infringed upon.

Article 26 of the 1951 Convention Relating to the Status of Refugees provides that "each Contracting State shall accord to refugees lawfully in its territory the right to choose their place of residence, and to move freely within its territory, subject to any regulations applicable to aliens generally in the same circumstance."[218] These rights have been set forth in many other of the conventions and treaties described above, although usually in the context of basic rights of "persons" and not of refugees in particular. See for example, the American Convention on Human Rights, ("Pact of San Jose") of 1969, which was signed by Mexico; and the Universal Declaration of Human Rights.

Mexican Law on Refugees

The legal framework in Mexico regarding foreigners is based on several laws regulating a person's activities. But, the larger-scale exodus of Central Americans constitutes a refugee phenomenon that exceeds the current legal and institutional framework. This exodus creates pressures on the government of Mexico, with its traditional policy of granting asylum, to move toward permitting the refugees to stay in national territory, on the basis of various legal categories regarding foreigners.

This section explores important elements of the laws governing refugees in Mexico.

The Political Constitution in Mexico

Within the Articles, Chapter 3 expressly discusses the existence of foreigners within national territory. Article 33 states that:

> Foreigners are those who do not possess the characteristics determined in Article 30. They have the right to the guarantees granted by Chapter I, Title One of the present Constitution, but the Executive of the Union will have the exclusive faculty of making any foreigner abandon the national territory, immediately and without necessity of prior judgement, whose permanence is judged inconvenient. Foreigners shall not, in any way, involve themselves in the political affairs of the Country.

The prologue of the Constitution, where the individual and social guarantees are defined, states:

> In the United States of Mexico every individual will enjoy the guarantees granted by this Constitution, which cannot be restricted or suspended except in the cases and with the conditions established by it.

Article 11:

> Any man has the right to enter the republic, leave it, travel through its territory and move residence without needing a letter of security, passport, safe conduct or other similar requisite. The exercise of this right will be subordinated to the faculty of the judicial authority in cases of criminal or civil responsibility, and to the administrative authorities for all that touches on the limitations imposed by laws on emigration, immigration, and the common health of the Republic, or on pernicious foreigners with residence in the Country.

The 15th precept indicates that:

> . . . it is not authorized to celebrate treaties for the extradition of political offenders, nor of those delinquents of the common order who, in the country where they committed the crime, have had the condition of slave; nor conventions or treaties by whose virtue are altered the guarantees and rights established by this Constitution for the man and the citizen. (Constitución Política de los Estados Unidos Mexicanos, pp. 1, 15, 16, 17 and 43.)

Organic Law of the Federal Public Administration

This law establishes the foundations and organization of the Federal Public Administration. Within this centralized administration are the Secretaries of State and the Interior Ministry (Gobernación), which according to Article 27, section XXV, is the agency responsible for "formulating and conducting the policy of population, save that of colonization, human settlements and tourism."

General Law of Population

This is the legal instrument that regulates the behavior and daily activities of foreigners within Mexican territory. It grants power to the Secretariat of the Interior (Article 3, secton VI):

> To subject the immigration of foreigners to the modalities that it judges pertinent, and to procure the best assimilation of these into the national medium and their adequate distribution over the territory . . .
> To subject the immigration of foreigners to the modalities that it judges pertinent, and to procure the best assimilation of these into the national medium and their adequate distribution over the territory . . .

The General Directorate of Migratory Services exercises these duties and also acts on the immigration, emigration, and repatriation of Mexican nationals.

This law considers three types of foreigners with residence in Mexican territory: a) nonimmigrant; b) immigrating; and c) resident. A nonimmigrant is a foreigner who enters the country temporarily with permission of the Secretariat of the Interior.[219] An immigrating person enters the country legally with the purpose of residing in it, and may do so upon acquiring the status of permanent resident.[220] Finally, a foreigner is considered a resident when the individual acquires the right to definitive residence in the country.

The General Law of Population and its more detailed regulations recognize political asylum, but not the migratory nature of political refugees. Moreover, the legislation grants individual rather than group treatment, making it inadequate for resolving the current problems of the refugees. (See Bravo, Guía del Extranjero).

Law of Nationality and Naturalization

Article IV concerns the rights and obligations of foreigners, and sets forth their individual guarantees, the activities they are prohibited from engaging in, and their legal obligations. For example:

> Article 30: Foreigners have the right to the guarantees granted under Chapter I, Title 1 of the Political Constitution of the United Mexican States, with the restrictions imposed by same.
>
> Article 31: Foreigners are exempt from military service; residents, however, have the obligation to do vigilance in matters of the security of properties and the maintenance of order in the same community where they reside.
>
> Foreigners and foreign moral persons are obligated to pay ordinary or extraordinary contributions and to satisfy any other monetary obligations, provided they are ordered by the authorities and are part of the general obligations of the place of residence. They are also obligated to obey and respect the Institutions, Laws and Authorities of the Country, subjecting themselves to the verdicts and sentences of the courts, accorded to Mexicans." (Bravo, Ibid.)

Accord Creating the Mexican Commission to Aid Refugees (COMAR)

On June 22, 1980, the Federal Government created COMAR in response to the influx of refugees. COMAR included those institutions whose area of responsibility covered the refugees. The Secretary of the Interior heads the commission, which includes representatives of the Secretariats of Foreign Relations and Labor. COMAR is responsible for direct assistance to refugees, determining needs, and developing programs of protection and assistance. The commission has declarative rather than executive power and is bound by the guidelines on refugees that the Secretariat of the Interior promulgates through the General Directorate of Migratory Services (Diario Oficial de la Federación, 1980).

Accord between the Mexican Commission of Aid to Refugees (COMAR) and the Office of the United Nations High Commission for Refugees (UNHCR)

This Convention took effect on March 2, 1981, with the aim of ensuring cooperation in developing and financing assistance programs for refugees and asylum cases. The Mexican authorities were to define a policy regarding the number of refugees, their reception, placement, occupation, and permanence and to develop programs for the refugees self-sufficiency during their stay in Mexico or until going to a third country (O'Dogherty, 1985:73-75).

Administrative Actions

Under this framework, the Secretariat of the Interior has taken actions restricting the scope of employment of foreigners, and creating obstacles for their entry into national territory, specifically from Central and South America (with the exception of Argentina). Similarly, it has sought to localize the refugees, specifying places to carry out detentions while investigations take place. The most significant action has been that of prohibiting foreigners from working in the Federal Public Administration.[221]

Other Documents and Events

Colloquium on Asylum and the International Protection of Refugees in Central America. This event took place in Mexico City from May 11 to 15, 1981, and was promoted by, among others, the Mexican government, the UNHCR, the Matias Romero Institute of Diplomatic Studies of the Secretariat of Foreign Relations, and the Institute of Juridical Investigations of the National Autonomous University of Mexico. The following conclusions and recommendations were reached:

> 1 To reaffirm that the universal and regional systems for protecting asylum applicants and refugees both recognize the international right of non-refoulement, including the prohibition of rejection at borders;

> 2 To indicate the necessity of making an effort proportional to the circumstances that have arisen in the region, one that would permit the

most favorable aspects of the traditional inter-American system to work in conjunction with elements provided by the universal system of protection for refugees and asylum cases;

3 To indicate the necessity in Latin America for the protection of the universal and inter-American provisions for refugees and asylum cases to be extended to all persons who flee their country because of foreign aggression, occupation or domination, massive human rights violations, or occurrences that seriously alter public order in all or part of the country of origin;

4 To recognize that the rules relative to the status of refugees and asylum cases, both universal and inter-American, constitute an adequate normative system of international protection, whose interpretation and application must be brought about in accordance with general principles of international law and international custom, while taking into consideration the progressive development of this material in the resolutions of the United Nations and the Organization of the American States.

Recommendations:

1) To exhort the States that have not yet done so to ratify or adhere to the Convention of the United Nations of 1951 and the Protocol of 1967 on the Status of Refugees; the Convention on Territorial Asylum (Caracas 1954); the American Convention of Human Rights of 1969 (Pact of San Jose); the Convention on Extradition (Caracas 1981); and further, to solicit the cooperation of the hemisphere with the UNHCR in actions within its competence;

2) To use appropriate institutions of the Inter-American system and its mechanisms, especially the Inter-American Commission of Human Rights and, in its consultative function, the American Court of Human Rights, for the purpose of completing the international protection of refugees and asylum cases (O'Dogherty, 1985:77–78).

Act of Contadora for Peace and Cooperation in Central America. In this document, the members of the Contadora Group (including Mexico) establish goals toward the resolution of the refugee problem. The following are most relevant to the present study.

FIRST. To carry out, if still not completed, the constitutional procedures required for adherence to the Convention of 1951 on the Status of Refugees and the Protocol of 1967 on the Status of Refugees.

SECOND. That all repatriation of refugees be of a voluntary nature, manifested individually and with the collaboration of the UNHCR.

THIRD. To strengthen the programs of protection and assistance to refugees, above all in area of health, education, work and security.

FOURTH. That programs and projects aimed at the self-sufficiency of the refugees be established.

FIFTH. To seek, with the collaboration of the UNHCR, other possible reception countries for Central American refugees. In no case will a refugee be moved against his will to a third country.

SIXTH. That once the bases for voluntary and individual repatriation have been agreed to, with full guarantees for the refugees, the host countries will permit official delegations from the country of origin, accompanied by representatives of the UNHCR and the host country, to be able to visit the encampment of the refugees.

SEVENTH. That the host country facilitate the exit process for refugees, for reasons of individual and voluntary repatriation, in coordination with the UNHCR.

EIGHTH. To establish measures in the host countries leading to the prevention of refugees taking part in activities aimed against the country of origin (O'Dogherty, 1985:83).

Act of Cartagena on Refugees, Colombia, November 19-22, 1984. This document comes out of the colloquium on the "International Protection of the Refugees in Central America, Mexico and Panama: Legal and Humanitarian Problems." Participants in this event arrived at the conclusion that many of the problems that have arisen in Central America, Mexico and Panama regarding refugees can only be solved by coordination at the national level. The following conclusions and recommendations were adopted:

1 To promote within the countries of the region the adoption of international norms that facilitate the application of the Convention and the Protocol and, if necessary, for procedures and internal resources to be established for the protection of refugees. Also, to propitiate the adoption of norms of internal law that are urged by the principles and criteria of the Convention and the Protocol, thus contributing to necessary process aimed at the systematic harmonization of national legislation on the matter of refugees.

2 To urge that the ratification of and adherence to the Convention of 1951 and the Protocol of 1967, with respect to those countries that still

have not done so, not be accompanied by reservations that limit the scope of said instruments, and to invite the countries that have formulated them to consider their readjustment as soon as possible.

3 To reiterate the importance and significance of the principle of non-refoulement (including the prohibition of rejection at borders), as the cornerstone of the international protection of refugees. This principle, operative in as far as refugees go, should be recognized, in the current state of the international community, as one of the cases of *jus cogens*.

4 To reiterate to countries of asylum the convenience deriving from refugee camps and settlements situated in border zone being relocated to the interior of the countries at a reasonable distance from the borders, aiming to improve the conditions of protection in their favor, to preserve their human rights and to put into practice projects intended for their self-sufficiency and integration into the host society.

5 To express their concern over military attacks on refugee camps and settlements that have occurred in various parts of the world and to propose to the countries of Central America, Mexico and Panama that they support the measures proposed by the Executive Committee of the UNHCR.

6 To urge the countries of the region to establish rules for the basic treatment of refugees, based on the precepts of the Convention of 1951 and Protocol of 1967 and the American Convention of Human Rights, also taking into consideration the conclusions emanating from the Executive Committee of the UNHCR, in particular No. 22 on the Protection of Applicants for Asylum in Situations of Large-scale Arrivals.

7 To study in the countries of the region that have a massive refugee presence, the possibilities of achieving an integration of the refugees into the productive life of the country, designating resources from the international community that the UNHCR channels for the creation or generation of jobs, thus making it possible for the refugees to enjoy their cultural, social and economic rights.

8 To reiterate the individual and voluntary character of repatriation of refugees and the necessity that this happen in complete security, preferably to the refugees place of residence in the country of origin.

9 To recognize that the reunification of family members constitutes a fundamental principle in the matter of refugees, one that should inspire both humanitarian treatment in the country of asylum, and the facilities that are granted in cases of voluntary repatriation.

FIRST. That the criteria and directives on the matter of refugees contained in the Act of Peace of Contadora, for the ten States participating in the Colloquium, constitute guidelines that must be necessarily and scrupulously respected in determining the line of conduct to be followed regarding refugees in the Central American area.

SECOND. That the conclusions adopted by the Colloquium (III) be taken adequately into account to solve the most serious problems raised by the massive flow of refugees in Central America, Mexico and Panama (O'Dogherty, 1985:84–88).

Seminar on the Productive Integration of Guatemalan Refugees in Southeastern Mexico. UNHCR-COMAR. Conclusions and Recommendations. Bacalar, Quintana Roo. April 19, 1985. During this event, the two most analyzed issues were the relocation of the refugees from Chiapas and their integration into the States of Campeche and Quintana Roo. Governmental policy on the matter of refugees defines refugees only as those persons in camps in Chiapas, and those who have been and are continuing to be relocated to the States of Campeche and Quintana Roo. No formal recognition is given, for example, to the existence of large numbers of Salvadoran refugees residing in Mexico.

The key conclusions and recommendations are as follows:

RELOCATION

1 By sovereign decision of the Mexican Government, the Guatemalan refugees located on the southern border of Chiapas must be relocated to the States of Campeche and Quintana Roo. The relocation of nearly 18,000 refugees has been accomplished with the support of the authorities of said States, and personnel of the COMAR and UNHCR.

2 The Office of the UNHCR respects the sovereign measure of the Mexican Government to remove refugees to a prudent distance from the border. The relocation of refugees away from the border is acceptable to the United Nations, as it guarantees the security of the refugees and favors the creation of long-term solutions.

3 It has been a fundamental concern of the Mexican Government to respect the human rights of the refugees, both during their relocation and upon securing shelter and work for them. Upon reaffirming that the relocation process would continue, using information and persuasions, it was recognized that the collaboration of the refugees themselves was necessary in the relocation efforts.

4 The relocation program at present is facing some difficulties arising from an unwillingness that, for various reasons, is being shown by some refugee groups. For that reason, the campaign of convincing the refugees will be intensified in the State of Chiapas. The Government will be especially watchful that refugees not be displaced from the camps they currently occupy without the knowledge of the authorities.

5 This unwillingness toward relocation is based on understandable reasons or on interests that transcend humanitarian questions. These are manifested in different forms depending on the types of camps where

they occur, as in some cases where for example, traditional relations are observed between Guatemalan and Mexican settlements near the border.

6 Despite the large number of refugees already transferred, the Seminar expressed its concern regarding the resistance to transfer that still persists among part of the Guatemalans settled in Chiapas. In effect, an eventual interruption of the relocation process, making it impossible for COMAR to complete the tasks conferred to it, could lead the Mexican government to take recourse through other legal means and channels that in the end would be harmful to the integration process being carried out in Campeche and Quintana Roo.

7 COMAR and the UNHCR reiterate their commitment to maintain the protection and basic assistance for all Guatemalan refugees in need of same in the southeast of the country.

8 It is reiterated that the policy of the Mexican Government is that all aid to refugees be proportioned through COMAR, since it is the organ with legal faculty to centralize and channel such assistance.

INTEGRATION

9 The process of integration of refugees in Campeche and Quintana Roo has advanced rapidly. This is demonstrated by the fact that, in less than one year, the initial stage of emergency has almost been overcome. It must be indicated, however, that the process is advancing unequally according to the refugee group's time of arrival.

10 The integration of the refugees into the two states has advantages both for the refugees and the reception regions. Among other things, the refugees finally have the opportunity to remake their lives, through access to land use and other forms of work, and by receiving health and education services. On the other hand, the reception regions benefit from an additional workforce and from the infrastructure produced for the requirements of the refugees. The cultural exchange is beneficial to both parties.

11 The goal of integration is the self-sufficiency of the refugees. Hence, it has been emphasized that not all productive activity implies self-sufficiency, nor does every form of self-sufficiency lead to integration. It was also insisted upon that integration and self-sufficiency are a gradual, long-term process that poses new and difficult challenges for the refugees, the COMAR, the UNHCR, the governments of the states and other interested entities.

12 In this sense, the disposition and motivation of the refugees to participate actively in productive projects was considered to be crucial. What was emphasized for bringing about such participation was the necessity of respecting the cultural expressions, organizational forms,

and initiatives of the refugees. There exists no incompatibility between the refugees' integration and the preservation of their culture. Interaction with the Mexican communities is beneficial and desirable.

13 Refugee participation and the integrity of a project are not mutually exclusive factors. On the contrary, it is considered indispensable for there to be refugee participation at all stages of planning and execution of the projects. This will have favorable repercussions on the success of their social and productive integration.

14 The integration process should be integral and gradual. The development of projects intended for the social, economic, cultural, civic, and legal integration of the refugees must be advanced.

15 To guarantee adequate, successful participation of the refugees, it is recommended: a) to establish training courses for refugees on aspects of administration and self-management; b) to organize refugee visits to those cultivation zones of the region not contemplated for the first agrarian cycle; c) to encourage secondary activities (pottery, shoe making, tailoring, etc). for self-consumption; d) to support all those initiatives of the refugees that contribute to the greater success of the integration programs or respond to needs not contemplated in the current projects.

16 The preceding considerations must be viewed within a framework of respect for Guatemalan cultural identity and its practical manifestations. The preservation of Guatemalan culture is a constant concern of those responsible for the refugees' integration into Campeche and Quintana Roo.

17 To initiate special projects aimed at preserving, reviving and developing the different Guatemalan cultural and ethnic expressions, including the production of their own clothing and domestic utensils and musical, dramatic, and dance expressions, and the development of their languages and narratives, etc.

18 To stimulate coexistence between Mexicans the Guatemalans through joint cultural and sporting activities (Alto Comisionado, 1985).

THE JURIDICAL FRAMEWORK CURRENTLY IN FORCE AND ITS OBSERVANCE

Background

The legal antecedents concerning refugees have their source in international laws, specifically the treaties on territorial asylum. These laws are influential in bringing about domestic legislation and in resolving disputes which arise. The first experience in this regard involved the Spanish asylum cases during the administration of President Lázaro Cárdenas, who passed a law receiving these refugees and regulating their stay in Mexico. The same law was applied to the Guatemalans who, because of a coup d'etat against the ruling democratic government, fled to Mexico in search of refuge in 1954. In the late 1960s and during the 1970s, Mexico continued to apply the same norms to the groups of Uruguayans, Chileans, and Argentines who fled to Mexican territory, thus dealing with the situation again using the individual concept. This same legal framework was again applied to the numerous groups of Nicaraguans that entered the country before the Sandinista Revolution.

Current Situation

The flood of Guatemalan refugees has overwhelmed the government institutions and the legal framework currently in force. Consequently, the Mexican government has taken on the regulation and control of the refugees in national territory.

There are important differences between Guatemalan and Salvadoran refugees. The great majority of Guatemalan refugees, for example, come from rural area (approx. 75 percent); the majority of Salvadorans come from urban areas and tend to settle in large and intermediate sized cities.

Refugee policy differs as it is applied across the country. Refugees are only considered to be those persons placed in the camps in Chiapas, Campeche, and Quintana Roo. To make up for the lack of a migratory category for political refugees, those who have already been relocated to camps in Campeche and Quintana Roo are being assigned to the category of nonimmigrant FM-3, visitor.

Here, the refugees are characterized as groups, following international law (the Convention of 1951 and the Protocol of 1967 on Refugees). These laws are supplementary to the Convention on Territorial Asylum of 1954, which the Mexican Government ratified in 1981.

But the refugees living in the Mexico City metropolitan area are treated differently. Cases are considered on an individual basis, adhering strictly to the General Law of Population and its regulations. Because of this, the great majority of refugees applying for asylum have their requests refused.

Refugees who file requests with the Mexican authorities generally do so once the UNHCR has recognized them as refugees and places them under its mandate. Once this has happened, the UNHCR directs them to the Secretariat of the Interior, specifically to the General Directorate of Migratory Services, with a letter presenting their case and requesting that, in conformity with the legislation and the traditional policy of asylum, the refugee be allowed to remain in Mexico until the causes leading to flight from the country of origin disappear.

Immigration authorities had been receptive in processing this type of request and, due to the lack of a migratory category for the refugee, had either assigned the political asylum nonimmigrant F-10; FM-9, student; or FM-3, visitor. Currently, however, approximately 80 percent of the cases are denied. The office that notifies a refugee of the rejection orders the person to leave the country within 30 to 40 days from the date of notification.

Regarding refugees located in the north of Mexico, those who manage to obtain migratory status (after having requested it and turned in a letter of presentation from the UNHCR) are few, owing to the governmental criterion that those in the north are economic migrants using the country as a passageway to the United States in search of work. Generally, refugees detained in the north are deported, without recourse to legal defense.

As the Mexican Government has not agreed to sign the Convention of 1951 on refugees or the Protocol of 1967, this gives it the flexibility to act in accordance with policies framed in a context of national security and, despite having granted to the UNHCR the necessary space for it to determine refugee status, it is not bound to grant the corresponding migratory status. Within the legal framework, refugees must meet requirements that the great majority cannot fulfill; subsequently the migratory authorities order them to leave the country.

Violations

There is contradiction between the policy followed by the Mexican government internationally and domestic actions concerning refugees. Consider some of the international forums Mexico has participated in and their conclusions (cited in O'Dogherty, 1985). In its first recommendation, the Colloquium on Asylum and the International Protection of Refugees in Central American calls for countries that have not done so to ratify the Convention and the Protocol on Refugees. On this same subject the Act of Contadora, also proposes that countries submit to the Convention and the Protocol. This is likewise stipulated in the conclusions of the Act of Cartegena. The Mexican government, however, has not adhered to or ratified the Convention or the Protocol regarding refugees.

The most detrimental action is defining as refugees only those people in camps in the State of Chiapas and those relocated to Campeche and Quintana Roo. This definition overlooks those living in intermediate and large cities, mainly Salvadoran refugees.

The actions carried out against the refugees in these cities, include locating foreigners for investigation and subsequent deportation; denying refugees entry at the airport, despite their arrival with immigration documents in order; and denying refugee family members from reuniting.

The Convention on the Status of Refugees of 1951, in its Article 2, establishes that:

> with respect to the country where they are found, all refugees have duties that, especially, involve the obligation to respect its laws and regulations, as well as those measures adopted to maintain public order. (Alto Comisionado, 1984:27)

In its Article 26, it establishes for those states adhering to that instrument that:

> every contracting state shall concede to those refugees found legally within the territory the right to choose the place of their residence in that territory and to travel freely through it, provided they observe those regulations applicable under the same circumstances to foreigners in general

The American Convention of Human Rights, in the chapter on the right of circulation and residence, Article 22, states in clause 1 that:

> every person *found legally* in the territory of a state has the right to circulate through it and to reside in it subject to the legal dispositions . . .

In clause 4 it indicates that "the exercise of the rights recognized in clause 1 can likewise be restricted by the law, in determined areas for reasons of public interest. . . ."

In the accord between the UNHCR and COMAR, both institutions agreed to cooperate on diverse programs, provided they are subject to the governmental policies regarding the number of refugees, their reception, location, occupation and permanency.

CONCLUSIONS

The relation between international law and domestic Mexican law on refugees is minimal, since the Mexican government has not subscribed to the Convention nor to the Protocol on refugees; neither has it legislated on the matter.

Among the international legal instruments on the matter of refugees, the Convention and Protocol relating to refugees provide a frame of reference regarding the form of regulating the refugees' behavior within the host country and protecting their human rights.

The legal precedent of the political asylum case is inadequate because it deals with individuals rather than groups.

The Mexican government is not complying with the Convention on Territorial Asylum when this migratory category is not granted to a requesting refugee.

It is a sovereign decision of the Mexican government to relocate refugees located in the state of Chiapas to other states, but the relocation should not be carried out in violation of the refugees' human rights.

APPENDIX D

Costs for Incorporating People into Development Poles

The process of building development poles is complex. Generally, there are three levels of activity: 1) immediate aid for displaced people (food, temporary shelters, medical attention, special assistance for orphans and widows, latrines, etc.); 2) organization of the new settlement (resource inventory and infrastructure design, manpower training, production planning, and construction of housing and urbanization); and 3) consolidation of socioeconomic development (credit, technical assistance, planting and harvesting, cottage industries, marketing, etc.). The average number of separate activities undertaken in four sample communities was forty-two, and the time period required to initiate activity on all three levels was twenty-five weeks. Each village program involved, again on the average, twenty-four different Guatemalan government agencies, plus numerous national and international, official, and private organizations.

The development poles require considerable human and material resources. The only data available is that published by the Guatemalan army, and it is partial and dated February 1985. Using this data, the next table presents a conservative calculation of a Q1,144 cost per person in a model village as outlined above. As a point of reference in predepression 1981, 51 percent of the Guatemalans, and almost all those in the rural area, had annual incomes of less than Q360.

**Guatemala: Estimated Direct Costs in 1986 for
Incorporating a Person Into a Model Village**

1. *Investment by government agencies*   Q574.0
   Based on the Q344,251.05 expenditures by 14 agencies for 600
   people in the Ojo de Agua model village reconstructed in late
   1984, the only detailed budget published by the army.

2. *Value of community labor*   Q102.3
   Based on the average 31 work (for food) days per person benefited

required for the reconstruction of five villages in the Ixil Triangle during 1984, calculated at Q3.30 per day, the minimum wage in agriculture.

3. *Credit to purchase agricultural inputs for 0.3 hectares per person benefited*   Q207.0
   Based on the National Agricultural Development Bank's 851 loans totalling Q2,150,502 granted to villages in development poles as of February 1985.

4. Total/person   Q880.0

5. Total/person adjusted for 30% inflation in 1985   Q1144.0

The Q1,144 figure could be pushed up or down by various factors. On the reduction side of the ledger, the government expenditures may be inflated, and food has been and could continue to be used to pay for community labor.

On the other side, additional costs could reasonably be included for land; the army emphasizes the importance of giving returning *campesinos* land title, and of the 4,335 families who had benefited from the model village program by the end of 1984, 2,480 had received provisional title to their land. The army's report gives land size information for 1,154 provisional titles, and these average 8.9 hectares each, enough land to maintain one family and in contrast to the less than one hectare average size of landholdings in the Indian highlands. There has been no expropriation of large landholdings, however, and although some of the development poles are in areas where the state owns most of the land, a large-scale demand by *campesinos* from *minifundia* areas would require either a broad-reaching agrarian reform, which is highly unlikely, or the purchase of considerable extensions of cultivatable land.

Another conservative element in the cost calculation is credit; obviously a gap between the 1.4 hectares per family (of five members) covered on the average by the agricultural loan figure and the amount of land being titled for each family. Inflation is expected to continue to rise, although it is impossible to project with any accuracy.

Lastly, the 30 percent inflation figure for 1985 is conservative.

The final arithmetic is easy and simply depends on the number of refugees to be reincorporated:

46,000 refugees	Q52,624,000
Or 150,000 people reputedly refugees in Mexico	Q171,600,000
Or 200,000 people refugees in all other countries	Q228,800,000
And up to 500,000 people displaced within Guatemala and considered "internal refugees"	Q572,000,000

These calculations assume the 36,766 people that were projected to be incorporated into model villages but had not been as of the beginning of 1985, have benefited in the course of 1985.

The government's budget for calendar year 1986 is still under discussion, but is reported to be Q20 million above 1985s Q1.3 billion. Once separated into operating (fixed) and capital (variable) expenditures by ministry, the significance of the cost of reincorporating refugees becomes apparent. In 1985 the combined capital investment of the ministries of education, health, and agriculture totalled Q46.2mn, and defense, Q35mn.

With a Q600mn budget deficit, the pressure will be to cut rather than increase expenditures, but nevertheless political pressures may be greater than financial. In September 1985, following the two weeks of price riots, the government gave civil servants an across-the-board Q50 per month pay raise, adding over Q100mn to the annual budget. Thus, any analysis of the economic feasibility of reincorporating refugees must be made from the perspective of the national socioeconomic situation and particularly with full account taken of the political implications of reincorporating or not reincorporating refugees.

Development and Service Poles and Their Model Villages, 1985.

Development poles and Model Villages, Planned/Completed.	Constructed	Families Benefited	People Benefited	People who Worked for Food
Ixil Triangle 16/8	1,826	1,826	10,221	4,150
1. Acul, Nebaj	450	450	2,700	1,500
2. Juil-Chacalté, Chajul	123	123	675	800
3. Tzalbal, Nebaj	315	315	1,890	900
4. Pulay, Nebaj	138	138	706	100
5. Ojo de Agua, Cotzal	100	100	600	100
6. Salquil, Nebaj	500	500	2,500	500
7. Santa Abelina, Cotzal	100	100	600	125
8. Bichilabá, Cotzal	100	100	600	125
Chisec 12/10	(1,865)	1,865	9,775	1,865
9. Chisec	(600)	600	(3,000)	600
10. Setzí	(180)	180	(900)	180
11. Sesajal	(81)	81	(405)	81
12. Saguachil	(134)	134	(670)	134
13. Sesuchaj	(131)	131	(655)	131
14. Semuy-Pecajbá	(63)	63	(315)	63
15. Carolina	(60)	60	(300)	60
16. Las Palmas	(50)	50	(250)	50
17. Semococh	(36)	36	(180)	36
18. Santa Marta	(80)	80	(400)	80
19. Acamal	(450)	450	2,700	500
Chacai 2/2	200	(18)	108	400
20. Chacaj				
21. Ojo de Agua				

Development and Service Poles and Their Model Villages, 1985. (cont'd)

Development poles and Model Villages, Planned/Completed.	Constructed	Families Benefited	People Benefited	People who Worked for Food
Senahú 1/1 22. Yallihux	160	(160)	(800)	200
Playa Grande 12/10 23. Cantabal 24. Xacbal 25. Trinitaria 26. San Pablo 27. San Francisco 28. San Jose la 20 29. Efrata 30. Santa Clara 31. Aldeas fronterizas 32. Salucuín	366	(366)	1,830	400
Yanahí 1/1 33. Yanahí	100	(100)	(500)	120
Total Estimated 49/33	4,517	4,335	23,234	7,135

Source: Guatemalan Army documents. Numbers in parentheses are estimates, based on army data. Completed villages are those actually finished or under construction by January 1, 1985. As of December 1, 1985 there was no official additional information on the villages under construction or those planned.

Refugee Letters

Refugee representatives developed a list of necessary conditions for repatriation. These were outlined in two letters sent to the President of Guatemala, Vinicio Cerezo. The first makes some of the following points:

> With regard to our returning to our homelands in Guatemala it is still, not yet the time, as you yourself, President Vinicio, have stated publicly in February of this year.

> At the present time we are not thinking of returning to our homes in Huehuetenango, El Quiché, San Marcos, Alta Verapaz and El Petén. What happened in those areas is the same that happened to us in the area of Kaibil Balam in the Ixcán (Chajul, Quiché). It was a Saturday around eight in the morning (2/27/82) as we were eating breakfast with our families. When the army took our village and executed 14 of our brothers, sisters, the elderly and children. Three days later they killed our animals. What wrong could the animals have done? At the same time they burned our village. A month later they returned to kill 14 more in their homes, on their lands, burning them in an oven used to make lime. One woman had just given birth. These acts were committed by the army under General Lucas García and General Efraín Ríos Montt.

> And they did the same thing in the villages of San Mateo Ixtatán in Huehuetenango, where countless of our Indian brothers and sisters were massacred during the month of June, 1982, and again the same on July 16th in the village of San Francisco where hundreds were killed.

> And again in the month of December, 1982, in our cooperative La Técnica in El Petén, where they killed the members of the cooperative and with them many others in the area. Women, even pregnant women, were raped by the army and often were tortured to death. Ever since that time there has been no peace in Guatemala, no liberty, no justice, nor security to insure human rights. Our freedom is to work the lands that have given us birth and daily sustanance for our families. We once lived free and like our national symbol of the Quetzal we can never live

as prisoners. Now we wait for the present government to do what it has promised and we ask the following questions:

> We would like to know if those responsible for the massacres, disappearances and torture—such as the Generals García, Ríos Montt and Majia Victores—have been brought to justice and punished?
> We would like to know if the concentration camps, called development poles have been removed?
> Have the civil patrols been disbanded?
> Have they returned the lands to the people as was promised by President Vinicio?
> Where are the 120 that disappeared during the period from January to May, 1986?

> And so we are not thinking of returning at this time. We would like to thank the President of Mexico who has received us with so much compassion and as human beings. We also thank the Mexican Commission to Aid Refugees (COMAR) which has assisted us in our needs. Also the United Nations (UNHCR) which has taken us under its protection. We would hope that Guatemala would respect these human rights that have been shown to us. In the meantime until Guatemala fulfills all of these we will not return.[222]

Another similar letter from refugee representatives in Campeche and Quintana Roo was sent to President Vinicio Cerezo. The following are some of the points they make:

> Many Guatemalans are living in Mexico because of the previous government's murderous campaigns.
> You can say this is the fault of other governments and that now there is democracy, but that's not true; besides, you are in agreement with the military assassins because otherwise they will throw you out, since they are free.
> We the Indians were treated worse than savage animals, we were despised, our wives were raped by the soldiers, we were tortured, and we were burned alive. That's why we are refugees.
> Its easy for you and your friends to tell us to return because there is democracy; for you its easy to say that we should forget the past; because you have never suffered what we have suffered; because we will never be able to forget when the military burned our villages, our cooperatives; we don't forget when we were celebrating our religious cults to God Almighty and the army closed the doors, threw gasoline, and burned children, women and men.
> We cannot forget the *calvario* as we fled through the mountains, and dying of hunger, and none of that appeared in the international news and, where were you Mr. President when they were killing us?
> We know that in Guatemala things have not changed and even if there is a new government that doesn't mean anything, because the

military assassins continue to rule and they have more power than you, and the day that you do something good for the people and try to change things, then the rich and the military will throw you out of power, that's why you have to play the game, that's why we don't believe in the democracy that they say there is in Guatemala.

The reasons the refugees give for not returning are:

1. There is no respect for human rights, because in the five months that you have been in the government more than 140 people have been assassinated and there are kidnappings.
2. There is no freedom of expression, of communication, only that which you want, in other words what you find convenient.
3. The paramilitary organizations continue, only their names have been changed and you authorized that.
4. Hunger and misery continues for the majority of the population because we don't have land nor real wages.
5. The civil patrols, development poles and model villages continue, where people are concentrated by force.

We the refugees have the firm opinion not to return to Guatemala, even though it is not the fatherland's fault, the fault rests with those that govern it. We love our country, but now we cannot return, because our lands, for example in the Ixcán — Zona Reyna — and Petén, have been given to other peasants.

In order for there to be democracy and for us to be able to return some day we ask, we demand the following:

1. That the military responsible for the massacres and all those who participated in the destruction of our villages be brought to justice and sentended;
2. That there be a true agrarian reform and no more large landowners, since only a few own the land and not those that work the land;
3. To terminate the civil patrols, because it is a paramilitary force, and it is obligatory;
4. To discontinue the model villages and the development poles, and that our culture be respected;
5. That we get paid for all the damages inflicted in our villages;
6. That our lands be returned to us;
7. That an international commission protect us at the time that we think of returning.

If you, Mr. President Vinicio Cerezo, respond (*cumple*) with all of this, then we will believe in you and if you don't, then you are the same as that Julio César Méndez Montenegro who was a puppet of the military. You have the opportunity to do something for Guatemala. Since you are such a good speaker, then let's see the truth because we are already tired of promises, of oppression and the *engaños de siempre de muchos años* (usual deception of many years).[223]

The Case of Cuchamadera: A Lumber Company in Huehuetenango

The Cuchamadera lumber company was formed by several powerful men, including the former governor and now Congressional Represenative, Franco O'Valle and a former commander of the Huehuetenango army base, Hernández Catalán, in the mid-1970s to exploit the pine forest which lies above San Mateo. The company estimates the value of the wood to be over three million dollars. The forest is considered sacred by many of the Chuj people and is viewed as vital to their survival. "We build our houses with it, cook our food, make the salt and earn a living by selling it to other people. It is also important for the *ocote* (pine heart wood) fires for saying our prayers." said an informant in San Mateo.

Outsiders had made attempts in the past to make money off the wood, all of which the people of San Mateo rejected. Thus, the Mateanos viewed this scheme as just the most recent outsider or government attempt to rob them of their livelihood and heritage.

Villagers were extremely upset when it was revealed that the elected mayor of San Mateo had signed away rights to the wood in 1977 without the permission or knowledge of the community. Their anger increased upon reports that he had received a substantial bribe. Two to three hundred people, including residents of the town and the villages gathered together and forced him to resign. They could not, however, invalidate the contract allowing the company to cut the trees.

The company claims a right to the trees because the contract was signed on the basis that a pine pest, the *gorgujo*, threatened the forest. The company agreed to fight the blight and improve the region, bringing in roads, etc. In the late 1970s, the company brought in engineers, consultants, and equipment and conducted an intensive study into the pest situation. The company claims that 400,000 *quetzales* were spent on the research. Legally if a township lacks the resources to properly care for a communal resource, a company might enter into a contract with that township to save the wood and be recompensed for its efforts. Thus, when the people of San Mateo first took the case to court the company defeated them.

A great deal of organizing centered on the attempt to get the company out of the region, and people were determined to resist the robbery of their wood at all costs, with their machetes if necessary.

In December 1980, before any trees were actually cut, the guerrilla forces of the EGP, already strong in the villages, entered San Mateo. The Cuchamadera company quickly pulled out. When the army reestablished control in 1982, the commander appointed a mayor who saw the Cuchamadera company as profitable for the municipality and himself. He agreed to renegotiate. When a new contract was signed, the villagers once again began to organize to save the forest. The leaders of the organization suffered repeated threats, but with the support of local religious workers and lawyers in Huehuetenango, they took the case to court again. After several trials, the villagers were able to obtain a *Recurso de Amparo* which has stopped all activity for the time being. The company claims, however, that the municipality owes it $400,000 for the study and has offered the alternatives of repayment or allowing the company to take the amount of trees that would recoup their losses.

Many people in San Mateo fear that their resistance will be answered with another massacre. For this reason, some say that they should simply allow the company to take the wood. Most of the people, especially in the villages, argue that without the wood they will die anyway and that there is a point where they must fight back. The fear is very great, however. One informant said:

> If they want that wood, they will have it. The *ladinos* and those people with university degrees, and the army, they will just come and massacre us. We will all die. A thousand pine wood fires and prayers will not save us.

While informants admitted that it has never been easy for Indians to defend their rights, the villagers' belief that they may be killed for opposing Cuchamadera is a direct result of the recent counterinsurgency campaign. It was difficult to find people willing to speak of the situation, and some of those involved in taking the case to court were considering leaving due to threats from the military.

Refugee Camps in Chiapas, Prior to Relocation

The main refugee camps and estimated population prior to the relocation in May 1984:[224]

Alvaro Obregón	79
Amparo Agua Tinta	1,258
Las Delicias	606
Bella Ilusión	36
Benemérito de las Américas	678
Cieneguitas	1,520
Chajul	3,150
Flor de Café	553
Frontera Corosal	470
Galaxia	62
Gallo Giro	158
Guadalupe Miramar	81
Ixcán	2,877
José Castillo Tielemans	210
La Constitución	212
La Democracia	49
La Gloria de San Caralampio	2,582
Las Ventanas	840
Loma Bonita	259
López Mateos	282
Maravilla Tenejara	149
Monte Cristo	93
Monte Flor	1,928
Niños Heroes	258

Nuevo Huistán	383
Nuevo Jerusalén	251
Nuevo Santo Tomás	333
Peña Blanca	131
Pico de Oro	1,750
Playón de la Gloria	201
Posa Rica	1,235
Puerto Rico	5,080
Quiringüicharo	808
Rancho Alegre	114
Reforma Agraria	363
Rizo de Oro	443
San Antonio los Montes	96
San Carlos del Río	76
San Juan Chamula	501
Santa Margarita Agua Azul	124
Santo Domingo las Palmas	148
Venustiano Carranza	270
Vicente Guerrero-Carman Xhán	268
Zacualtipán	68
44 Camps	**31,033**

Additional Camps:

Agual Azul	Nuevo Porvernir
Barrio Cuernavaca	Nuevo Refugio la Noria
Bella Vista del Norte	Nuevo San Juan Chamula
Benito Juárez	Ojo de Agua
Cablotal	Ojo de Agua Chicharras
Cuauhtémoc	Pacayalito
El Bosque	Paso Hondo
El Cobán	Rosarito Linda Vista
El Poblado	Sabinalito
Emiliano Zapata	Santiago El Vértice
Francisco I. Madero	San Antonio Buena Vista
Gpe. Grijalva	San Caralampio
Guadalupe Victoria	San José Bella Vista
Heselchakán	San José Belén
Ignacio Allende	San Vicence
Jaboncillo	Santa Elena El Lagartero
J. Miguel Gutiérrez	Santa Marta
Jemel	Santa Polonia
José María Morelos	Santa Rosa

La Gloria   Santa Teresa Llano Grande
Las Lajas, Chicharras   Sinaloa
Nanzalito   Tierra Blanca
Nueva Libertad   Tsiscao
Nuevo México   Villa La Rosas

Estimated Population   15,000

Total (approximate)   46,000

Tables

TABLE 1
Guatemala: Central Government Budgeted Expenditures, 1985
(In millions of quetzales)

	Operating Expenses	Capital Expenses	Public Debt Payments	Total
TOTALS	726.8	333.8	221.5	1,282.1
National Constituent Assembly	4.1	–	–	4.1
Judiciary	8.4	–	–	8.4
Executive				
Chief of state (Presidency)	28.6	19.8	–	48.4
Foreign Relations	11.0	–	–	11.0
Government	50.4	–	–	50.4
Defense	163.4	35.0	–	198.4
Public Finances	117.7	49.1	221.5	388.3
Education	165.3	5.9	–	171.2
Health	80.6	16.1	–	96.7
Labor	2.7	0.3	–	3.1
Economy	4.2	–	–	4.2
Agriculture	29.7	24.2	–	53.9
Communication	50.4	181.1	–	231.4
Energy and Mines	3.9	2.3	–	6.2
Attorney General	0.9	–	–	0.9
Elections Board	1.9	–	–	1.9
Comptroller	3.7	–	–	3.7

Source: Diario de Centroamérica. Guatemala.

Appendix H 221

TABLE 2
Refugees in the Ixcán Camp Sept. 1982

Community of Origin	Adult Male		Adult Female		Minor Male		Minor Female		Total
	Num.	%	Num.	%	Num.	%	Num.	%	
Ixtahuacán-Chiquito	120	25.53	134	28.51	114	24.25	102	21.70	470
Mayalán	50	19.23	56	21.53	102	39.23	52	20.00	260
Mónaco	55	30.72	34	18.99	53	29.60	37	20.67	179
Cuarto Pueblo	35	29.41	26	21.84	32	26.89	26	21.84	119
Sto. Tomás	10	9.01	11	9.91	16	14.41	74	66.66	111
Los Angeles	25	25.51	28	28.57	30	30.61	15	15.30	98
Pueblo Nuevo	8	14.03	10	17.54	18	31.58	21	36.84	57
Flor del Café	7	18.42	7	18.42	10	26.31	14	36.84	38
Xalbal	7	23.33	6	20.00	10	33.33	7	23.33	30
TOTAL	317	23.27	312	22.91	385	28.27	348	25.55	1362

Source: Delegación de Asuntos Migratorios, Ixcán, Chiapas. Cited in Centro de Estudios (1982).

TABLE 3.
Quetzal-Edzná and Maya Tecún Population

	Quetzal-Edzná	Maya Tecum	Total
Families	972	1,543	2,515
Persons	4,803	7,531	12,334
Births	4	2	6
Deaths	0	2	2
Total Population	4,813	7,534	12,347
Econ. Active	1,164	1,544	2,708
Widows/Widowers	173	201	374
No. of Leaves	1	3	4
No. of Entries	7	6	13
No. of Promoters	139	247	386

Source: Statistical data provided by Comisión Mexicana de Ayuda a Refugiados (COMAR) 1985.

TABLE 4
Camp: Los Lirios General Population Census

Group	Population	Families
San Jose Xoxlac	112	22
Zunil	52	11
Jacaltenango	151	29
San Antonio Chiquito	212	49
Maravilla Tenejara	73	16
La Constitución	90	16
Dolores	174	43
Monte Cristo	148	25
Peña Blanca	25	5
Santo Domingo	105	17
Nuevo Jerusalén	77	14
Santa Margarita	130	24
Zacualtipán	46	10
La Unión	349	69
Xinabajul	90	16
Gallo Giro	134	26
Total	1,968	392

Source: Statistical data provided by Comisión Mexicana de Ayuda a Refugiados (COMAR) 1985.

TABLE 5
Camp Los Ranchos: General Population Census

Group	Population	Families
Xalbal	219	48
Flor Todos Santos	210	41
Niños Heroes	51	9
Palmera P. Blanca	139	30
Zunil	113	18
Mayalán	507	115
Loma Bonita	93	19
San Antonio Tzejá	128	27
Cuarto Pueblo	436	75
Pueblo Nuevo	374	74
Nuevo Santo Tomas	159	42
Los Angeles	155	33
San José	85	18
Candelaria	213	50
Nuevo Huixtán	400	67
Total	3,482	666

Source: Statistical data provided by Comisión Mexicana de Ayuda a Refugiados (COMAR) 1985.

TABLE 6
Maya Tecún: Literacy in Percentages

Age		Illiterate			Literate	
	M%	F%	Total%	M%	F%	Total%
5-9	14.41	13.50	27.91	2.72	2.12	4.84
10-14	9.44	8.14	17.58	19.07	8.58	27.65
15-19	3.69	5.46	9.15	15.23	7.47	22.70
20-24	3.37	5.42	8.79	12.92	4.64	17.56
25-29	2.81	4.41	7.22	4.75	2.52	7.27
30-34	3.22	3.80	7.02	5.85	0.91	6.76
35-39	2.45	3.69	6.14	3.63	0.20	3.83
40-44	2.50	2.33	4.83	3.23	0.20	3.43
45-49	1.98	1.64	3.62	1.92	0.50	2.42
50-54	1.57	1.02	2.59	1.41	0.61	2.02
55-59	1.01	0.74	1.75	0.81	0.00	0.81
60 +	1.96	1.44	3.40	0.61	0.10	0.71
Totals	48.41	51.59	100.00	72.15	27.85	100.00

Source: Statistical data provided by Comisión Mexicana de Ayuda a Refugiados (COMAR) 1985.

TABLE 7
Camp: Quetzal-Edzná: Literacy in Percentages

Age Groups		Illiterate			Literate	
	M%	F%	Total%	M%	F%	Total%
5-9	16.34	16.32	32.66	3.58	2.05	5.63
10-14	8.97	9.76	18.72	15.61	7.29	22.90
15-19	3.20	4.16	7.36	12.40	7.55	19.95
20-24	2.85	4.66	7.51	11.76	6.40	18.16
25-29	2.70	4.76	7.46	6.77	2.56	9.33
30-34	2.40	4.08	6.48	6.90	1.92	8.82
35-39	2.13	3.01	5.14	2.81	.64	3.45
40-44	2.10	2.10	4.20	3.2	.64	3.84
45-49	1.61	1.98	3.59	2.43	.25	2.68
50-54	1.30	1.16	2.46	2.55	.51	3.06
55-59	.99	.91	1.90	.65	.25	.90
60 +	1.56	.96	2.52	1.16	.12	1.28
Totals	46.14	53.85	100%	69.82	30.18	100%

Source: Statistical data provided by Comisión Mexicana de Ayuda a Refugiados (COMAR) 1985.

TABLE 8
Maya Tecún Languages in Percentages

	M%	F%	T%
Spanish	15.99	12.72	28.71
Maya Language	16.93	20.24	37.17
Bilingual	16.42	17.72	34.14

TABLE 9
Quetzal-Edzná: Languages

Language	Male %	Female %	Total %
Spanish	29.48	28.7	58.18
Maya Language	11.87	13.47	25.34
Bilingual	9.94	6.54	16.50

Source: Statistical data provided by Comisión Mexicana de Ayuda a Refugiados (COMAR) 1985.

TABLE 10
Quetzal-Edzná and Maya Tecún: Employment Outside the Camps (Number of Workers)

Month	Quetzal-Edzná	Maya Tecún	Total for Campeche
January	500	373	873
February	294	189	483
March	350	466	816
Total	1,144	1,028	2,171

Percentage of Workers

January	55%	31%	41%
February	33%	15%	23%
March	39%	37%	39%

Source: Statistical data provided by Comisión Mexicana de Ayuda a Refugiados (COMAR) 1985.

Maps

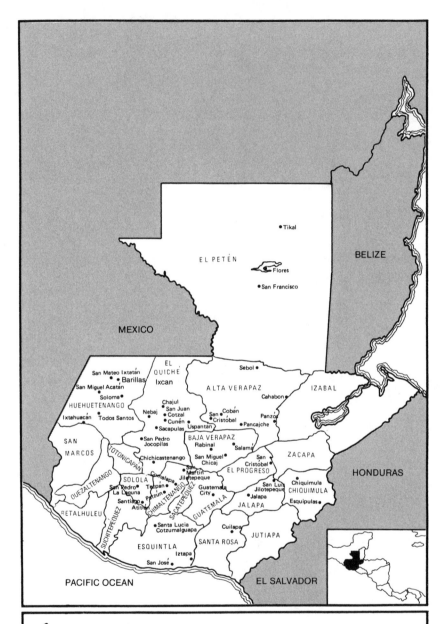

1   MAP OF GUATEMALA

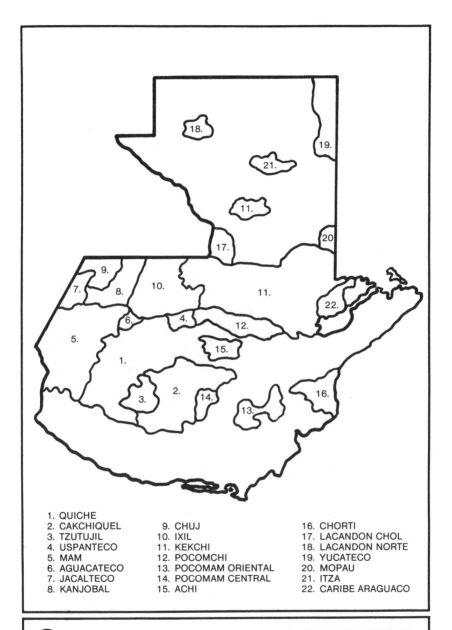

1. QUICHE
2. CAKCHIQUEL
3. TZUTUJIL
4. USPANTECO
5. MAM
6. AGUACATECO
7. JACALTECO
8. KANJOBAL

9. CHUJ
10. IXIL
11. KEKCHI
12. POCOMCHI
13. POCOMAM ORIENTAL
14. POCOMAM CENTRAL
15. ACHI

16. CHORTI
17. LACANDON CHOL
18. LACANDON NORTE
19. YUCATECO
20. MOPAU
21. ITZA
22. CARIBE ARAGUACO

2   MAP OF THE INDIGENOUS POPULATION

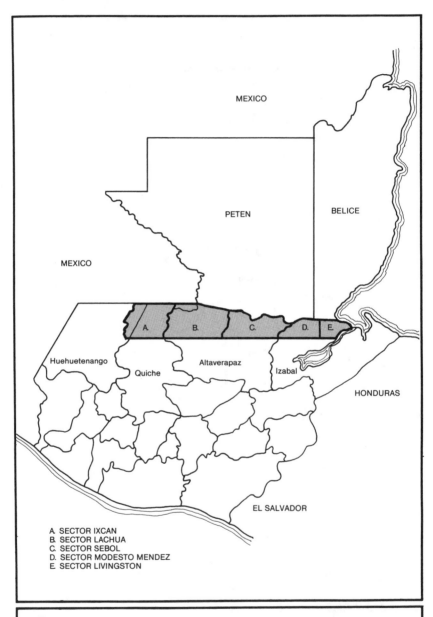

A. SECTOR IXCAN
B. SECTOR LACHUA
C. SECTOR SEBOL
D. SECTOR MODESTO MENDEZ
E. SECTOR LIVINGSTON

3 LOCATION OF THE NORTHERN TRANSVERSAL STRIP (FTN)

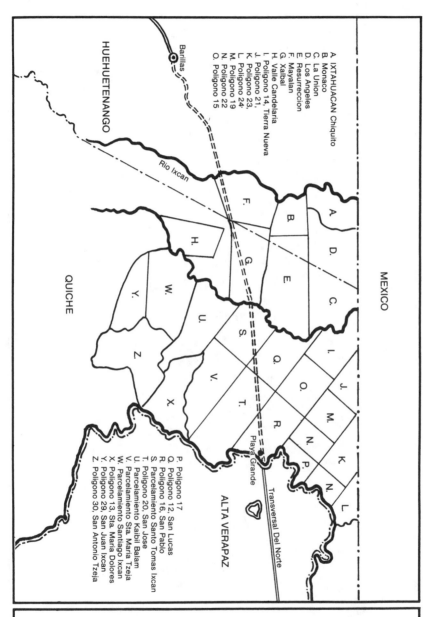

HUEHUETENANGO

Barillas

Río Ixcan

QUICHE

MEXICO

A. IXTAHUACAN Chiquito
B. Monaco
C. La Union
D. Los Angeles
E. Resurreccion
F. Mayalan
G. Xalbal
H. Valle Candelaria
I. Poligono 14, Tierra Nueva
J. Poligono 21,
K. Poligono 23,
L. Poligono 24
M. Poligono 19
N. Poligono 22
O. Poligono 15

P. Poligono 17
Q. Poligono 12, San Lucas
R. Poligono 16, San Pablo
S. Parcelamiento Santo Tomas Ixcan
T. Poligono 20, San Jose
U. Parcelamiento Kaibil Balam
V. Parcelamiento Sta. Maria Tzeja
W. Parcelamiento Santiago Ixcan
X. Poligono 13, Sta. Maria Dolores
Y. Poligono 29, San Juan Ixcan
Z. Poligono 30, San Antonio Tzeja

Playa Grande

Transversal Del Norte

ALTA VERAPAZ

4

SECTOR
IXCAN

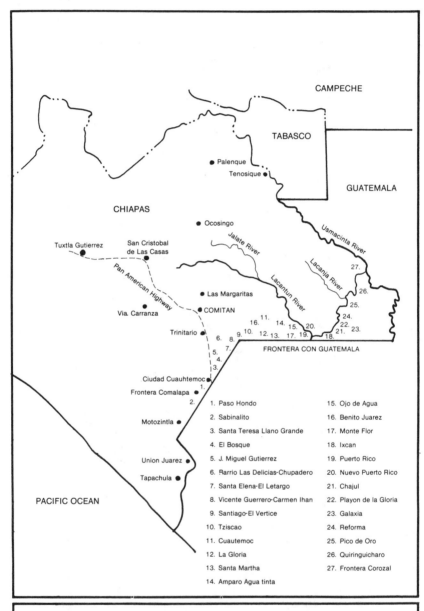

CAMPECHE

TABASCO

GUATEMALA

CHIAPAS

Palenque
Tenosique

Ocosingo

Tuxtla Gutierrez

San Cristobal
de Las Casas

Jalate River

Usmacinta River

Pan American Highway

Lacantun River

Lacanja River

27.

26.

25.

Las Margaritas

COMITAN

Via. Carranza

Trinitario

11.
16.   14.   15.   20.
10.   12. 13.   17. 19.
9.   18.
8.
6.
5.   7.
4.
3.

24.
22.   23.
21.

FRONTERA CON GUATEMALA

Ciudad Cuauhtemoc
1.
Frontera Comalapa
2.

Motozintla

Union Juarez

Tapachula

PACIFIC OCEAN

1. Paso Hondo	15. Ojo de Agua
2. Sabinalito	16. Benito Juarez
3. Santa Teresa Llano Grande	17. Monte Flor
4. El Bosque	18. Ixcan
5. J. Miguel Gutierrez	19. Puerto Rico
6. Barrio Las Delicias-Chupadero	20. Nuevo Puerto Rico
7. Santa Elena-El Letargo	21. Chajul
8. Vicente Guerrero-Carmen Ihan	22. Playon de la Gloria
9. Santiago-El Vertice	23. Galaxia
10. Tziscao	24. Reforma
11. Cuautemoc	25. Pico de Oro
12. La Gloria	26. Quiringuicharo
13. Santa Martha	27. Frontera Corozal
14. Amparo Agua tinta	

5 MAP OF MAIN GUATEMALAN REFUGEE
CAMPS AND TOWNS IN CHIAPAS

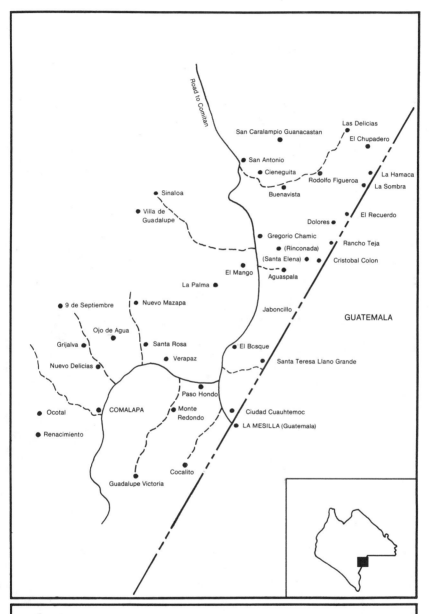

Road to Comitlan

Las Delicias

San Caralampio Guanacastan

El Chupadero

San Antonio

Cieneguita

Rodolfo Figueroa

La Hamaca

La Sombra

Buenavista

Sinaloa

Villa de Guadalupe

Dolores

El Recuerdo

Gregorio Chamic

Rancho Teja

(Rinconada)

(Santa Elena)

Cristobal Colon

El Mango

Aguaspala

La Palma

9 de Septiembre

Nuevo Mazapa

Jaboncillo

GUATEMALA

Ojo de Agua

Grijalva

Santa Rosa

El Bosque

Verapaz

Nuevo Delicias

Santa Teresa Llano Grande

Paso Hondo

Ocotal

COMALAPA

Monte Redondo

Ciudad Cuauhtemoc

Renacimiento

LA MESILLA (Guatemala)

Cocalito

Guadalupe Victoria

6   **"PASO HONDO" ZONE**
PRINCIPAL REFUGEE CAMPS

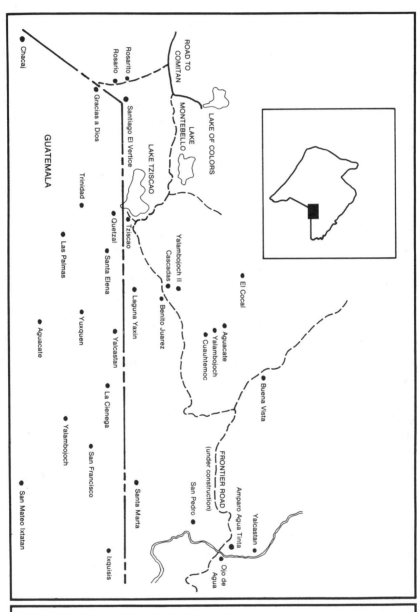

7   "TZISCAO" ZONE

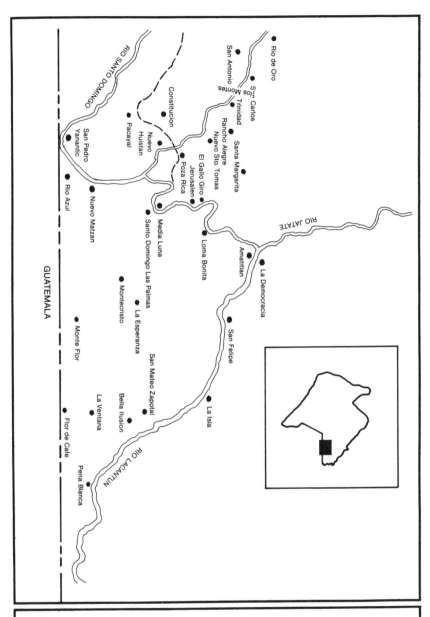

8

"POZA RICA" ZONE (MARGARITAS)

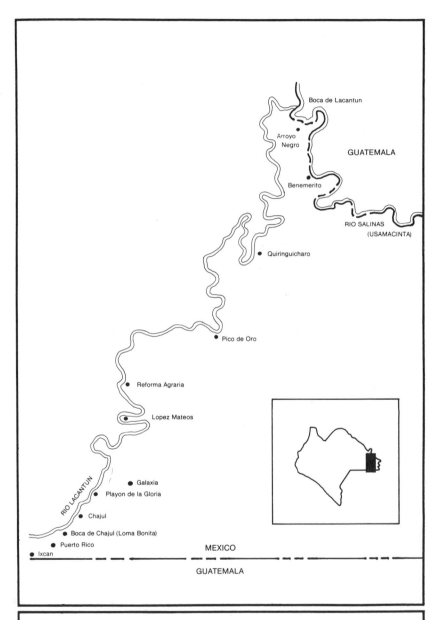

Boca de Lacantun

Arroyo Negro

GUATEMALA

Benemerito

RIO SALINAS (USAMACINTA)

Quiringuicharo

Pico de Oro

Reforma Agraria

Lopez Mateos

RIO LACANTUN

Galaxia

Playon de la Gloria

Chajul

Boca de Chajul (Loma Bonita)

Puerto Rico

Ixcan

MEXICO

GUATEMALA

9 ZONA MARQUES DE COMILLAS

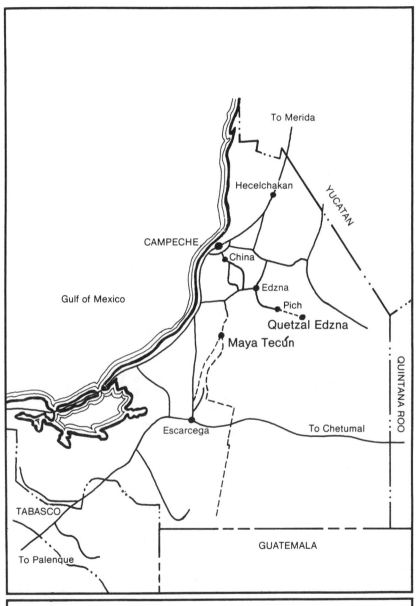

To Merida

Hecelchakan

YUCATAN

CAMPECHE

China

Edzna

Gulf of Mexico

Pich

Quetzal Edzna

Maya Tecún

QUINTANA ROO

Escarcega

To Chetumal

TABASCO

GUATEMALA

To Palenque

10   MAP OF REFUGEE RESETTLEMENT
CAMPS IN CAMPECHE

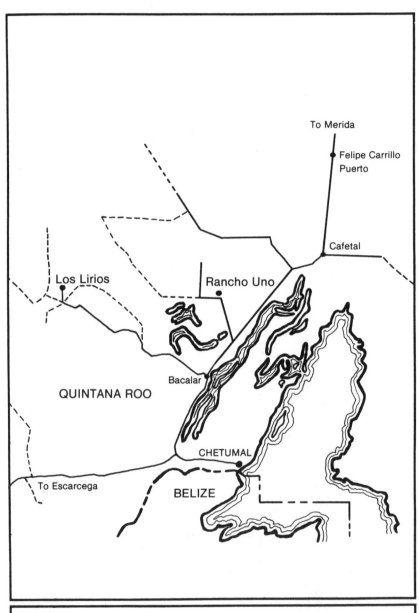

11

PRINCIPAL REFUGEE CAMPS
QUINTANA ROO STATE

Notes

CHAPTER ONE

1. During the 1980s, political violence and repression have led to a surge of over two million displaced people in Central America, according to some observers.

2. The system set up by the colonists awarded local political authority to former Indian noblemen. This system of indirect rule assured tribute to the Spaniards while Indian communities were able to retain a measure of local political autonomy.

3. Indigenous communities were linked to the national economy earlier and to a larger degree than they were integrated into the political life of the country.

4. This resulted, among other changes, in the many agricultural cooperatives formed in northeastern Huehuetenango, northern El Quiche and western El Peten in the late 1960s and 1970s.

5. For more information on Guatemalan society during this period see Adams (1970) and specifically on the 1954 coup, see Immerman (1982) or Schlesinger and Kinzer (1982).

6. See McClintock (1985) for background on state terrorism and the U.S. role in Guatemala.

7. Arana had spent some time in exile for his role in kidnapping the Archbishop of Guatemala in 1968.

8. Guatemala's membership in the Central America Common Market (CACM) attracted dozens of factories and brought new employment opportunities, although industrial workers still represented only 13 percent of the workforce.

9. For a detailed account of the Spanish missionary's work in the department of El Quiché, see *Cronología* (1986). This one hundred page manuscript written by three protagonists, evaluates and analyses the pastoral work of the Catholic Church in El Quiché from 1960 until 1980, when as a result of military persecution, the clergy left the Diocese. Most of the priests from El Quiché left the country and formed the Guatemala Church in Exile. Fourteen priests have been assassinated in Guatemala.

10. Management and government efforts to destroy a union at Coca-Cola galvanized CNUS, which organized widespread support for the workers involved. Between 1976 and 1980 workers struck throughout Guatemala in industries as diverse as meatpacking and banking. Moreover, workers organized broader pro-

tests, occupying workplaces, calling hunger strikes, and marching crosscountry, demanding an end to repression as well as improved economic conditions for themselves. CNUS garnered support throughout the population, becoming a central voice for grass roots groups for several years.

11. The English translation of the names of the guerrilla groups are the Guerrilla Army of the Poor (EGP), the Organization of the People in Arms (ORPA), and the Rebel Armed Forces (FAR).

12. The *Partido Guatemalteco del Trabajo* (PGT), the communist party, is not part of the URNG. It's primary base is among the urban labor and student movements.

13. The Panzós massacre took the lives of more than 100 Kekchí Indian men, women and children who had gathered in the town square to demand that rights to their lands be respected. The army and local *finqueros* (plantation owners) opened fire on the unarmed crowd. A year and a half later a group of peasants from El Quiché and their urban supporters occupied the Spanish Embassy to call attention to violations of their land rights and to the army's repression in their communities. The police broke into the building against the wishes of the Spanish Ambassador. Incendiary chemicals set the building aflame. Thirty-nine people were burned alive as local television crews filmed the scene. The Ambassador managed to escape before the fire broke out. There was one survivor; he was kidnapped from his hospital bed and his body later tossed out on the campus of the National University. See Burgos (1984) for a personal account of growing up in this period.

14. The large scale spending program launched by the Lucas García administration between 1977–1981 multiplied the budget deficit seventeen times.

15. During the first four months of 1982, the guerrillas were still inflicting some 250 casualties per month on the army.

16. Following the March 23 coup, the military named three officers to rule the country: General Ríos Montt, General Maldonado Schaad, and Colonel Gordillo. Ríos Montt became the first among equals and then declared himself sole head of the government in June. Mejía came to power on August 8, 1983.

17. Occasional massacres of entire communities occurred in this period. The massacres in the Chajul, Nebaj, and Uspantán regions of Quiché in 1979 were some of the events that led the group of peasants from that area to occupy the Spanish embassy in January 1980.

18. For a more complete analysis of the civil patrol system see Americas Watch (1983) and Americas Watch (1986).

19. Elections were held in November 1985 to elect municipal officials, Congressional representatives and a President and Vice president. Run-off presidential elections were held a month later since no candidate had won a clear majority of the votes in the November balloting, as stipulated by the Constitution.

20. Within this context, the 1985 elections were part of the culminating stage of a cycle of counterinsurgency. The elections could not have been held in 1983. The army was still involved in finishing its major operations against the insurgent's social base, then in turning its guns more directly against the guerrillas and especially, in efforts to militarize life in conflict areas. From the army's point of view, the country wasn't yet ready for elections. In addition, the army itself

had not fully regained its institutional coherence, seriously eroded during the Lucas years (1978-1982) and only partially restored under Ríos Montt (1982-1983). By mid-1984, the military situation and the rural population were sufficiently under control and the army's internal coherence and hierarchy largely reestablished. The army then sought political, social, and economic measures to consolidate gains won on the battlefield. The elections were a major component of these measures to return the country to constitutional rule, to diminish the polarization, and to lessen the social conflicts that derive from the country's structural injustice (without changing the structures).

21. There have been other plans to modernize the nation, whose contents were not so very different from the "National Project, 1986-1991." National Development Plans for each four-year period beginning in 1970, AID strategy and projects for the country and, most recently, the Kissinger Commission Report have been formulated using similar logic.

22. On the part of some of the country's economic elites, one indication of a search for a new political model is the electoral debacle and total fragmentation of "old right" forces, who had always reflected the traditional positions of those elites. The Movimiento de Liberación Nacional (MLN)–Partido Institucional Democrático (PID) alliance, representing the most traditional rightist forces, won only 12.6 percent of the votes in the first-round presidential elections and only 12 seats in Congress. The vice presidential candidate for the MLN, Héctor Aragón Quiñonez, and several other congressmen, recently elected as MLN candidates have left the party, claiming that it is too rigid, that its historic leader, Mario Sandoval, is more interested in his own power than in the party's success or failure. Until the early 1980s, the MLN was the best organized and most solid political party in the country (SIAG Boletin, No. 53 and Inforpress, No. 667).

23. Continued violence and instability throughout Central America hamper Guatemala's economic recovery by limiting the effectiveness of the Central American Common Market.

24. Six months into Cerezo's term there was a mix of apprehension, expectation, and disillusionment. A woman in Guatemala City voiced a common feeling: "The deception is so big because the hopes were so big."

25. Interview with Andrés Girón, Nueva Concepción, Escuintla. June 1986.

26. For more information on GAM see, (Americas Watch, 1985).

27. Interview with Nineth García, Guatemala City, June 1986.

28. In Guatemala, the percentage of the national budget that is generated through taxes is one of the lowest in the world. The Christian Democrats had made structural tax reform one of their economic priorities for the five-year plan. Nonetheless, for the time being, they have only proposed new, one-shot taxes on export earnings and limited their discourse to the need to make the tax collection more effective.

CHAPTER TWO

29. Statistics on human rights violations have been difficult to compile because human rights organizations were not allowed to operate in the country and fear of reprisal prevented many from reporting the deaths or disappearances of family members or friends. Many informants during the fieldwork in 1985

refused to speak of the violence or to identify its perpetrators out of fear. Those who did, made it clear they were risking their safety by speaking, repeatedly asking that extreme caution be used to hide their identities and their communities. Those who decide to speak out publicly, such as GAM members, are subject to threats and possible assassination.

30. Juvenile Division of the Guatemalan Supreme Court figures. Inforpress No. 629 (Feb. 21, 1985) uses the official figure of 100,000 "orphans" (one or both parents dead) and calculates 30–40,000 parents killed through the following estimates: 3 to 4 children per family, 80 percent of children lost one parent and 20 percent lost both.

31. Nineth de García, a leader of GAM, was quoted in the daily Guatemalan paper *El Gráfico* March 31, 1986 as saying that 40,000 people had disappeared as of March 31, 1986.

As throughout much of Central and South America, to "disappear" has a special meaning. For the victim it generally means being dragged from one's home or car, grabbed from the street or school or work area never to be heard from again. At times the bodies appear, sometimes near a highway hundreds of miles from the victims' homes, often with signs of rape and mutilation. The majority never turn up, leaving the families in a state of constant uncertainty as to the fate of their loved ones.

32. One example appeared in the *New York Times*, July 28, 1985. In less than seven months more than sixty people were killed or disappeared from the village and surrounding area of Patzún, Sololá.

The role of the Guatemalan press is not dealt with in this report. They rely on the military or police for information (reporters rarely travel or "investigate" stories). For an example of this see, Manz (1986). Sometimes the press is directly curtailed, as during a July 1985 "wave of violence and criminality", when the government "asks the press not to publish notices of violence," (*La Razón*, July 8, 1985) because 'the press alarms people." In this case the debate was public (*El Gráfico* responded with an indignant editorial saying "we only transmit what happens" July 9, 1985), but shortly thereafter press coverage of violence dropped sharply.

33. *The New York Times* of July 28, 1985 quotes General Mejía Víctores' views: "The army has never committed a single human rights abuse." The article then describes his opinions in this area in more detail: "People said to have disappeared have really travelled abroad or become guerrillas. Dead peasants were actually guerrillas executed by other rebels for desertion and refugees are "cowards" whose stories of army brutality cannot be believed. The 11 University (of San Carlos) students reported killed or missing were victims of common crime caused by drug addiction."

34. In March 1986 Vinicio Cerezo told the members of the GAM to "stop being masochistic" and give up their search for their loved ones (Nairn and Simon, 1986). Cerezo has backtracked on a commitment to establish an independent commission to investigate documented cases of disappearances. In early June, the president announced he had reconsidered the matter and the commission was unnecessary since its proposed tasks fall within the jurisdiction of the judiciary. Most observers took Cerezo's turn-around on this matter to be the result of army pressure.

35. See *Washington Post*, July 6, 1986. In the article, President Cerezo contends the total number of murders in the period is 560 of which 40 are politically related. The article cites one diplomatic source as saying that murders have risen 10 percent over last year. The news agency IPS reports 109 murders (excluding deaths in counterinsurgency operations) in the one-month period, June 20 to July 22. Reported in *Boletín ACEN-SIAG, no. 66*, August 3, 1986.

36. A disturbing new phenomenon is the emergence of large numbers of disorganized urban youth with few prospects and no hope for the future. This lumpen element is prone to random acts of violence and other antisocial behavior.

37. See Nairn and Simon, 1986 *op. cit.*, for an analysis of the ways in which repression has become a routine part of the military's activities.

38. The motives in this case are being disputed as to whether it was the security forces or personal union activity. In early 1986 another union leader was kidnapped and badly beaten in the capital. He reports that men told him that he and his friends had better stop their activities. *Prensa Libre*, May 13, 1986 reported that a student leader in Quetzaltenango who had been kidnapped three days earlier was found alive but his body showed signs of abuse. The young man was refusing to say anything. The same daily reported on May 16 the disappearance of an Engineering student of the national University of San Carlos.

39. The government eliminated the old secret police (DIT), considered to be responsible for much of the urban terror, although most elements were integrated into other police forces after "retraining." The government has also actively sought foreign funding and training for its police, seeking support especially from Venezuela and West Germany, both now headed by Christian Democratic governments.

40. The service requirements and restrictions on movement, however, are not new. The vagrancy laws during the Ubico regime (1932–1944) required peasants with small land parcels to give 100 days unpaid labor. After the 1954 coup, new forms of control were instituted. In the Ixil region, for example, the 1966 field notes of Colby, Lincoln, and van den Berghe describe how passes were needed by the population for certain travel purposes, that literate men were required to vote (and bribed to vote for the *ladino* mayoral candidate), and that the *contratista/*migration system effectively restricted the population's activities to conform with the coastal plantation labor needs.

41. Although several informants stated this, we received the impression that some exceptions must be made for the routine traveling between the municipal capital and the close-by villages. Nor did we witness thorough civil patrol checks for people traveling to San Mateo Ixtatán's market day. The main concern seemed to be with long-term or far away travel with particular emphasis on controlling movement to and from the villages to the northeast that are also the entrance to the Ixcán region.

42. Most army checkpoints demanded the presentation of women and men's documents, whereas civil patrol checkpoints generally only affected men. The day before the elections women were included in a rigorous check by the army when they unexpectedly stopped the bus. In Huehuetenango many rural women from isolated communities do not have papers. In the Ixil region, people stated that virtually all women living in the towns and villages were documented.

43. The consequences of former Indian soldiers seeking to reintegrate into their communities is a subject that has received little attention from social scientists.

44. Given an opportunity to choose in the future, communities conceivably might retain the civil patrol, given the overall context in the country. The reasons might vary. For many, the consequences of voting against maintaining the civil patrols could be a consideration. For others, if the system could be modified to be less onerous, they might prefer it to having the army keep direct tabs on the village. In either case, villagers would be mindful that a vote for the patrols would be interpreted as an expression of loyalty.

45. One informant in the Ixcán had in his possession two passes allowing him to leave the Ixcán. One pass from Playa Grande read as follows: "[*Aldea's* name and date] The commander of the Civil Defense Patrol of the Aldea of XX, Playa Grande, Quiché, through this means makes evident that XX is a member of this community, identified with his I.D. number XX and registration number XX. He is headed for the capital city for fifteen days, and upon return will continue giving his service here in this community. I request the civil and military authorities to give him the consideration of the case. Signed, XX [Under the signature is the stamp of the] Jefe de la Autodefensa Civil, XX, Playa Grande, Quiché." He also carried a similar pass from the Zone 22 military base. This note stated that he was going to the capital for medical treatment and that he had not registered to vote because he had been ill.

46. The specific duties and weapons of the patrols vary somewhat. Although never heavily armed, in Huehuetenango patrollers were sometimes armed only with sticks in the shape of rifles. In the Ixil area, the army orders patrollers to capture and bring in any internal refugees found on a sweep.

47. In the current economic crisis army supplies of building materials are limited. The resettlement of some areas has been delayed until building supplies are available.

48. In the Ixil area this rapid mobility has been made possible by several years of compulsory labor on the part of internal refugees and inhabitants of the model villages in construction and upgrade of the area's roads.

49. In some instances the army has relied on religious organizations to stave off disaster when it has been unable or unwilling to provide the necessary resources to internal refugees or those it has settled in the model villages. Often it will then claim the credit for the work done.

In one instance in the fall of 1984 refugees were settled in a pre-model village in the Ixil region. The army provided materials to build *galeras*, (open sheds used as living quarters) but was unable to feed the refugees. Local religious workers noticed shock and malnutrition setting in and donated enough corn and beans to keep the people alive until the next harvest.

In the Ixil area internal refugees brought in from the mountains were relocated in a holding camp near the town of Nebaj. While the army claimed to provide for the needs of these people the help seemed sporadic. Religious workers in the area tried to provide some basic foodstuffs, clothing, and mats for sleeping. They were unable, however, to help everyone.

50. Acul, near Nebaj, serves this function. One day during the fieldwork, international journalists arrived in two planes and a helicopter for an afternoon

of investigation and interviews with the inhabitants, leaving before twilight. The civil patrol commander of Nebaj (in charge of Acul) said he did at least one interview a week with foreign journalists.

51. These companies are made up of men and women, many bilingual, who are experts in community organization, social promotion, rural development, health, nutrition, education, and agriculture. Apparently, a good number have been hired from civilian life.

52. This novel administrative model for the next phase of the counterinsurgency program may have built-in problems. First, while government agencies and even the civilian population may have to go along, nongovernmental organizations balk at working under military control. Second, no one who serves on a coordinator is paid directly for that work, which over the long-term could cramp the machinery. Third, the government may have difficulty generating new sources of money to support more credit, public works, health care, educational services, and so forth.

53. *Instituto de Investigaciones Económicas y Sociales, Universidad de San Carlos de Guatemala.*

54. As part of the National Economic Reordering Program, proposed by the president, "harmonized" with the private sector and finally approved by Congress with some minor adjustments, a one time only tax, ranging from 33 percent to 40 percent depending on the product, will be charged in 1986.

55. Inforpress Centroamericana, based on 1980–1983 data from the United Nations Economic Commission for Latin America and 1984 data from Dirección General de Estadísticas and Banco de Guatemala.

56. These readily available *jornaleros* can be employed through local contractors who provide their transportation, freeing the plantation owner from the obligation of providing food and housing for the workers or their families.

57. During the period of field work when the quetzal fluctuated from 2.8 to 3.8 per dollar, prices in the highlands for certain basic goods were:
corn: Q11.00–15.00 for 100 pounds (quintal)
beans: Q65.00 for 100 pounds
machetes: Q3.00–6.00
standard *cortes*: Q35.00–55.00
Standard wages in the highlands for agricultural labor were Q1.25 to Q1.50, often without the midday meal. In May 1986 the government approved new price ceilings for several fixed price goods. Affecting the highland population was an increase in *incaparina*, a soy-based formula, from Q0.25 to 0.42 per pound. Corn, beans and other basic consumer items in the rural areas have no price guarantees (*El Gráfico*, May 21, 1986).

58. *El Gráfico*, April 14, 1986 reports Guatemala's need to import basic grains from the U.S. and Europe. Planned imports are 23,000 metric tons of corn, 2,300 of beans, and 10,500 of rice.

59. Throughout the country, women have been led to prostitution in record numbers. This phenomenon is particularly unprecedented in Indian areas. In Nebaj, where 700 soldiers are based, there are now three houses of prostitution.

60. The *judiciales*, or plainclothes policemen, routinely monitor these commercial activities. Checking petty traders for papers has become a method of tracking down those displaced for political reasons. Arresting someone on a

charge of illegal trade is often an excuse to officially arrest those under suspicion for organizing or activism. Those interviewed described cases of internal political refugees disappearing in 1985, some located through the use of army informants (*orejas*) recruited from their home communities. The fear of being "found out" in hiding and subsequently disappearing imposes serious limits on income earning possibilities.

61. *Prensa Libre*, May 7, 1986: Alfonso Cabrera, secretary of the Christian Democrats and President of Congress, related the rise in diesel fuel to the likelihood of continued increases in basic goods although he stated that a "just solution to the problem will be sought."

62. See U.S. AID (1982:7) and Inforpress (1986). Inforpress also refers to 70,000 farms of 0.4 hectares.

63. The amount of land needed for an average family varies with the quality of land. Estimates range from 3.5 hectares of unirrigated land estimated by some, or 3.9 hectares of first class land estimated by AID researchers to ideally support a family. See, AID (1982) *op. cit.*, pp. 14–15 and table p. 18.

64. Land seizure may be widespread and for obvious reasons people do not discuss it. In recent history army officers became large landowners in Indian areas. The most notable is the case of General Lucas García's large estate in Alta Verapaz.

65. This publication also suggests: "Refugees returning from Mexico to regain their property will find that they have no legal right to do so and will be forced to resettle elsewhere. The potential magnitude of this problem is staggering and must be taken into consideration."

66. The San Mateo municipal buildings were burned by the guerrillas in 1981.

67. In the November 3, 1985 first round election the Christian Democrats received 38.65 percent (648,681 votes) against eight contenders. In the second round on December 8th the Christian Democrats won 68.37 percent of the votes (1,133,517) against the Union of the National Center.

68. The primary goal appeared to be electing officials rather than the meaning of the party program.

69. The census in Ixcán reports 17,000 adults, but only about 3,000 voted.

70. Among those who are sympathetic toward the refugees, there is, however, some apprehension about their return, fearing that having them back might attract the army and more killings.

71. Informants described their personal experiences with resisting the patrols: "We didn't want the patrol but when we saw that they were killing the people who didn't obey, we had to comply (*cumplir*) with the orders." In 1984 the Guatemalan press cites various examples of petitions for the dissolution of the patrols. In November of 1984, the Independent Agriculture Workers, a group in Chichicastenango, asked the government to disarm the patrols because patrol members "threaten the population and falsely denounce citizens to the army." (*Central America Report*, Vol. X, no. 46). This same group, in mid-1985, suffered harassment, as reported in the Guatemala press (June 1, 1985, *El Gráfico*). One member was shot at in the street and others harassed and intimidated in their homes by "unknown people."

72. Teachers went on strike in all the departments except El Quiché where reportedly the military disrupted teachers' planning meetings, warning against their participation. One informant commented that El Quiché, "is just too militarized" to have participated (with the exception of Chichicastenango). Two elderly men on the streets of Santa Cruz del Quiché were overheard commenting on those "great teachers in Chichi, as least they have some spine left!"

73. *Prensa Libre*, April 29, 1986. The organizer, Father Andrés Girón, has been provided with body guards by the government after several death threats.

74. In April 1986 the Guatemalan press reported demonstrations by those of Colomba, Quetzaltenango, San Andrés Itzapa, Chimaltenango, and city workers as well as the Esquintla marchers. The Grupo de Apoyo Mutuo also holds weekly vigils and demonstrations.

75. A group of over 30 people captured in the Ixil area in May/June 1985 were called "guerrillas" by army spokespersons. Over 20 of them were children.

76. For example, a group of 38 brought to the Nebaj military base in June, 1985, were described as: "peasants displaced by the delinquent subversives who sought the protection of the army." *Diario de Centroamérica*, June 28, 1985.

77. The first two or three years were difficult. People died of starvation and illness. Children could not endure the lack of food, the walking and the constant need for absolute silence. The daily twenty-four hour cycle had to be adapted to their condition as internal refugees: cooking and moving at night, staying still in the daylight hours.

Currently, they reportedly have had a good harvest of corn, and some domestic animals. Daily activities take place in the daylight hours. Children attend classes. But the entire community must be ready to flee at a moment's notice. Children have been socialized to this reality.

78. Ambrose Evans-Pritchard, "Guatemala: Despite Army Boast, Rebels Still a Force," *The Boston Globe*, January 12, 1986. Evans-Pritchard reports of the peasants he saw visiting the guerrilla encampment: "Asked if they would fight when called upon, they said '*Claro*,' of course." As an overall assessment he states: "The [civilian] resistance is impressive."

79. In Xix (Chajul, Quiché), one of the most militarized areas in the entire country, members of the EGP held a "meeting" for the resident population in August, 1985, to state their case, and then left, without confrontation. The army arrived in Xix after the local patrol notified them. There was some army-guerrilla fighting in the surrounding mountain area, which was bombed three days later with planes that arrived from the capital. In the same municipality, earlier in the year, Finca La Perla was the site of another army-guerrilla confrontation. The seventy soldiers based there, at the request of the plantation owners, were at breakfast when the guerillas attacked in April 1985. The guerrillas took supplies from the army garrison and escaped after a shootout in which three townspeople died.

80. *Central America Report*, Vol XIII, no. 23, and May 3, 1986 *Prensa Libre*. Two weeks later, General Lobos Zamora (now ambassador to Panama) contradicted his successor saying the insurgency is a small bother now, being confused with common delinquency and drug trafficking (*PL*, May 19, 1986).

81. Different government officials and some peasants would give virtually a word-for-word description as to how the people had been taken in by the false

promises of the guerrillas. Frequent mention was made of the fancy cars that had been promised. In an interview cited in *Insight*, a conservative magazine published by affiliates of the Unification Church through the Washington Times, José Orive, a Guatemalan government spokesman is quoted, "Campesinos who joined the guerrilla forces were promised Mercedes" (England, 1986:24).

CHAPTER THREE

82. For those with poor and insufficient land, the fertile lowlands of the Ixcán seemed like the promised land, yielding two crops a year of corn, as well as cash crops like cardamom and coffee (see Ixcán section).

83. In 1982, when the guerrillas were still strong in much of the area, a catechist reportedly denounced someone to the army in a northern village of Huehuetenango, resulting in the latter's death at the hands of the army. In response, the community and the guerrillas came to punish him. When he could not be found, the guerrillas killed the man's father and brother. The father had been the first in the town to convert to Catholicism, and informants believed that a deep anger at those who forsook the community and betrayed the old ways was also a factor in these murders.

84. See *La Palabra*, July 2, 1985 for accounts of a reported guerrilla-army skirmish in the municipality of Nentón (bordering on San Mateo) where a soldier was killed and a supposed cache of guerrilla weapons found, in caserio Santa Rosa, Nentón. In May 1986, Jaime Hernández, Defense Minister, included Huehuetenango in his report of the country's (five) most conflictive areas.

85. Documented cases of army terror in the study area during the period in question are abundant. The following is a partial list to illustrate the army's methods and the terror these methods generated:

May 31, 1981; "Armed men attack San Mateo Ixtatán, Huehuetenango, killing 36 persons, including four women and eight children. Five people disappear, and others escape into the mountains" (Davis and Hobson, 1982:50–1).

July 19, 1981; "200 soldiers attack the village of Coyá, San Miguel Acatán, Huehuetenango, killing more than 150 people. Helicopters surround and bomb the village, while soldiers throw grenades and fire machine guns on women, children and old people."

August 17, 1981; "Armed men kill 15 people in the village of Suntelaj, San Miguel Acatán, after forcing them to dig their own graves. The victims, including three of the mayor's children, were chosen from a list of people who had contributed funds to the building of village schools."

July 17, 1982; "I will tell my brothers here what happened to us there in San Francisco (plantation in the municipality of Nentón). We left there when the army came to massacre our entire family. They came about 11 in the morning and first asked for two bulls to eat. The people wanted to give them their animals so they brought them in order to give the army something to eat . . . Finally we gave them the bulls and killed them. Then they called all the families and said they were going to share the food with us. But when we didn't go to get our families, they went and got them from the houses to come to a meeting. They gathered everybody and made the women and children go into the church. They put us, the men, in the courthouse.

"They had killed the bulls and eaten them. When they finished eating, they divided up into two groups. About 70 or 80 of them went to search our houses and take our things. Even though we are peasants we manage to get what we need. There is always a little money in the houses and they took that, and radios and cassette recorders, watches, and clothes. They took every thing. We had a community cooperative there where we had Q10,000. From the houses, they got maybe another Q10,000. Whatever we had, they took. They took the watch from my wrist and Q20.00 from my pockets . . .

"When finished robbing, they took the women in groups of 20 and left the little children outside. They put the women in the empty houses and shot them and threw grenades to kill them. Then they set the houses on fire. Then they took other groups of 20 and threw grenades and shot them and burned them. Anything that moved was burned and all the houses became ashes. They finished off the women and then the children, children of 12, 15, 10 years; of 7, 8, 10, 12 months. The 8 and 10 month olds they took out in their arms and carried them to a house and there they slugged them. They cut the intestines out of them and they were still screaming. And even though they were still alive, they just threw them into a house and piled them up. When they finished killing the little ones, they began with us.

"First the women, then the children and then the old people. They took the old people and killed them with knives like animals. They kept crying out. What crime did they commit? When they finished with the old people, they went for the working men. They took them out all tied up and shot them four times each in groups of ten and threw them back in the church. They piled them up in the church. And they were getting everyone. But God is greater. When there were only about 20 to 25 of us left, God inspired one of us to open the window of the courthouse. It was already on fire and feeling the heat, the soldiers got to one side and left the window open. One companion escaped through the window and saw that there was no one on that side. About six got out and finally it occurred to me to get out too. They shot at us with bursts of bullets, but by the grace of God I got away. We were saved, but everything else was lost. What crime have we committed? Certainly we are peasants, but hard workers." (At least 302 people were killed in the massacre. See Krueger (1982) for testimony; pp. 15–16; Cultural Survival (1983) for details and interpretation.

July 12–14, 1982 (Massacre and destruction of the village of Petenac, San Mateo Ixtatán); "At 11 o'clock on July 14 about 80 army soldiers came to our village and killed about 80 men, women and children. We also found out that on the 12th and 13th, they killed people in Xelbep, a village near to ours. There, they killed 38 people. On the 14th, they left Xelbep and went to Yocultac and killed 8 people there.

"They also went to Patalcal by way of Uayisna and came to our village. They surrounded the village. When we saw the army coming, some of us left our village, but many people could not get out. Our village is in a place where there are no weeds to hide in. That made it easy for the soldiers to shoot anyone who tried to get out. They took a rope out of one of the houses, cut it up into sections and used it to tie all the men's hands behind their backs. Then they put them in one of the houses where they shot them and then burned the house down. Afterwards, they rounded up all the women with their children in another house and did the same thing again. Finally, they set fire to the rest of the town" (Krueger, 1982:10).

July 19, 1982; "At 2:30 in the afternoon, I saw smoke from Yalcastán. This village is close to the Mexican border. Those burning the houses were soldiers. I drew nearer and realized that they were leaving. I heard screams of their prisoners and a shout from the officer. I could see from where I was that they were going up the mountain toward Yaltoyá, about 60 of them.

"Yaltoyá is another village to the south of Yalcastán, and about 10 kilometers from the Mexican border. I went further along the road and before getting to Yaltoyá, I saw 12 people dead in the road, among them two small children about eight months old. Many of their heads were split. They were carrying tortillas like they were going on a trip. Everything was strewn around. One woman's intestines were also lying out in the road. The heads were smashed and the teeth were broken. Most of them were women. At the most there were three young men, maybe about 19 years old. One woman was about 30; another about 20. They were the ones carrying the eight month olds. They were killed by machetes and blows from something heavy, like a rock, because their faces were all broken up. The women were naked with their blouses thrown on top of them. The soldiers had raped them and then thrown some bushes on top of them" (Villages of Yalcastán, Yaltoyá, Aguacate; Nentón) (Krueger, 1982:14).

July 21, 1982; "The army massacred 40 people in Yalambojoch (Nentón) using the same type of arms and methods as in San Francisco. 45 houses were burned. I've never seen anything like it. So many dead. I was overwhelmed; I wanted to cry. I could only stay there a little while. The bodies were already three or four days dead. They had torn the intestines out of some of them."

"They left a 13-year-old girl alive who was without food, she was a cripple. She couldn't walk and she was alone in the house, one of the few that they didn't burn. She told me that members of her family had been killed. She had no food when I got there. There were a great number of dead animals, pigs, chickens. The houses had been made of wood slats and the roofs were of straw. The machetes and the hatchets that they used to kill the people were thrown around, covered with blood. Some were stuck upright in the ground next to the bodies.

"Many of the women had been raped. Many of them were nude and many had their skirts up. An 8 year old boy had his teeth knocked out from beating, and one could tell that they had killed the kids by beating them; they grabbed them and they hit them with something hard, you could tell. The bodies that were outside the houses were those that had been decapitated. In Yaltoyá two of the bodies had been completely cut in half" (Krueger, 1982:19).

86. During the fieldwork when the army arrived without warning in San Mateo, the characteristic hubbub of the town (it was a fiesta day) was diminished and people stayed in their homes. Young men went into hiding in the hills in fear of being forcibly drafted into the army. One woman said, "I hope they don't start shooting again!"

87. Some informants described how soldiers dress up like guerrillas, trying to engage people in conversation to see if they will criticize the army.

88. In one instance, soldiers entered a town in the region, stole many things of value and kidnapped three local officials. The hostages were freed on the con-

dition that they sign a statement claiming that "nothing had occurred" and assuring that they would not press charges or attempt to recover the stolen goods. Although this occurred in the fall of 1984, to date townspeople will not speak of the incident.

89. According to informants, in Barillas, the local army commander's abuses became so blatant around 1984, that a large delegation from the municipality went to the Huehuetenango army base to complain; the commander was removed. In a village north of San Mateo a similar incident occurred, but the commander in Huehuetenango refused to replace the local commander. He finally conceded that if *everyone* from the village came to Huehuetenango he would remove the man. As the trip costs more than 8 quetzales per person and could take three days, this became impossible.

90. But others may also be chosen. A San Mateo municipal staff member in 1985, known as a "friend" of the army, had a great deal of control over the community. Many people said that to cross his will or to challenge his authority was tantamount to crossing the army. When this local official extorted a large amount of money from a town resident, witnesses chose not to press charges or to make any accusations because of his close ties to the military.

91. Officially the army does not recruit married men with children (although it may); so in one town a commissioner reportedly handcuffed a young man who had been taken for the draft, marched him to the priest's house, and forcibly married him to the woman he had lived with for three years (they had two children).

92. Stories abound about the training process of young recruits that converts Indian boys into soldiers willing to kill their own people on command. A soldier in Huehuetenango said, "I am not an Indian, I am a soldier." Many after this experience find it difficult to return to their home communities to live a normal life.

93. The IIC is meant to include all government institutions, such as DESACOM, INACOP, INTA, INAFOR, BANDESA, etc. (Community Development, Cooperatives, Agrarian Transformation Institute, Forestry Agency, Agricultural Development Bank, respectively), representatives of the civil patrol, the military commissioner, the school system, the hospital and health organizations, cooperatives, churches and other nongovernmental organizations (NGOs), as well as an army representative.

94. In Santa Eulalia, through 1985, he was the mayor and the military commissioner. In San Mateo he also holds the posts of Police Chief and Military Commissioner.

95. Letter by Father Ron Hennessey, December 20, 1984 to his family in the states.

96. Sweeps are, at times, even called on major traditional holidays. The day before the first round of the election, part of the All Saints' Day holiday, an all-day sweep was called by the army.

97. This seemed to be a personal decision of the civil patrol commander in San Mateo who claimed it was too big a bother to try to make them serve.

98. On the south coast we even heard rumors of patrol commanders acting as *contratistas* sending down civil patrol *pelotones* to work for the plantation owners.

99. There were reports of commanders using patrollers' labor for their own benefit as well, gathering firewood, or weeding their fields.

100. In one very small village, an order came for everyone to join in a region-wide sweep. The village declined to send anyone, explaining that no one was left to send. There were no reprisals.

101. When discussing land tenure in Huehuetenango, as any place in Guatemala, the status of titles must be kept in mind. In the Indian communities of the highlands, much of the land is still held in communal titles, many of which are not accepted by INTA as legal. Others are still paying for their land and do not yet hold titles. Those who held private titles and fled may still have trouble reclaiming their land because many records were lost, burned in their homes or municipal buildings, or left behind when they fled.

102. Information on rents varies. Everyone asked said that land rents for Q1–2.00 per *cuerda* per year, but some held that it would cost between Q100.00 to 200.00 to rent enough local land to feed a family for a year.

103. For example, thirty people returned to Yolcultac in late 1984, with a population of over a thousand. They were held in San Mateo for several weeks and then allowed to return on the recognizance of members of their family who had remained. But in a lowland village of Barillas where most of a community fled, when one family returned, the man's brother refused to give them their land back. They took him to court and finally to the military base trying to reclaim their land. The base commander, however, ruled in favor of the man who had remained. The returning family was forced to clear less fertile municipal land, and now they are having problems obtaining titles for that. In another instance in the village of Soloma a returning refugee killed the new occupant who took over the land in his absence and refused to vacate it. The refugee is in jail.

104. These are villages we either visited or had information from reliable informants. For more information on the state of villages in Northern Huehuetenango, see PAVA report (1984), *op. cit.*

105. Informants told us in December 1985 that all of the inhabitants were heavily indebted to BANDESA. Many received credits for an irrigation system that does not work.

106. Todos Santos has always suffered from a scarcity of arable land. Many residents have a small plot of land in or near the village and another in a neighboring village. Many Todos Santeros also took advantage of land distribution on the south coast area of La Máquina and also in the Ixcán. While the land on the coast may still be in their hands, most people have lost the land they had in the Ixcán.

107. While the high price of thread has caused some women to begin to dress their children in Western clothing, most women still spend the six months or more necessary to embroider the large and elaborate *huipiles* that they wear. These are primarily for their own use and most women have more than one. While San Mateo *huipiles* are for sale in Huehuetenango, Chichicastenango, Guatemala City and other tourist spots, there did not seem to be a working system for widespread export. In San Mateo *huipiles* that took pounds of expensive thread and months of work would sell for Q45–60. In tourist centers, they were going for more than Q130.

108. The constant discussion of economic problems doubtless stems from the difficulties caused by the crisis. But, in the current political situation, criticisms of anything else can be very dangerous, and people may in fact be attempting to reveal their feelings about a general situation of injustice in a more acceptable mode. For instance, when asked about the elections for a civilian government, several informants said, yes, they thought that would help because, "the army only knows how to make soldiers, and finances get worse and worse."

109. In addition, the army forced families to leave any isolated houses beyond towns and villages, even those on major roads, and has not yet permitted new or returning residents.

110. There is no reliable total figure available. The United Nations High Commissioner for Refugees (UNHCR) data only include those who have returned officially under their auspices and were tabulated beginning in mid-1984, with the Mexican decision to relocate refugess out of Chiapas: 1042 total (mid-84 to March 31, 1986). Army figures regarding the numbers of people processed were not available.

111. The priest was later refused permission to travel to and say mass in a village where there is a large army base because the commander there was angry that he had made them "give up the guerrillas."

112. The form reads: "*Srs.* _____ (name of refugee) *son libres y tienen el derecho a volver a sus hogares, después de sufrir la ausencia por culpa de la violencia de la guerrilla. Confiesan que no eran parte de la guerrilla y sólo huyeron para salvar sus vidas.*" ("Mssrs. _____ are free and have the right to return to their homes after suffering the exile caused by guerrilla violence. They confess that they were not part of the guerrilla and only fled to save their lives."

113. Even the relatives of refugees still in Mexico face harassment from time to time. In Huehuetenango a man whose son and daughter-in-law had gone to Mexico several years ago was visited by soldiers who said they were going to kill him. He protested that he hadn't seen his son for four years, but they spent several hours threatening him. Another family complained to a religious worker that their house was being watched and that they were being harassed by army and civilian officials. They were sure that if their family members returned they would be taken away.

CHAPTER FOUR

114. Aside from the army, U.S. Evangelicals based in the area repeatedly use the term "Ixil Triangle," in their literature. More recently, scholars and academics have also adopted the term. It is not a term that the people have used to describe themselves.

115. Population figures from the early 1970s.

116. The coffee plantations local to the Ixil area, a sector dominated by the Brol and Arenas families, hired laborers on both a permanent and seasonal basis. Finca San Francisco, for example, a 93 *caballería* plantation to the east of Cotzal, in 1966 employed some 600 workers and their families on a permanent basis. This constituted a village of 2000–3000 people, including *ladinos* (40 percent), Ixiles, and some Quichés from the town of Uspantán to the south. A foreign visitor in this period observed "squalid poverty," (relative to the surrounding area). For the

seasonal coffee harvest the plantation would hire an additional 150–300 workers. Their wages in the late 1960s were 80 centavos per day, some rations and minimal shelter (Colby and van den Berghe 1969a).

117. Ray and Helen Elliot, with the Wycliffe Bible Translators, arrived in Nebaj in 1963, and have remained, on and off, ever since. Paul Townshend, another Wycliffe Bible Translator/Summer Institute of Linguistics worker, has lived in Cotzal since 1972 and currently sponsors literacy workers, bible translators, health promotion, construction projects, and large-scale relief work in the surrounding area.

118. Ríos Montt a "born-again Christian" maintained close links to U.S. fundamentalist churches throughout his rule. His Verbo Church or Church of the Word is closely tied to Gospel Outreach, based in California. Several of the Church Elders and his personal advisors were U.S. Gospel Outreach members.

119. Additionally, these groups portray the situation in the Ixil region in a positive light. While General Ríos Montt brought the period of mass terror to the countryside and particularly to the Ixil area, Alfred Kaltschmitt, director of FUNDAPI stated "that the Ríos Montt government is doing more to help the poor and bring justice to the Indian people than any previous Guatemalan president" (Guatemala Task Force, 1983). A press release, by the Guatemalan Task Force of Gospel Outreach, in Whittier, California states: "The reality of Guatemala is completely different than what is being reported." The counterinsurgency operations in the Ixil region were reported by the Evangelicals as a "basic plan to help the Indians hardest hit by the communist guerrilla warfare . . . they build roads, involve themselves in community projects such as portable water systems for villages, or sawing lumber for what will eventually be their own houses. All the work is designed to benefit them." *Ibid.* Perhaps because of their support for the army, these groups have been allowed to carry on their work, even in the most difficult of times.

120. The following is a selective chronology of the violence in the Ixil region, taken from (Davis and Hodson, 1982).

appendix C:

1976: February 20, Army helicopters and troops occupy Chajul, in response to a supposed guerrilla threat.

March 19, A group of armed men in civilian clothes driving two Toyota vehicles pass through a military roadblock and kidnap nine men from Cotzal, Chajul, and Nebaj.

March 28, Armed men kill three brothers aged thirteen, eighteen, and twenty-two in Nebaj and execute three other men in their homes in the village of Chicel, San Juan Cotzal.

1977: February, An army base is set up near San Juan Cotzal. In one year the killings have included sixty-eight cooperative leaders in the nearby Ixcán, forty community leaders in Chajul, twenty-eight in Cotzal, and thirty-two in Nebaj.

August, Peasants from San Juan Cotzal denounce the persecution they have experienced since 1976.

1978: February 21, Army helicopters and troops circle northern El Quiché, occupying the towns of Chajul and Cotzal. Soldiers set up camp on the highway between Uspantán and Nebaj and establish numerous roadblocks.

March 9, Police arrest thirteen peasants in San Miquel Uspantán, El Quiché, accusing them of destroying property on Finca San Francisco.

June 12, Inhabitants of all three municipalities in the Ixil area again denounce the militarization of their communities. According to their statement, the military continues to support large landowners in the region while killing and kidnapping peasants.

1979: October 3, Closely following a rash of kidnappings and subsequent protests in Uspantán to the south, more than 2,000 gather in the town square of Cotzal to protest recent kidnappings and to demand the expulsion of the army from Chajul. Officers accuse the protesters of being "communists" and use their machine guns to turn the protesters back.

November 2, One-thousand special forces arrive heavily armed to the base in Jaboncillo, Chajul.

November, Army surrounds, bombs area near Salquil Grande, Nebaj, also heavy bombing around Chajul.

December, Army actions, intimidations, kidnappings in the area; group kidnapped from Uspantán publicly killed in Chajul.

1980: March 2, Troops surround Nebaj on market day, forcing 3,000 people to stand in line to receive identity cards, subsequent disappearances.

August, Sixty men publicly assassinated by the army in Cotzal.

September 6, Army attacks Chajul, over fifty people killed, including priest.

1981: April, Soldiers kill nine in Nebaj, sixty-eight in village of Cocobob, Nebaj. (from Amnesty International: "Massive Extrajudicial Executions in Rural Areas Under the Government of General Efraín Ríos Montt")

1982: April 5, One-hundred people killed in village Nangal, and others in Chel, Jua, and Amachel in northern El Quiché.

121. According to Sgt. Miguel Raimundo, stationed in Nebaj, as cited in (Nairn, 1983).

122. *Ibid.*, Nairn observed in his 1982 visit stockpiled bombs in the base munitions dump in Nebaj that included U.S. made 50-kilogram Ml/61As.

123. The army has since withdrawn its permanent presence from Acul.

124. During our time in the region, several civilians were pointed out to us as working for the army in some unofficial capacity.

125. According to one civilian official in Cotzal, the entire structure was in trouble. He blamed this on the fact that little was accomplished at the meetings; thus, agency representatives got bored and refused to come to meetings.

126. These *garitas* are generally located along each road entering town, or in the center of town.

127. There are reports of patrollers in the past being forced by the army to kill defenseless civilians, including children. When the army carried out sweeps in the mountains, often patrollers would be made to participate in killings with machetes. Today, social workers state, the traumas of those experiences are deeply felt.

128. This count is according to the *Diccionario Geográfico* data taken from the 1964 and 1973 censuses. However, some of the hamlets had undoubtedly grown enough to be considered villages. Residents stated that there were originally

"thirty villages of Nebaj and now there are only six." The eight counted here are: Río Azul, Pulay, Acul, La Pista, Tzalbal, Salquil, Palop, and Las Violetas (La Pista and Las Violetas are new).

129. The road continues on to Salquil, and is wide, well-packed, graded and graveled in some places, as are the roads running halfway to Chajul and all the way to and beyond Cotzal (there are two: toward both Ojo de Agua and to Finca San Francisco).

130. Along with the military, publications of the Wycliffe Bible Missionaries laud the army development of the Ixil area. In a March, 1983 special report on the activities of Love Lift International, FUNDAPI, and other Evangelical groups' activities, is the statement by FUNDAPI director Alfred Kaltschmitt: "The roads, for instance, will help [the Indians] bring to market products like coffee and corn that they used to have to haul out by horse or on their own backs" (Guatemala Task Force, 1983).

131. There are six development poles: The Ixil Triangle (El Quiché); Chacaj (Huehuetenango); Playa Grande (El Quiché); Chisec (Alta Verapaz); Senahú (Alta Verapaz) and Yanahí (El Petén). The program has been endorsed and supported by the new civilian government as an important component of its development strategy.

132. As part of the Food-for-Work program, the 100 construction workers reportedly received their houses at no additional cost.

133. He is the only priest in the entire region.

134. According to Gall (1981), in 1973 Acul had a total of 342 houses housing approximately as many families. Army statistics record 450 housing units and as many families, totaling 2,700 people (Ejército, 1985a).

135. One impractical item that was plentifully provided was medicine for constipation although the primary problem with children is diarrheal diseases. Also included was a spray-can of antilice formula specifically meant for use in bedclothes and not on skin. This information was only provided in English however and the health worker was barely literate in Spanish.

136. The first resettlers in Salquil Grande were involved in a "Development Committee" and the Salquil residents still in La Pista wanted to participate but were not permitted to (by the residents who had first returned). Although the causes were not well understood by informants, the resulting division between "old" and "new" settlers (many of the "new" still living in La Pista) has caused many problems.

137. In July 1985, a Pulay resident was assassinated while on patrol duty. He was a *principal* of the town and was doing literacy work through DESACOM, a government community development agency. There was speculation on both sides as to who had killed him because he had been "helping the people," (and therefore an army target), but also "working with the government," (and so a guerrilla target).

138. Although in early 1986, the EGP was able to attack the army in these areas.

139. According to informants, he went to the mountains about seven years ago and apparently was killed.

140. One man living there said that his original village was a twelve hour walk away. Three years ago when the violence was very bad, his community fled to a neighboring department. But the people there were poor and had nothing to spare for the refugees, this informant said. They also felt uncomfortable trying to deal with a different language and customs. "So we came to Nebaj, where at least the people are *our* people and might lend us a little land." They were placed under the jurisdiction of the army in Nebaj and were resettled at Ax'ctumbal.

141. Sample prices in the region varied: Ojo de Agua and other villages of Cotzal reputedly had land available for sale at Q25 or Q30 per *cuerda*. In the center of the town of Cotzal it is possible to pay Q300 for the same size plot, but on the outskirts of town, land is being sold to displaced widows at Q25 per *cuerda* (see description under "Cotzal"). Rental prices generally ranged from Q1-3 per *cuerda* per year. In some cases land availability is less of a problem than having the money to rent or buy it.

142. There were rumors which could not be substantiated of army corruption and misuse of aid funds and goods. Of course, it is always risky to accuse the army of anything, but the suspicions engendered by gross governmental misuse of donations after the 1976 earthquake, combined with the general tendency for men who enter public office or become ranking military officers to emerge as millionaires, serve to foster such allegations.

143. During the period of fieldwork in 1985, a group of 72, a group of over 30, and a few smaller groups were brought to Nebaj, within the space of a few weeks. In 1986 the refugees continue to come: "According to official reports, two groups of *campesinos* turned themselves over to the army in April and May: the first group, 33 men, women and children from the villages of Sumal and Bicalama in the township of Nebaj; the second group, of 23 men, 17 women and 46 children came from the rural areas surrounding Batzumal, Nebaj. Both groups were received by the army's Victory Task Force in Nebaj" (*Central America Report*, Vol. XIII, No. 23, p. 180).

144. To counter this, the refugees have devised appropriate survival strategies. They tend to stay mobile, to farm on land in small plots where the army dare not go and live in ingenious camouflaged huts and sometimes in caves.

145. While people in the major towns often seemed to know when a group of refugees was brought in, it is nevertheless difficult to document disappearances.

146. For example, a church worker had been caring for a child who disappeared one day. Two weeks later she found him tending sheep and badly malnourished, living with a family that needed extra labor.

CHAPTER FIVE

147. In terms of the number of refugees, the Ixcán is followed by the western section of El Petén. This part of the country has been known for its rich archaeological sites, including the famous Maya center of Tikal, the most impressive of Maya archaeological sites. In recent history, this inhospitable rain forest has been sparsely populated. Since the 1960s, however, El Petén has been the scene of many changes. Along the Usumacinta and La Pasión rivers a number of

cooperative communities were established; the Rebel Armed Forces (FAR) based their operations in this area; large deposits of oil were discovered in the mid-1970s; an important east/west road in the Franja Transversal del Norte (FTN) was constructed in the south edge of El Petén in the mid-1970s; large land owners, particularly military officers linked to the Lucas García administration, acquired extensive estates in the general region. The government set up the FYDEP (Petén Development Agency), now under military administration, to administer the needs of the Petén. Thus by the late 1970s El Petén acquired a new social, economic and political importance in Guatemala. The military has also targeted the region in the development programs. The Yanahí development pole, housing very few families, is located in the central-west section of El Petén.

A member of the research team went to a number of communities in western El Petén, along the Usumacinta and La Pasión rivers, site of refugee home communities. According to FYDEP, the population of El Petén has risen from 30,000 to almost 300,000 since development of the area began in the 1960s. FYDEP, which has been in existence for twenty-seven years, is currently giving land parcels of forty-five hectares to new settlers. Informants stated that there had been an increase in guerrilla activity in the last year, with heavy fighting and damages to the oil companies operating in the area. In comparison to Ixcán, the standard of living and general health of the population is much better. Civil patrol service is performed rather casually, though officially it is twenty-four hours every fourteen days.

148. *Aldea* is a village. Names are not given to protect the villagers.

149. For a detailed account of the colonization of Ixcán Grande up to the mid-1970s see (Morrissey, 1978).

150. This is not to say that there were no social problems in the settlements. The role of the priest, particularly in an isolated area, can be overwhelming. Father Guillermo Woods who directed the Ixcán project from 1969–1976, has been described by Morrissey (1978) as arrogant and authoritarian. His role, attitudes, and personality invariably left a profound imprint on the project. Today, the new Italian Salesian priest, Father Tiziano Sofía, is regarded by some to have a similar authoritarian personality. But ultimately the difference between a priest's authority and the military's power can hardly be compared.

151. For an ethnohistorical background on the Quiché-Maya, see Carmack (1973) and (1981). Falla (1978) presents a study of the changes in one municipality in El Quiché from 1948 to 1970.

152. The land parcels were 30 hectares, making it possible to plant cash crops in addition to the subsistence crops.

153. In a recent interview Archbishop Prospero Penados del Barrio declared that he was worried about the increasing violence in Guatemala. He recalled that "already fourteen priests have been assassinated, and many have disappeared, and religious workers have had to flee Guatemala. Hundreds of catechists suffered violence due to their delicate and sensitive work among marginalized peasants." *Prensa Libre*, June 4, 1986.

154. In April 1982 men from Ixcán managed to reach Guatemala City where they brought some news about the events unfolding in the area and to ask for help

to stop the killings. This is what they described as having taken place between February and April:

1. The soldiers started killing in Santa María Tzejá and Santa María Dolores, result unknown.
2. Polígono Trinidad, San Pablo. On February 12 and 13 all peasants disappeared. All the homes were burned.
3. San Lucas. Feb. 14, six people including two women were taken by the military.
4. Santo Tomás. On Feb. 15, 16 and 17, more than 150 people were massacred, then the soldiers put all the bodies in the church and burned the building.
5. Puente Xalbal de la Resurección. On Feb 19, ten people were killed by the soldiers near the river.
6. Rio Xalbal. On Feb. 24, fifteen people were captured by the army.
7. Tierra Nueva del Norte. Between Feb. 25 and March 10, the soldiers burned homes and killed many people (exact number unknown.)
8. La Unión (also known as Cuarto Pueblo). On March 14, a Sunday market day, soldiers arrived and massacred the population until Tuesday the 16th. The people were "not killed with bullets, but with knives and machetes." Reportedly about 300 people were killed, including children. An additional 80 children were left orphans. According to the source, the soldiers were particularly vengeful, because on April 28, 1981 the guerrillas had killed many soldiers in La Unión.
9. Los Angeles. On March 25 the army entered this *aldea*. No one was massacred. They told the people from now on they have to live in the center and not on their parcels.
10. La Resurrección (also known as Pueblo Nuevo.) On March 26 more than 300 soldiers entered this *aldea*. Warned by two sentries the entire village escaped. The soldiers stayed till the 28th. Animals were killed and homes destroyed.
11. Centro Galileo. One person killed, animals killed and one home destroyed. Four men were taken tied together by the soldiers.
12. Nuevo Progreso. On March 29, the soldiers burned five houses.
13. On the road to La Resurrección. On March 30 soldiers burned 38 houses, and the coffee crop. They kidnapped two adult men and one 12 year old boy.
14. Xalbal. On March 31 soldiers arrived in Xalbal, destroying all the homes and killed one catechist with his whole family. The rest of the villagers had fled.

155. According to the army 1,300 families have received assistance in the newly created Playa Grande Development Pole. The 1,300 houses constructed are distributed in 15 communities. The *aldeas* are Xacbal, Cantabal, San José la 20, Efrata, Santa Clara, San Pablo, San Francisco, Trinitaria and a broad category referred to as *aldeas fronterizas*. Included in the Playa Grande Development Pole is Salacuín, though it belongs to the Department of Alta Verapaz. The investment in El Quiché between August 1983 and December 1984 was Q2,505,783.87, according to army documents. This is the highest expenditure of any department in the country, except for the department of Guatamala, which was slightly higher. Likewise the food distribution, through the National Reconstruction Committee/World Food Program was the highest in El Quiché. Records show that 3,011,260.91 rations were distributed (Ejército, 1895b).

156. *El Gráfico*, July 28, 1985; *El Gráfico*, August 25, 1985; *El Gráfico*, September 24, 1985; *La Hora*, November 15, 1985.

157. Villagers claim the *aldea* had close to a thousand head of cattle.

158. Informants stated the S-5 officer is changed rather frequently.

159. One hears quite matter-of-factly the expression "they gave me fifteen days" (permission to leave the village), as if they were prisoners out on parole.

160. Father Tiziano Sofía, for example, sometimes must spend a month on foot or horseback, visiting communities in the parish because there are no roads.

161. Interview with Ing. Gustavo Adolfo Búcaro González, Guatemala City, April, 1986.

162. Interview with Lic. Raquel Blandón de Cerezo, Guatemala City, June 1986.

163. The cooperative had legal standing since September 23, 1970.

164. The Diocese donated the land to INTA to be distributed to the cooperative. This three-way arrangement—the Catholic Church/INTA/Cooperative—had been worked out with INTA to exempt the sellers from paying taxes for idle land. The Diocese bought this land for $100,000 with a loan from a German foundation. To repay this loan the Diocese charged $80.00 per parcel. The title for all the land was in the name of the Ixcán Grande Cooperative, composed of: Mayalán, Xalbal, La Resurrección, Los Angeles, Cuarto Pueblo and Zunil.

165. In early 1978, for example, just two days after the expulsion of Father Karl Stetter, the defense vice minister went to Ixcán to distribute 1,444 land titles. INTA also gave national lands directly to the cooperative. On another occasion, the government mediated a dispute of the Mayalán cooperative (Second Center) and the Cooperative Ixcán Grande in May 1978. It recognized not only the titles but improvements made such as housing, cultivation of coffee, cardamom, sugar cane, fruit trees, etc., which amounted to $76,490. The Cooperative Ixcán Grande in this instance bought off the grievers (those who were disputing), paying for the improvements from loans obtained from Catholic Relief, CARITAS, the Instituto para el Desarrollo Económico Social de América Central (IDESAC) and the Diocese of Huehuetenango. In another case in September 1980, the Petromaya oil company reportedly paid about $80,000 indemnity for damages to the cooperative members. The cases document the labor and money invested in these cooperatives.

166. The number of the registry of the three properties mentioned in *"La contrainsurgencia y la tierra"* are: (1) n.2076, f.274, libro 6 de Bienes de la Nación. Measurement 6,284 hectares. (2) n.4621, f.74, libro 31 de Huehuetenango, measurement 908 hectares. (3) n.4539, f.182, libro 33 de Huehuetenango, measurement 905 hectares. Property Registry, Quetzaltenango.

The study concludes with an indemnity argument in favor of the refugees, for a total of Q27 million.

Minimum salary established in 1980 - Q3.20

Average number of years - 11 years

Working days per year - 310 days

Number of adult peasants

(2000 coop members + 500 sons) - 2500 men

Total indemnity - 27,280.000

CHAPTER SIX

167. Tens of thousands of Indians moved to Guatemala City or the south coast, where they have become part of a large marginal unemployed population.

168. For an overall background to the Guatemalan refugees in Mexico, see Americas Watch (1984).

169. The first communities that refugees fled from were El Arbolito, Monte Sinaí, Tichán, Yaxchilán, Quetzal, Técnica, Felicidad, Bethel, Bonanza, Bella Guatemala, Flor de la Esperanza, Ixmucané and Laureles.

170. The communities that received the refugees were: Benemérito, Frontera Echeverría, La Fortuna, El Tigre, Macachi Rochen and Canán.

171. For a comprehensive report on the Central American refugees in Mexico, see Aguayo (1985).

172. The Mexican government granted asylum to only fifty-eight of two thousand Guatemalans who were subsequently repatriated to Guatemala in 1981.

173. Interview with Pierre Jambor, Mexico City, November 1982.

174. *Uno Mas Uno*, August 28, 1985. This figure includes refugees in camps as well as the much larger number of "unofficial" refugees not living in UN recognized camps.

175. The population of a camp varied. Puerto Rico reached 6,000 at one point. At the time of our first field visit to the Lacandón area camps in Nov. 1982, more than 500 refugees arrived at this camp. Already highly experienced in community organization, the camp representatives organized a supply of food (they collected a tortilla per household, and for the next days everyone contributed some corn so that the new arrivals could make their own tortillas), they provided them with temporary shelter made with nylon tarps, palm fronds, and cane and wooden slats for a sleeping platform. Some of these refugees would move to other less crowded camps or to camps where they might find relatives or members of their own communities.

176. The Guatemalan government repression drew the attention of humanitarian organizations, especially from Europe and the United States. Many foreigners went to Chiapas to offer help, collect information and verify the devastation brought about by the repression in Guatemala. The Diocese supplied aid received from international donations, raising an estimated one million dollars yearly to assist the refugees.

177. In a November 4, 1982 article, *Uno Mas Uno* referred to 100 deaths in a four month period.

178. Interview with Ambassador Oscar González, Mexico City, August 1984. A number of additional options might also have been possible. One alternative was to leave the refugees where they were, taking steps to protect them from incursions. Another more realistic option was moving the camps closest to the border to a safer distance within Chiapas.

179. Conflict over land is tense in Chiapas. Hundreds of land evictions have occurred in recent years. The government unveiled a plan to develop Chiapas (the Plan Chiapas), but this has barely gotten off the ground. Moreover, organizations among impoverished peasants in this state linked to the Mexican socialist party (PSUM) are becoming a concern to the Mexican ruling party, the Revolutionary Institutional Party (PRI). One Mexican government official stated that the government was indeed concerned with the PSUM inroads in Chiapas and

declared in jest that in Campeche (where the refugees were being relocated) there are "soviet style elections, where the PRI wins 98 percent of the vote."

180. The political consciousness and organizational experience of the Guatemalans was impressive even to UNHCR and Mexican officials.

181. Because of its inability to respond quickly to the needs of the refugees, the Mexican government found it necessary to cede important aspects of relief work to voluntary organizations. Yet Mexico continued to resent the involvement of nongovernmental organizations (national and international) in refugee relief.

182. As early as October 1982, the State Department appeared concerned about the location and lack of control over the camps. They made this concern known to UNHCR and COMAR officials:

> We indicated that in the view of the USG [United States Government] better control over the camps was necessary . . . and suggested that moving them to sites further inland and more accessible to the relief effort would solve both the safety and the logistics problem. Mr. Witschi anticipated our request and agreed to inform Geneva of our discussion.

State Department Memorandum, October 25, 1982.

183. The optimal solution would be to repatriate the refugees. A 1984 *State Department memo* states: "If large groups [of Guatemalan refugees] return from Mexico, we are prepared to assist in meeting their basic needs for food, shelter, and medical treatment . . ."

184. As of June 1986 these refugees are still in La Gloria de San Caralampio.

185. Not all went well for the refugees in their relations with the Chiapas population. There were incidents when refugees were stoned, hit, denounced, extorted, abused, and exploited. These incidents, however, were the exception, not the rule.

186. There were even cases, such as the case of Juan Moreno, the best-known dissident leader of the La Gloria camp, whose family had lived in Mexico, then moved to Nentón, Huehuetenango, only to return to Mexico as refugees.

187. The refugees at the Puerto Rico camp had fled across the Lacantún River to avoid being relocated.

188. The Mexican authorities reluctantly agreed to a visit by Americas Watch at the beginning of August. This delegation, (the first outsider's visit since the relocation process began) composed of Eliecer Valencia and Beatriz Manz, was allowed to visit the Lacandón Forest camps and, with Robert Goldman, interview a number of Mexican government officials. See Americas Watch (1984).

189. During this period, Mexican authorities temporarily kidnapped four Mexican citizens who were involved with the Guatemalan refugees: a medical doctor, two nuns and a prominent journalist. Several Guatemalans were also kidnapped in the Federal District and in Chiapas.

190. UNHCR cable from Mexico, April 11, 1986.

CHAPTER SEVEN

191. In Guatemala, the people lived in very small villages (often 50–200 families); their houses were situated on extensive lots and scattered rather randomly across the terrain.

192. For details on the COMAR-UNHCR plans for the refugees, see the documents presented as part of a meeting held by COMAR, the UNHCR, and invited guests in April 1985 at Bacalar, Quintana Roo, printed as mimeo (Alto Comisionado, 1985).

193. *Minsa* is industrially prepared corn flour and has a very different taste and texture than corn when made into tortillas. This interview was conducted during the first camp visit, several months before the first harvest was in.

194. ". . . *Por eso se desespera uno. A veces pienso regresar a Chiapas, a la felicidad. Sembramos milpa a nuestro gusto, con las facilidades que nos daban los Señores Mexicanos allá.*"

195. The figures are as given to us by refugees. In Campeche, before the first harvest, some informants complained that the food they were given did not generally last the entire week. We did not hear similar stories when we returned in early 1986 (after the harvest). People also commented that even when they were receiving powdered milk, it was old and unusable; it caused diarrhea independent of the manner in which it was prepared. The Catholic religious workers in Quetzal Edzná helped set up a yogurt project (part of the weekly mass collection goes to buy the milk) that the women run collectively and that provides about a half cup of yogurt per day for each member of the several hundred families that participate. People also complained about the quality of the soap, saying that it is useless for washing dishes and pots and useless against lice (of epidemic proportions among the children), that they must buy detergent if they really want to keep things clean.

196. When discussing model villages (where most of them would be placed, according to Guatemalan government plans, if large groups are repatriated), several men commented on what they see as similarities to their present camps: they are not free to travel as they like, their work opportunities are limited by the decisions of authorities, they have been placed there against their will. They are quick to acknowledge, though, that there is a life and death difference between having COMAR as the authority, or the Guatemalan army, and that the internal organization is much freer than in the Development Poles, or even in most communities in rural Guatemala.

197. In addition the materials provided by the Church's pastoral agents in Chiapas are considered by the refugees to be of higher quality than those they receive through COMAR. During the course of the field visits to Chiapas, refugees there explain that the Church provides them with some goods that are not on the COMAR list (coffee, for example) and with others also provided by COMAR, but that are of such poor quality (milk and soap are commonly cited) that cannot be used. According to informants and our own field observations, the role of pastoral workers in developing camp infrastructure and services has been supportive, nonimposing, and respectful of the refugees' initiatives and decisions.

198. There are other important factors, as well. Many of these people have cleared land, built homes, clinics, and schools (and then seen them destroyed), and left behind family, friends and community several times in the past five to fifteen years. Informants close to the refugees say that for many, the destruction of their camps in the Lacandón area, their lack of options, and the physical hardships of the move made the relocation especially traumatic.

199. In Quintana Roo, one group representative explained that when questions about food rations have been raised after cuts were implemented or families were left without food for several days, COMAR officials would often respond that the refugees have been getting aid for three years and "don't deserve it anymore," or that the UN is no longer sending money or that the problem is that they've become "big eaters" (*comelones*). An informant in Campeche told of meetings with COMAR in which refugees raised questions about chronic water shortages; they were told to be quiet and to be more careful not to waste water. Several told of another incident in which one COMAR official reproached people because they weren't keeping things clean enough, told them to bathe their children more often and to wash their clothes better. Yet, the same official had not been able to resolve the problems with the camp's well or to assure a constant, adequate water supply to the refugees in the more than two years since the camps were established. And a woman explained that COMAR officials often get angry if "the men lodge complaints when they are robbed on the job" [paid less than the contractual agreement; a very common problem for seasonal agricultural workers on plantations]. They have been told simply, "If it's work you wanted, it's work you got."

In fact, an underlying cause of some tension in the camps may be the reported UNHCR budget cut.

200. A few midwives continue to practice quietly, but receive no equipment or supplies from COMAR.

201. In a July 1985 interview, a COMAR official acknowledged that the problem had not been resolved, although they were drawing up plans to put in a second pump and hoped the situation would soon be better. The problem is related in large part to difficulties in regulating and supplying electricity for the pump.

202. An *ejido* is a land-holding community established under the Mexican agrarian reform law and is a common land tenure system throughout the country.

203. Informants explained that it is often hard to hold meetings or get community projects going, in part because of difficulties with collective farming projects and in part, because when the water trucks arrive, the women drop whatever they'd been doing to get in line for water so they can do chores like cooking and washing that they'd left undone when the water ran out.

204. Almost all of this work is for men, although if the group is large and contracted for a longer period of time, a woman or two may be hired to go along to cook. Women may also occasionally find jobs on their own as domestic workers in nearby Mexican communities. Pay tends to be extremely low, about 200 pesos a day in fall 1985 (about $.40 US). All dollar equivalents are based on exchange rates at the time of fieldwork.

205. To give some idea of how far money might go in the camps, in early 1986, a young pig cost 5–6000 pesos (depending on size), live hens about 600 pesos/kilo, a dress about 1800–2000 pesos and men's pants about 2500 pesos.

206. According to a camp representative, these kinds of abuses were somewhat less common during the second work season.

207. Many had learned sewing or carpentry skills in Guatemala. Some were able to carry their sewing machines from Guatemala (mostly those from towns in

Huehuetenango, located a few kilometers from the Chiapas border) or somehow acquired them in Chiapas.

208. Fieldwork in Quintana Roo was done before the system was fully implemented: thus, we cannot compare the situation in the two areas. The discussion that follows refers only to Campeche.

209. It is not clear why COMAR insisted so strongly on this matter, whether it was a question of expedience or of mistaken criteria regarding how to encourage community development.

210. Refugees were generally surprised at the size of the yields. The thin, rocky soil hadn't given them much hope that their work would be fruitful.

211. In some cases, then, precisely those people with the least possibilities for earning cash (*i.e.*, widows, the elderly) will have to buy staple grains during part of the period.

APPENDIX A

212. See the various publications of the Washington based Refugee Policy Group. Also, Fagen and Aguayo (1986).

213. According to COMAR, there are 200,000 Guatemalan refugees in Mexico, making these figures unusually conservative for all refugees in Mexico.

214. For an extensive analysis of Cambodian and Vietnamese refugees, see Shawcross (1984).

APPENDIX B

215. *Vienna Convention in the Law of Treaties*, May 23, 1969, Art. 18. See also Sklar, Hing and Silverman (1985: 4008).

216. It is noteworthy that the Organization of African Unity (OAU) Convention on the Governance of Aspects of Refugee Problems in Africa, 1969, includes in its definition of refugees, "every person who, owing to external aggression, occupation, foreign domination or events seriously disturbing public order in either part or the whole of his country . . . is compelled to leave his . . . residence in order to seek refuge . . . .".

217. See, Sharry (1984). Sharry suggests that this question has been raised by the UNHCR.

218. The refugees in Chiapas would be considered lawfully present, given the formalization of their status and issuance of visas by the government of Mexico (Grahl Madsen, 1973: 357). "He may also be lawfully in the territory even if he does not meet . . . requirements, provided that the . . . authorities have dispensed with any or all . . . and allowed him to stay . . . anyway."

APPENDIX C

219. The foreigner enters in one of the following ways: Tourist (FM-T), Transient, Visitor (FM-3), Advisor, Diplomatic Asylum (FM-10), Student (FM-9), Distinguishing Visitor, Local Visitor (FM-8), and Provisional Visitor.

220. This category includes: Administrator (FM-2), Investor, Professional, Private Agent, Scientist, Technician and Relative.

221. See (O'Dogherty, 1985: 36–7):

a) Memorandum No. 6, of April 15, 1983, expedited by the Delegate of the General Directorate of Migratory Services.

b) *Oficio* No. 9865, of April 19, 1983; General Directorate of Migratory Services.

c) *Diario Oficial de la Federación*, June, 1983.

APPENDIX E

222. The letter is from refugee representatives of the Quetzal-Edzná camp in Campeche. June 27, 1986.

223. Letter from refugee representatives from Campeche and Quintana Roo, sent to President Vinicio Cerezo, dated July 1, 1986.

APPENDIX G

224. See Americas Watch (1984). Data provided by COMAR, IMMS, Diocese of San Cristóbal de las Casas, and the refugees.

Bibliography

Alto Comisionado de las Naciones Unidas para Refugiados (ACNUR). *Recopiliación de Instrumentos Internacionales Relativos a los Centroamericanos en México* (versión provisional). Geneva: 1984.

Alto Comisionado de las Naciones Unidas para Refugiados (ACNUR)/ Comisión Mexicana de Ayuda a Refugiados (COMAR). *Seminario Sobre Integración Productiva de los Refugiados Guatemaltecos en el Sureste de México; Conclusiones y Recomendaciones.* Bacalar, Quintana Roo: April, 1985.

Adams, Richard. *Crucifixion by Power: Essays on Guatemalan National Social Structure 1944–1966.* Austin, Texas: University of Texas Press, 1970.

Aguayo, Sergio. *El Exodo Centroamericano.* México: Foro 2000, September, 1985.

American Convention on Human Rights. San Jose: November 22, 1969.

Americas Watch. *Guatemala: A Nation of Prisoners.* New York: 1983.

Americas Watch. *Guatemalan Refugees in Mexico 1980–1984.* New York: September, 1984.

Americas Watch. *Guatemala: The Group of Mutual Support.* New York: 1985.

Americas Watch. *Civil Patrols in Guatemala.* New York: 1986.

Amnesty International. *Massive Extrajudicial Executions in Rural Areas Under the Government of General Efrain Rios Montt..* London: 1982.

Atchison, Roberta. "Repatriating Refugees to Ethiopia: A Model Calling for Assessment." *United States Comission for Refugees.* Survey. Washington: 1984.

Avebury, Lord Eric, Beatriz Manz, and Georges A. Fauriol. *Hearings Before the Subcommittee on Western Hemisphere Affairs of the Committee on Foreign Affairs.* United States House of Representatives, February, 1985.

Black, George. "Under the Gun." *North American Congress on Latin America, Report on the Americas*, New York: November/December, 1985.

Black, George, Milton Jamail, and Norma Stoltz Chinchilla. *Garrison Guatemala*. New York: Monthly Review, 1984.

Bossen, Laurel H. *The Redivision of Labor: Women and Economic Choice in Four Guatemalan Communities*. Albany, New York: State University of New York Press, 1984.

Bravo Caro, Rodolfo. *Guía del Extranjero, Ley General de Población*. México: Editorial Porrua.

Brintnall, Douglas E. *Revolt Against the Dead: The Modernization of a Mayan Community in the Highlands of Guatemala*. New York: Gordon and Breach, 1979.

Burgos, Elisabeth. *I . . . Rigoberta Menchu*. London: NLB (U. S. Distributor, New York: Schocken Books) 1984.

Carmack, Robert. *Quichean Civilization: The Ethnohistoric, Ethnographic, and Archaeological Sources*. Berkeley, California: University of California Press, 1973.

Carmack, Robert. *The Quiche Mayas of Utatlan: The Evolution of a Highland Guatemalan Kingdom*. Norman, Oklahoma: University of Oklahoma Press, 1981.

Centro de Estudios Económicos y Sociales del Tercer Mundo. *INFORME: Relaciones México-Estados Unidos*. Vol. I, No. 3, México: 1982.

Cerquone, Joseph. "Vietnamese Boat People, Pirate's Vulnerable Prey." *United States Commission for Refugees*. Survey, Washington, February, 1984.

Chichini, Malak El. "Nicaragua: Priority to Rural Integration." Geneva: *Refugee*, September, 1984.

Cifuentes H., Juan Fernando (Capitán de Navío DEM G-5.) "Apreciación de Asuntos Civiles (G-5) para el Area Ixil." *Revista Militar*, Guatemala: Centro de Estudios Militares (CEM), September/December, 1982.

Colby, Benjamin, and Pierre van den Berghe. Field Notes. 1969a.

Colby, Benjamin, and Pierre van den Berghe. *Ixil Country*. Berkeley, California: University of California Press, 1969b.

Constitución Política de los Estados Unidos Mexicanos. México: Editorial Trillas.

Convention Relating to the Status of Refugees. Geneva: July 28, 1951.

Convention on the Status of Aliens. Sixth International Conference of American States, Havana, February 20, 1928.

Convention on Territorial Asylum. Tenth International Conference, Caracas, 1954.

Cronología de una Experiencia Pastoral: Veinte Años de Vida y de Muerte, de Fe y Esperanza Cristianas. México, 1986.

La Contrainsurgencia y la Tierra. Mimeo, September 15, 1985.

Cultural Survival, Inc. and Anthropology Resource Center. *Voices of the Survivors, The Massacre at Finca San Francisco.* Boston, 1983.

Davis, Shelton H. *Land of our Ancestors: A Study of Land Tenure and Inheritance in the Highlands of Guatemala.* Ph.D. Dissertation, Department of Anthropology, Harvard University, 1970.

Davis, Shelton, and Julie Hodson. *Witness to Political Violence in Guatemala: The Suppression of a Rural Development Movement.* Boston: Oxfam America, 1982.

Democracia Cristiana Guatemalteca. *Proyecto Nacional, 1986-1991; Primera Parte: Lineamientos Generales.* Guatemala, July, 1985a.

Democracia Cristiana Guatemalteca. *Proyecto Nacional, 1986-1991; Segunda Parte: Políticas, Programas, y Proyectos.* Guatemala, November, 1985b.

Dennis, Phillip A., Gary S. Elbow, and Peter L. Heller. *Final Report: Playa Grande Land Colonization Project, Guatemala.* Texas Tech University, January, 1984.

Diario Oficial de la Federación. Mexico, July 22, 1980.

Diario Oficial de la Federación. Mexico, June, 1983.

Ejército de Guatemala. *Polos de Desarrollo y Servicios: Filosofía Desarrollista.* Guatemala: Impreso en Editorial del Ejército, 1984.

Ejército de Guatemala. *Guatemala: Revista Cultural del Ejército.* Edición Especial dedicada a los Polos de Desarrollo. Guatemala, January/February, 1985a.

Ejército de Guatemala. *Guatemala: Revista Cultural del Ejército.* Pensamiento y Cultura. Guatemala: January/June, 1985b.

England, Robert. "Peasants fight and buy stock to save belieguered plantation." *Insight.* June 16, 1986.

Fagen, Patricia Weiss and Sergio Aguayo. *Fleeing the Maelstrom: Central American Refugees.* Occasional Paper No. 10. Central American and Caribbean Program. School of Advanced International Studies, Washington: John Hopkins University. March 1986.

Falla, Ricardo. *Quiché Rebelde.* Guatemala: Editorial Universitaria, 1978.

Gall, Francis. *Diccionario Geográfico de Guatemala.* Guatemala: Instituto Geográfico Nacional, 1981, 1983.

Goodwin-Gill, Guy. "Entry and Exclusion of Refugees." *Transnational Legal Problems of Refugees, Michigan Yearbook of International Legal Studies.* 1982.

Grahl-Madsen, Atle. "Refugees and Refugee Law in a World in Transition." *Michigan Yearbook of International Law,* 1982.

Grahl-Madsen, Atle. *The Status of Refugees in International Law.* The Netherlands: A. W. Sijthoff-Leiden. Volume 2, 1972.

Guatemala Task Force of Gospel Outreach. *Radiance Monthly.* Whittier, California: Gospel Outreach, March 1983.

Hamilton, Virginia. ed., "Cambodians in Thailand, People on the Edge." *United States Commission for Refugees.* Survey. Washington: December, 1985.

Hartling, Poul. "Refugee Aid and Development: Genesis and Testing of a Strategy." *United States Commission for Refugees. World Refugee Survey*, 1982.

Hawkins, John. *Inverse Images: The Meaning of Culture, Ethnicity, and Family in Postcolonial Guatemala.* Albuquerque, New Mexico: University of New Mexico Press, 1984.

Hutchinson, Maria. "ICARA: Where Does it Stand Now?" *Refugee*, Geneva, April, 1985.

Immerman, Richard H. *The CIA in Guatemala: The Foreign Policy of Intervention.* Austin, Texas: University of Texas Press, 1982.

Inforpress Centroamericana. *Guatemala: Elections 1985,* Guatemala, 1985.

Inforpress Centroamericana, Informe Especial. "Resurge el Problema de la Tierra en Guatemala." June 19, 1986.

Johannessen, Piers. "Refugees in a New Country." *Refugee*, Geneva, August, 1985.

Jones, Allen K. "Afghan Refugees, Five Years Later." *United States Commission for Refugees (USCR) Survey*, January, 1985.

Krueger, Chris (editor). *Guatemala: Government Against the People.* Washington: Washington Office on Latin America, 1982.

Manz, Beatriz. "Guatemalan Refugees: Violence, Displacement and Survival." *Cultural Survival Quarterly*, 7:1, 1983.

Manz, Beatriz. "The Forest Camps in Eastern Chiapas." *Cultural Survival Quarterly*, Fall, 1984.

Manz, Beatriz. "A Guatemalan Dies and What it Means." *New York Times*, Op-ed. July, 14, 1986.

McClintock, Michael. *The American Connection: State Terror and-Popular Resistance in Guatemala, Volume II.* London: Zed Books, 1985.

Millet, Artimus. *The Agricultural Colonization of the West Central Peten, Guatemala: a Case Study of Frontier Settlement by Cooperatives.* Ph.D. Dissertation, Department of Geography, University of Oregon, 1974.

Morrissey, James. *A Missionary Directed Resettlement Project Among the Highland Maya of Western Guatemala.* Ph.D. Dissertation, Department of Anthropology, Stanford University, 1978.

Nairn, Allan. "The Guns of Guatemala." *The New Republic*, April 11, 1983.

Nairn, Allan, and Jean-Marie Simon. "The Bureaucracy of Death." *The New Republic*, June 30, 1986.

Nash, Manning. *Machine Age Maya: The Industrialization of a Guatemalan Community*. Glencoe, Illinois: Free Press, 1958.

National Immigration Project, National Lawyers Guild. *Project Report, Attachment C*. February/March, 1986.

O'Dogherty, Laura. *Algunos Documentos Relativos al Asilo y Refugio en México*. México, D.F.: Academia Mexicana de Derechos Humanos, May/June, 1985.

Organization of African Unity. *Convention on the Governance of Aspects of Refugee Problems in Africa*. 1969.

Organization of American States. *Report on the Situation of Human Rights in the Republic of Guatemala*. Washington D.C., 1983.

Oxfam America. *Project Report on Guatemala*. Boston: 1984.

Programa de Ayuda para los Vecinos del Altiplano, (PAVA.) *Final Report*. Washington D.C.: USAID Project No. DR-520-84-04, 1984.

Protocol Relating to the Status of Refugees. New York: United Nations Treaty Series. January 31, 1967.

Rubin, Gary. "Refugee Protection: An Analysis and Action Proposal." *United States Commission for Refugees*. Survey, Washington, 1983.

Rubin, Gary E. "The Asylum Challenge to Western Nations." *United States Commission for Refugees*. Washington: December 1984.

Sabatier, Patrick. "Hong Kong: Boat People in Search of a Haven." *Refugee*, Geneva: September, 1984.

Schlesinger, Stephen and Stephen Kinzer. *Bitter Fruit: The Untold Story of the American Coup in Guatemala*. New York: Doubleday, 1982.

Sharry, Frank. "Displaced Persons, Humanitarian Challenge in Central America." *United States Commission for Refugees*. Survey. Washington, 1984.

Shawcross, William. *The Quality of Mercy*. New York: Simon and Schuster, 1984.

Sklar, Helen, Bill Ong Hing and Mark Silverman, editors. *Salvadoran and Guatemalan Asylum Cases, A Practitioner's Guide*. San Francisco: Immigrant Legal Resource Center, 1985.

State Department Memorandum. Washington, October 25, 1982.

State Department Memorandum. #7400N, Washington, October 25, 1984.

Tedlock, Barbara. *Time and the Highland Maya*. Albuquerque, New Mexico: University of New Mexico Press, 1981.

Torres-Rivas, Edelberto. *Report on the Conditions of the Central American Refugees and Migrants*. Washington D.C.: Center for Immigration Policy and Refugee Assistance, Georgetown University, July, 1985.

Unidad Revolucionaria Nacional Guatemalteca. *Planteamientos de la URNG Sobre la Situación de los Refugiados Guatemaltecos en México.* June 18, 1985.

United Nations. *Declaration on Territorial Asylum,* 1967.

United Nations. *International Covenant on Civil and Political Rights,* 1966.

United Nations. *Statute of the Office of the United Nations High Commissioner for Refugees, Annex to Resolution 428 (V).* December 14, 1950.

United Nations. *Universal Declaration of Human Rights, 1948.*

United States Agency for International Development. *Land and Labor in Guatemala: An Assessment.* Washington, D.C., 1982.

United States Committee for Refugees. *World Refugee Survey.* 1984.

Vienna Convention in the Law of Treaties. May 23, 1969.

Warren, Kay B. *The Symbolism of Subordination: Indian Identity in a Guatemalan Community.* Austin Texas: University of Texas Press, 1978.

Winter, Roger and Joseph Cerquone. "Horror on the Water: Pirate Attacks Against Vietnamese Boat People." *USA Today,* Society for the Advancement of Education. NY: November, 1984.

Index